Didn't You Kill My Mother-in-Law?

'There was this drunk homosexual Pakistani squatter trade unionist takes my mother-in-law to an Irish restaurant . . . says to the West Indian waiter, "Waiter, waiter, there's a racial stereotype in my soup" . . .'

TONY ALLEN

'I don't use comedy to make a point under any circumstances . . . I use comedy to be funny.'

BEN ELTON

'We did another night at the Comedy Store to the Thames Valley River Police who were out on a stag night: "Get 'em off, show us your tits." '

DAWN FRENCH

'I can't make stuff up – I can't write jokes, I can only do it from my own perspective.'

CLAIRE DOWIE

'Didn't you kill my brother?'

ALEXEI SAYLE

Didn't You Kill My Mother-in-Law?

The Story of Alternative Comedy in Britain
from the Comedy Store to Saturday Live

ROGER WILMUT and PETER ROSENGARD

Methuen

Also by Roger Wilmut

Tony Hancock 'Artiste'
From Fringe to Flying Circus
Kindly Leave the Stage
No More Curried Eggs For Me (*editor*)
Son of Curried Eggs (*editor*)

The Goon Show Companion (*Robson Books*)
The Illustrated Hancock (*Queen Anne Press*)

First published in Great Britain 1989
by Methuen London
Michelin House, 81 Fulham Road, London SW3 6RB

Part One Copyright © Peter Rosengard 1989
Part Two Copyright © Roger Wilmut 1989

Printed and bound in Great Britain
by Butler & Tanner Ltd, Frome and London

ISBN 0 413 17390 9

Contents

Illustrations

viii

Acknowledgements

The authors are very grateful to the many people who assisted in the making of this book. Firstly, for giving interviews to Roger Wilmut, thanks are due to Keith Allen, Tony Allen, Mark Arden, Jim Barclay, Arnold Brown, Lee Cornes, John Davy, Andy de la Tour, Claire Dowie, John Dowie, Jenny Eclair, Adrian Edmondson, Ben Elton, Simon Fanshawe, Dawn French, Stephen Frost, Ronnie Golden, Malcolm Hardee, Jeremy Hardy, John Hegley, Kit Hollerbach, Paul Jackson, Dillie Keane, Maria Kempinska, Jenny Lecoat, Helen Lederer, Norman Lovett, Rik Mayall, Pauline Melville, Roland Muldoon, Jean Nicholson, Nigel Planer, Nick Revell, Peter Richardson, Jennifer Saunders, Alexei Sayle, Don Ward and Victoria Wood.

The script extracts quoted in the text are an essential part of the story, and thanks are due for permission to quote them: for extracts from their acts – Keith Allen, Tony Allen, Mark Arden & Stephen Frost, Jim Barclay, Arnold Brown, Andy de la Tour, Claire Dowie, John Dowie, Jenny Eclair, Simon Fanshawe, Jeremy Hardy, John Hegley, Kit Hollerbach, Jenny Lecoat, Helen Lederer, Norman Lovett, Pauline Melville, Nick Revell, Gerry Sadowitz and Alexei Sayle. Thanks are also due to Victoria Wood for 'Had it up to here with men', *Lucky Bag* and *Victoria Wood As Seen On TV*; to Rik Mayall for 'Theatre/Vanessa'; to Nigel Planer for 'Neil'; to Nigel Planer and Peter Richardson for 'AC-DC-10'; to Rik Mayall and Adrian Edmondson for 'Dangerous Brothers'; to Jim Barclay for *Four Minutes to Midnight*; to Dawn French and Jennifer Saunders for 'Psychodrama', *The Entertainers* and *French and Saunders*; to Ben Elton for 'Nudie Sunbathing', *Happy Families*, *Filthy Rich and Catflap* and *Saturday Live*; to Rik Mayall and Colin Gilbert for 'Kevin Turvey'; to Rik Mayall, Ben Elton and Lise Mayer for *The Young Ones*; to Ben Elton and Richard Curtis for *Blackadder 2*; and to Lenny Henry and Kim Fuller for 'Delbert'. Dillie Keane's 'Radiating Love' and 'Whites Blues' are quoted by permission of Sweet 'n' Sour Songs Ltd; the extract from the Central Television series *Girls on Top*, produced in association with Witzend Productions and written by Dawn French, Jennifer Saunders and Ruby

Wax, is reproduced by permission. For the extracts from the *Comic Strip* films, thanks are due to Channel Four Television and: to Peter Richardson and Pete Richens for 'Five Go Mad in Dorset', 'Five Go Mad on Mescalin', 'Gino', 'The Supergrass' and 'Strike'; to Peter Richardson, Pete Richens and Rik Mayall for 'A Fistful of Travellers' Cheques'; to Adrian Edmondson for 'Bad News Tour' and 'Eddie Monsoon – a life'; to Peter Richardson and Keith Allen for 'The Bullshitters'; to Dawn French and Jennifer Saunders for 'Consuela'; and to Alexei Sayle, Pauline Melville and David Stafford for 'Didn't You Kill My Brother?'.

For the loan of audio and video tapes, special thanks are due to Jim Barclay, Ben Elton, Paul Jackson, Norman Lovett and particularly Nigel Planer; with thanks also to Tony Allen, Arnold Brown, Peter Copeland, Andy de la Tour, Sarah Fairburn, Simon Fanshawe, Jenny Lecoat, Helen Lederer, Nick Revell, Alexei Sayle, Geoffrey Strachan and Maureen Vincent; and thanks to John Hegley for the book of poems and John Dowie and Ben Elton for the LP's.

Finally, thanks are due to Helen Thomas for compiling the index, to Tim Smith for checking through the typescript, and to Peter Copeland for research assistance and criticism of the typescript as it progressed.

Roger Wilmut
Peter Rosengard
December 1988

For permission to reproduce photographs, thanks to Peter Rosengard (pp. xx and 7), The Richard Stone Partnership (pp. 19, 123 and 208), Linda Sayle (pp. *i*, 25, 51 and 268), William Alford (pp. 26, 31, 33, 72, 120, 143, 156, 159, 201, 206, 225, 227 and 231), Andy de la Tour (p. 39), Lindsay Cameron (pp. 43 and 265), Trevor Rogers (p. 64), Christopher Pearce Photography (p. 60), Garry Hunter (p. 59), London Weekend Television (pp. 69, 84, 129, 194/5, 234 and 249), Lee Cornes (p. 82), Tony de Meur (p. 89), Ben Elton (p. 92), BBC Television (Frontispiece and pp. 96, 102, 162, 163, 166, 169, 188 (top and bottom), 191, 240, 245 and 252), Channel Four Television (pp. 110, 113, 114, 127, 136, 148, 149, 150, 153, 175, 176, 179 (top and bottom), 181, 182, 257, 258, 263 (top and bottom) and 277), Simon Fanshawe/Jenny Lecoat (p. 133), Ian MacQuillan (p. 140),

Central Television (p. 173), Noel Gay Artists Limited (p. 184), Paul Fulton (p. 202), Malcolm Hardee (p. 212), Maria Kempinska (p. 221), Rick Rogers, Pavilion Books (p. 278) and Time Out Magazine (p. 78).

The publishers have made every effort to trace all copyright holders; apologies are due for any errors or omissions in the credits, which, if they come to light, will be corrected in future editions.

Introduction: An alternative to what?

'Alternative Comedy' is a phrase that few of those involved in that area of comedy in Britain seem to like. The other journalistic label – 'New Wave Comedy' – is not much more popular. One of the problems with the first label is that it lends itself to the jibe that the style is an alternative *to* comedy, at least from those who do not appreciate it; but if labelling an area of comedy is to be done at all, this label is perhaps as good as any.

Certainly the style is an alternative to the bland prolefeed of the situation comedies which form the staple diet of television entertainment; and its exponents themselves see it as a rejection of the easy techniques of racist or sexist jokes on which so many mainstream television and club comics rely. In this they share common ground with the best comics in any tradition, who have always managed to avoid the easy but offensive laugh.

But in another way, 'alternative' comedy is simply a rejection of the preceding fashions in comedy – just as each new generation of comics has sought to build their own style rather than stay in the well-established mould. In this sense the latest generation of comics, who came to prominence in the early 1980s, can be seen as another stage in the continuing story of British comedy since the birth of widespread and organized popular entertainment in the form of the Victorian music-hall.

The early music-hall had a strong tradition of social satire; it portrayed, often with considerable sharpness, the real lives of ordinary people. Only as, very gradually, the halls became 'respectable' was this style replaced by a blander and less challenging sort of humour; but by the end of the First World War the evolution of music-hall into variety – a purely theatrical entertainment, rather than an adjunct to food and drink, and with the comic emphasis on nonsense rather than social realism – was complete, and set the style which held for twenty years.

The agent of the next change was the Second World War; a whole new generation of performers arose in the entertainments organized by the armed forces from their own ranks – the Forces Gang Shows, for example, which provided a training-ground for so many of the comedians of the 1950s. With the return to peace, these comics came to dominate the entertainment profession, taking over from the tradition of variety. Their comedy was sharper and more pungent than that of the thirties; the finest and best remembered of them were the splendidly surrealistic creators of *The Goon Show* and Tony Hancock's superbly realistic comedy.

With the beginning of the 1960s came yet another cycle of comedy, dominated by the so-called 'Oxbridge Mafia', who had emerged from the student stage revues of Oxford and Cambridge and went on to dominate radio and television comedy for the next twenty years. The watershed had come with *Beyond The Fringe* in 1960, which established techniques of comedy including direct political satire, hitherto unheard of on the stage or television; it also killed London stage revue for the next twenty years. Of all these shows, *Monty Python's Flying Circus*, which did for (or to) television what the Goons had done for radio, left a legacy of comic brilliance coupled with extremism of approach which was a hard act to follow.

By the end of the 1970s this generation of comic performers had begun to move away from stage, radio and television into other fields, leaving something of a vacuum which came to be filled by the latest wave of young comedians. Though widely divergent in style, approach, and indeed quality, they shared a rejection of most of what had gone before – not only the sexist and racist element already mentioned, but also the erudite middle-class approach of the university wits.

The main concern of the new comics was life as it was experienced by their audiences – many of them young, radical, working-class . . . and perhaps also unemployed and somewhat disenchanted. Political satire was an important part of their style, but usually looking at the way the behaviour of the government directly affected the lives of the audience, especially in terms of the then rapidly rising unemployment and increasing poverty among young people in particular.

Since their comedy not only commented directly on the experiences of the underprivileged, but was also performed in pubs, clubs and small cabarets rather than to well-to-do audiences in theatres, the new generation of comics was in many ways returning to the beginning of music-hall. However, their immediate descent was not from music-hall and variety (both long since dead), but more from the continuing tradition of rock concerts which had built up since the emergence of rock-and-roll in the 1950s; indeed some of them started their careers filling out rock concerts with a little comic relief. Because of this link, they picked up some of the terminology of musicians; two terms in particular will recur throughout this book –

'gig', for a particular event, and 'set', originally meaning a group of musical numbers played without an intermission, but coming to mean any individual uninterrupted stand-up routine.

Although there were the small beginnings of alternative comedy in existence before 1979, the explosion of new comics emerged initially from one particular cabaret club, the Comedy Store, with the most interesting of them going on from there to inter-react and to work in cabarets, television and films. In order for this reaction to happen there had to be a catalyst; in this case in the unlikely form of Peter Rosengard (who can accurately be accused of being a catalyst in the strict chemical sense of something which enables a reaction to take place while itself remaining unchanged). Though Rosengard had nothing to do with the entertainment world, and indeed had no experience of performing even on an amateur level, he provided the conditions under which this particular new generation of comics could appear.

Just as he kicked off the new wave in comedy, so Peter Rosengard kicks off this book with his own first-hand story of the beginnings of the Comedy Store – how it came to happen, and the chaotic and heady early days when a new and exciting form of comedy was being unleashed. He takes his narrative to the point where, in 1981, he severed his connection with the club. Roger Wilmut then takes up the story, examining the spilling out into the outside world of the performers who made up *The Comic Strip Presents ...*, *The Young Ones* and other television programmes, and the rise of the now well-established cabaret circuit in pubs and other venues in London and elsewhere.

It is a rather sprawling subject, and in the nature of things the narrative cannot be strictly chronological; sometimes a particular subject will be followed for a while along its own time-path before the story moves back a little to follow some other aspect. It has also not been possible to mention every single performer on the new cabaret circuit – there are after all probably about a couple of hundred people in the business, and the population is ever-changing as new people come in and others give up and fade away; so the book attempts to look at the most interesting figures, particularly those who have been established for a reasonable period of time. Their own stories and viewpoints – often told in their own words – are illustrated with excerpts from their acts, although since most performers' material is constantly if slowly changing, what is quoted is, of necessity, one frozen moment out of a changing reality.

Peter Rosengard was an unlikely person to start all this off. He was born in 1946, as Peter Rose, reverting to the original family name of Rosengard in the early 1970s. His early career was somewhat chequered; abandoning a course at London University Dental School, he found himself working for a bubble-bath company. He left when they transferred him to the mothball department. He spent three months working for a company which had developed a prototype for bank cash-dispensing machines (his job was to try to find ways to break into them); then in June 1967 he went to Israel as a volunteer for the 'six-day' Arab-Israeli war. Fortunately for him it was almost over by the time he got there, and after a period picking peaches and washing dishes on a kibbutz he returned to England, working as the assistant to the managing director of a pram factory in Altrincham. Sacked for extending his weekends in London, he capitalized on a long-standing fascination for clubs and discos by becoming a disc-jockey in Soho's au-pair mecca, 'Die Fledermaus' club. He admits to having been a terrible DJ, and was sacked for scratching the records. He then went to Sweden and spent a year as a dish-washer-cum-disc-jockey; fed up with sleeping on floors during a Swedish winter he returned to England in early 1969, taking up a job as a life assurance salesman. This seems to have been his niche, because he was successful at it and has stuck to it ever since – once he created a world record by selling a hundred life policies within one month.

(He has found time for digressions as well; in 1984, while eating a pizza in Kings Road, Chelsea, he asked the barman the name of a song being played; it was a demo tape, and he was pointed in the direction of the four young men who had brought it in. Within five minutes he had persuaded them that a) he should be their manager and b) they should change their name to Curiosity Killed The Cat, the name of the song he'd just heard. In 1987 they had three top ten hits, a number one album, and sold over a million records worldwide.)

It was, however, Rosengard's life-long love of comedy, together with an entrepreneurial streak, which led him to open the Comedy Store in 1979 as a venue for aspiring comedians. The whole story of its inception and huge success is a comic epic in itself, and a strange beginning to a number of careers. Although it is perfectly possible that those involved would have eventually found their way into professional performing through the application of their own talents, it is unlikely that they would have formed quite the combinations they did, sparking off each other to produce some of the best comedy of the 1980s. What made it all possible was not only Peter Rosengard's entrepreneurial drive, but also his self-confessed innocence and inexperience in dealing with the volatile world of performers. As the (theatrical) angel who rushed in where fools fear to tread, he achieved the near-impossible; anyone with any experience of the theatre, clubs, cabaret or comedy would have known better than to attempt such an idea – common sense would have prevailed, and nothing would have happened. Without Peter's naïvety London would never have had a *Comedy Store*, and there might just never have been *The Young Ones, The Comic Strip Presents..., Saturday Live, French and Saunders, Alexei Sayle's Stuff*, and all the other manifestations that grew out of it. And that would have been a pity.

Peter Rosengard
in 1979 . . .

and in 1989

Part One
'GONG!!'
by Peter Rosengard

In 1978 I went on holiday to Los Angeles. One hour after arriving, I'd decided I would like to leave London and live there. I looked up an estate agent in the Yellow Pages and twenty minutes later I was up in the Hollywood hills being shown round a series of beautiful sun-drenched, pool-sided, Jacuzzi-integrated, astro-turfed, three-bedroomed, six-bathroomed homes by a certain Morty ('please call me Mad-Dog') Weinberg.

'Mad-Dog' Weinberg was definitely not one of the pin-stripe, public-school brigade of London estate agents. This became even more apparent when around 5 pm and some half a dozen increasingly palatial homes later ('You just push this little button, Peter, and the whole roof slides off...') he said he was sorry but he had to go as he was auditioning at the Comedy Store club later that evening and had to rehearse his act. I thought this was really unusual because in England you just didn't meet estate agents who were also stand-up comedians.

The next night we asked the hotel porter to recommend somewhere that would be fun to visit and he asked if we had been to the Comedy Store. So we went along. The compère introduced the acts – all young comedians – one after the other, each performing for about ten minutes, like a comedy conveyor belt. They were great and I had never laughed so much in my life. I had never been to a comedy club in London. In the late seventies there wasn't one. Where did you go to laugh in London? I'd spent too much time going to discothèques over the years and I was fed up with the sight of the 'cool' – i.e. miserable-looking – posers. I couldn't even remember ever having seen anyone laugh in a disco. (I'd never been 'cool' myself, even for a minute, as I could never say 'yeah man ...' with the right lack of enthusiasm.)

I had always loved comedians. My father is a doctor, a Hebrew Highlander from Glasgow. His grandfather's family were gentle Jewish fisherfolk from Poland who'd set sail for California in the 1890s and by faulty navigation had landed up in Glasgow. My father came south after the war, with his war wound – a vivid scar running the length of his arm (a lorry overturned on a sand dune in Syria

1

and everybody inside was thrown out, landing on top of him, their Medical Officer). He settled as a family GP in East Acton, West London – not exactly a centre of Talmudic learning. Our synagogue in Ealing was a converted church. We were very liberal Jews. My father was a great joke teller and would always be surrounded at family parties by groups of laughing men.

The only comedians I'd ever seen in England were on television. I'd grown up with Tony Hancock, Peter Cook and Dudley Moore, and later Monty Python. I was a big fan of Woody Allen, but I'd been too young to see Lenny Bruce when he came to London to the Establishment Club in the early sixties. I had never liked the northern club comics and their mother-in-law jokes on TV. After years of Benny Hill I'd had enough of *double entendre* jokes to last a lifetime.

The young comics that night at the Comedy Store in Los Angeles were doing really creative, intelligent comedy and I loved it. When we left the club, I said 'I must open a place like that in London so I can have a place to go to laugh in.'

When I got back I found the Nell Gwynne Club as my venue, through somebody who knew somebody who knew Don Ward, who ran the club together with a downstairs room called the Gargoyle. When we met I explained that I wanted to open a Comedy Club like the Comedy Store in Los Angeles. He had also heard of it and amazingly had once been a professional comic himself. He liked the idea and said I could use his premises on a Saturday night. The Gargoyle club's members were mostly businessmen who were only in town during the week and so he closed at weekends. It was perfect. We shook hands on the spot. I would find the comedians and promote and put on the shows and he would supply the premises, drinks and staff. I had already decided to start off with a Saturday and Sunday night only and see how it went from there.

The Gargoyle had opened as the Blue Room in 1926 and was one of London's oldest night clubs. At that time it was a favourite watering hole of the Prince of Wales. There was a mural by Matisse, who had also designed the beautiful staircase which led down into the club. The room itself was L-shaped and intimate, with a stage at one end and two raised tiers with tables and little gilt chairs, around a tiny dance floor. Walking down the stairs into it for the first time was like stepping back into the thirties, slightly faded but unchanged. Unlike most night clubs, which are usually in basements, the Gargoyle was three floors up and could only be entered by taking a tiny lift into which two people could be wedged face to face. You had to take the lift to the fourth floor, which housed the Nell Gwynne strip club, walk through their topless waitress bar and then down

Matisse's staircase to the Gargoyle. It gave a new meaning to the phrase 'hidden away'.

As a self-proclaimed promoter of non-sexist comedy, I was to have a bit of trouble explaining away the topless barmaids to some of the aspiring comedians when they started coming to audition. 'Look, they definitely won't be there when we open. They are nothing to do with me, really, they belong to the strip club, and it's closed when we're open,' I blustered. I soon found out that Don Ward had other ideas, but after several heated discussions, during which I attempted to point out to him that the tits in question could seriously get in the way of any credibility we might stand a chance of having as pioneers of a new kind of comedy, he finally agreed that the contentious boobs could disappear into the new Comedy Store T-shirts I'd had made up, but only after midnight, when we opened. A lot of people thought I was crazy to open there. 'Who wants to go to Soho at midnight on a Saturday to a sleazy strip joint to watch a bunch of amateur comics?'

So it's February 1979 and I am sitting in an empty strip club in Dean Street, Soho. It's six o'clock in the evening and I've been waiting there for an hour for 'any aspiring comedians, comedians or frustrated dentists' who had read my one-line ads in *Private Eye* or *The Stage* to turn up to audition for my new comedy club which, I had announced at a press conference a week earlier, would be opening in April. This was the first time I had done anything like this. I wasn't in 'showbiz'. I was a thirty-three-year-old life assurance salesman. I had been selling life assurance ever since performing the one heroic act of my life, walking out of dental school because I discovered I didn't like teeth.

I had been sitting in the Nell Gwynne strip club every evening after work for nearly a month, waiting for an English Lenny Bruce or Woody Allen to walk in, and I was still waiting. My first mistake had been to put my ad in *The Stage*. I'd been besieged by every out-of-work Butlins Redcoat in Britain, as well as by everybody who wanted to be a Redcoat. Also a lot of semi-pro northern club comics sent me their glossy ten by eight photos (Kenny 'Cheekie Chappie' Smith), together with their own ads ('Dougal Donovan is back from his sensational tour of South Africa and the Far East and has some unexpected dates free before his annual summer season on the Cunard Princess').

The *Evening News* had run a story about the club and now a lot of people were turning up whose wives or girlfriends had said to them, 'Go on John . . . you tell some terrific jokes down the pub . . . you're really funny after eight or ten pints.' It seemed as if almost everybody wanted to be a comedian, although I don't think an estate agent ever turned up. Chauffeurs, builders, labourers, policemen, bank clerks. They were all terrible, but I didn't know that you didn't applaud at auditions and after every act I would clap enthusiastically. I started having nightmares about an opening night's show composed entirely of these people one after the other, an endless stream of unfunny people, hundreds and hundreds of them stretching off the stage into the distance ... before a silent, appalled audience.

One morning I auditioned someone at my insurance office in the sales training room. His name was Lee Cornes and he was the first aspiring comedian I'd met who actually did look funny. He reminded me of Marty Feldman with his crossed staring eyes and a slightly manic manner. He did two mime sketches. The first was a surgeon performing an operation who removed every possible organ except the one he was meant to take out. In the other he finished up foaming at the mouth with rabies and at that moment my boss put his head round the door. 'This is Lee,' I said. 'He's thinking of joining us, aren't you, Lee?'

He'd made me laugh for the first time since I'd embarked on what was increasingly seeming to be a hopeless enterprise. If England was full of brilliant undiscovered young comedians, they were certainly doing a good job at remaining undiscovered. I told Lee he was booked for the opening night and not to leave the country without telling me! As the day of the opening came closer and closer, the auditions were getting worse and worse and I realized that there were very few more depressing experiences than sitting in an empty strip club watching unfunny people, most of whom thought they were hilarious.

The procession was sometimes enlivened by the odd 'speciality' act – the sixty-year-old housewife who sang, 'I'm Only a Bird in a Gilded Cage' with her head in a bird cage. She followed it up after a quick change with 'Any Old Iron' in a dress with bits of iron and lumps of metal hanging from it. Then there was the man who called me about his saxophone act. He played 'I'm Forever Blowing Bubbles' whilst sitting at the bottom of a glass tank full of water. He didn't manage to audition because he couldn't get his tank into the lift. I've always thought that was a shame.

One Thursday evening in March, having sat through another dozen terrible acts with a frozen smile on my face, although I'd stopped applauding by this time, there was only one person left to get up on stage and then I could thankfully go home. He was a stocky, tough-looking young man in a leather jacket with a Liverpool accent. He'd seen my ad in *Private Eye*. His name was Alexei

Sayle and five minutes later, after a brilliantly surreal and hilarious monologue involving a violent encounter in a cake shop, I knew I'd found my compère. Even if he had to introduce twenty-two of the world's worst comedians, I would definitely be opening as planned.

I'd always known the choice of compère would be crucial to the success of the club. I knew that I didn't want a traditional compère of the: 'A big hand, ladies and gentlemen, for the tremendously talented...' type. More the: 'Well, that was John, taking another giant step from mediocrity to obscurity' school was what I was looking for. I instinctively knew that I'd found him in Alexei Sayle. Physically he reminded me of John Belushi from the American TV series *Saturday Night Live* – one of the most brilliant of the new young comedians whose work I admired.

As the opening night loomed up we were joined by Arnold Brown. He was a forty-year-old Scottish Jewish accountant working in the rag trade in London, and of course he wanted to be a comedian. 'Why not?' he would ask – the question was soon to become his catchphrase. He was so incredibly nervous and hesitant on stage that it was difficult to know whose ordeal would be the greater – his or the audience's. However, he had a very original way of looking at life, and he'd head off in the direction of being funny, unfortunately mostly never quite making it. But he took the while thing extremely seriously and would spend hours agonizing over every word.

I'd sent out over three hundred invitations to the first-night party on 19 May 1979. The club was only licensed to hold a maximum of 120 people, but I was told that most people probably wouldn't want to come. They all did and it was packed. We had stocked up with an enormous quantity of champagne and a terrific buffet. I had invited the press and heads of all the major television companies. A TV crew from the BBC *Nationwide* programme and several radio reporters came. There was a lot of excitement and anticipation as everybody waited to see these great new comedians I had discovered.

I was extremely nervous and was rushing about trying to marshal my twenty-five 'comedians' – and I use the inverted commas advisedly – into some kind of running order. I had asked them to wait in the kitchen. The dressing-room was even smaller than the tiny lift, but most of them seemed to have joined the party and I kept grabbing them and pushing them back into the kitchen. They seemed to have been enjoying the champagne rather too much. Ian Hale, a civil servant from Hanwell, arrived at the last minute with his bicycle clips still on, hauling a huge suitcase full of props that I never saw him use in his act. He bore an unnerving resemblance to Norman Wisdom.

So my motley bunch of chauffeurs, builders, labourers, housewives with bird cages on their heads, and one accountant prepared for – in nearly all cases – their first ever public performance before the cream of Britain's entertainment industry, most of whom seemed to be getting pissed out of their brains. Earlier in the evening I had realized that I hadn't got a spotlight to flash on and off from the back of the club to signal the comedians that they should wind up their act and get off stage. Somebody had told me that comedians will never leave the stage willingly and the spotlight was how they did it in the Californian clubs.

I had asked my friend, Ashley 'Billy the Kid' Roy, to pop out to a hire shop and rent one for the night. He arrived back, just before the first guests were arriving, with what looked like the gong from Rank films. It was at least three feet across and hung from a solid wooden frame. A massive gong stick came with it. 'What the hell is that?' I asked. 'They didn't have a spotlight, so I got this,' Billy said. 'We can just tap it gently and then they'll know it's time to go.' It was too late to change it, so we set it up on the side of the stage.

The audience, who were sitting, standing, shouting and drinking champagne from the bottle, were getting very impatient. I could tell that because they'd started to chant 'Why are we waiting?' and stamp their feet. The whole place was like a matchbox waiting to be lit. Sweating profusely, fearing some of the worst comedy ever was about to be performed, I reluctantly told an unnaturally relaxed Alexei to start the show.

The comics never stood a chance. The first one had hardly been on for two minutes before somebody shouted, 'Get him off.' Then the rest of the audience joined in and the poor man on stage, a look of terror in his eyes, was totally thrown and seemed about to cry. I gestured desperately to Billy to tap the gong. A deafening 'Gong' rang out. It was almost as if Big Ben were in the room. The first victim, I mean comedian, slunk from the stage. Alexei brought on the next one. He didn't fare any better. 'Good evening, ladies and gentlemen' is a strange line to finish on. This time somebody shouted 'Gong, gong!' and Billy hit the gong again. It seemed impossible to strike it so that it rang softly, and now everybody seemed to join in, yelling 'Gong him! Gong him!' Things were not going well. They were like cannon fodder, one after the other, on, off, on, off. At the rate we were going the whole twenty-five would have been on and off in fifteen minutes. It was a comedy massacre. The *Guardian* journalist, Tom Tickell, was there to perform and then write about it in the next morning's paper. (Ironically he was the *Guardian*'s insurance reporter.) He lasted longer than most of the others – about three minutes.

A huge American restaurateur called Bob Payton was helping Alexei out as compère during the night. I'd met him when I was searching for venues a couple of months earlier. He was just about to open his first restaurant, the Chicago Pizza Pie Factory, and had somehow persuaded me it would be very funny if he came along and read out his old High School book to the audience. Why not?, I now thought, as he proceeded to do just that to the incredulous mob. It was a crazy night. Amazingly, nobody appeared to be walking out. In fact they seemed to be having a great time! Unfortunately, as far as I was concerned, for all the wrong reasons. Alexei was, however, a terrific success, handling comedians and audience alike with equal contempt, whilst unleashing his manically threatening stream of violent invective at both parties throughout the evening. Without him it would have been a total disaster. Finally we ran out of comedians and champagne and Alexei threw everybody out into a deserted Soho. It was 3 am and had been quite a night. Shattered, and suffering from acute nervous exhaustion, I drove home.

Tom Tickell's column the next morning accurately captured the night's events. 'All Rosengard has to do now to make the Comedy Store a success is find some comedians.' So what else was new? Probably the only thing that saved us over the next three or four months was the fact that we were only open on Saturday and Sunday nights. We were one of the first of the new 'one-nighter' clubs that were to revitalize London's night life over the next five years. Most of the old discos had found the going very tough in the late seventies, after the *Saturday Night Fever* mania had run out of steam. Then along came punk, and kids were going to live gigs again. Many of the clubs were empty throughout the week, surviving only on their traditional Saturday night business. Now a new breed of young entrepreneurs were approaching the disco owners and telling them they could fill their clubs for one night every week, giving it a new name and identity for the night, taking the door money and leaving the club owner to keep the bar revenue.

It was difficult enough to find a dozen people to perform for two nights, let alone six nights a week! To my amazement we got some good write-ups over the first few weeks and people turned up for the shows. But every night I was worried that either no comedians would show up or no audience. Sometimes the audiences were outnumbered by the comedians. It was touch and go for the first few months whether we could make it. In 1979 Soho wasn't the hip area it became five years later. When the Comedy Store opened, it was still full of porno cinema clubs, rip-off bars and girlie magazine shops.

I kept trying to get well-known comedians to come down to try out new material, but their agents weren't very enthusiastic. Jasper Carrott and Billy Connolly never came down. Rowan Atkinson promised to, but got lost and went into a sauna massage parlour by accident, asked if it was the Comedy Store, got punched in the stomach, was sick and went home. Les Dawson was an exception. He performed a couple of times and was very well received, even though his first act was very different from the type of comedy the young audience was expecting. But he is a very funny man. Lenny Bennett came once, was heckled, and sneered, 'Listen, luv, when I drive home in my Rolls Royce, you'll be standing in the rain waiting for the bus.' Alexei gonged him off. 'I'm not a violent person, but I keep being provoked,' said Alexei.

We managed to survive the summer and then some new and very funny people started to appear. Tony Allen, Jim Barclay and Andy de la Tour all turned up at about the same time. Tony had been running an alternative cabaret at the Elgin pub in Maida Vale. Soon we had a nucleus of half a dozen regulars who were tremendous. Within six months they were joined by two brilliant double-acts, Twentieth Century Coyote (Rik Mayall and Ade Edmondson) and The Outer Limits (Peter Richardson and Nigel Planer). The place was now packed every weekend, by word of mouth, and stayed like that, with people queuing round the block to get in hours before we opened. We didn't have to advertise any more. The press loved the place and a steady stream of rave reviews appeared. It became the most talked about club in London, the 'hottest place in town'.

The audience was young, early twenties to early thirties, and from all walks of life – students to dockers, lords to dustmen. Everybody had to queue, even if they were celebrities who thought they should just walk to the front. There was always an electric atmosphere in the club before the midnight show. People were crammed in everywhere, almost hanging from the ceiling. The first tables were set up only six inches from the front of the stage. The audience never knew who was going to show up to perform and I was never sure either. One night I didn't go for the first time since we'd opened almost a year earlier and the American comedian Robin Williams walked in and did an hour of incredible comedy. I was his number one fan and I missed him. I'd followed his career since he'd been in *Mork and Mindy* on TV and for me he was one of the top two or three comedians in the world. The next Saturday he came again and did another hour of brilliance. It was the first time he had ever performed in England.

I had an audience spot at the end of every show where anybody could get up and perform for five minutes, and every week there were three or four people trying out – although sometimes it was just to tell their only joke. After some months I couldn't stand the stress of hoping the comedians would just drop in, so I started booking them a week ahead.

Very early on I realized two very important things were helping our success. Firstly, it was OK – in fact it was essential – to have very bad performers along with the few good ones, not only to fill the show out to at least two to two and a half hours, but also because I noticed the audience took a perverse pleasure in watching the people who were hopelessly and embarrassingly bad. Secondly, the gong. From the first night when the audience had screamed 'Gong!' I had realized that it was a great audience participation device, and it soon became enshrined in the Comedy Store legend: 'Have you been to the club with the gong?' In much the same way that the early music-halls had a man with a shepherd's crook pulling the unwilling performer from the stage, the gong was our shepherd's crook. We set it up on the stage and Alexei was the gong master. At the beginning of every show he would explain the rules to the audience. If you couldn't stand the comedian any more, you shouted 'Gong', and if there were enough people shouting 'Gong', a clear majority, then Alexei would strike the gong and the comedian had to leave immediately. This was the Christians versus the lions all over again and it had to be the toughest club in the world to play. If you could survive the gong at the Comedy Store, you could definitely play anywhere. Incredibly, the comedians kept coming back for more, and so did the audiences.

One night in early 1980 during the 2 am audience spot, a short stocky young man with a severely cropped haircut got up and unleashed a blisteringly aggressive monologue of surreal brilliance on the packed room. Alternating between seemingly being on the edge of violence and an icy calm, he gripped everybody with his mesmeric presence. Driven by an 'intense hatred of Max Bygraves', Keith Allen performed many more times over the next year – becoming a Comedy Store legend within weeks of his arrival. Always unpredictable, he didn't seem to care whether he was funny or not, but when he was on stage there was always an air of danger that was unique. Once David Hancock of the *Evening Standard* came to see him. Keith turned the fire extinguisher on him. Undeterred, Hancock came back for more the following Saturday.

In autumn 1980 Ben Elton came down from Manchester University, and by early 1981 had joined earlier Manchester graduates Rik Mayall and Ade Edmondson at the Store. He soon became one of the regular compères. His super-fast aggressive hectoring delivery combined with prolific writing ability quickly made him one of the most popular acts.

From the beginning I'd based the club on the original Store in Los Angeles where the idea was for it to be both a showcase for new talent and a place for professional comics to drop in to try out new material. None of the performers got paid, although I was very tempted to charge some of them! Alexei as the compère got £5 a show. I had hoped that agents, TV producers and journalists would regularly come to discover new people. This didn't happen. The showbiz establishment regarded us as a threat. They didn't see any wider audience for a bunch of foul-mouthed amateurs. TV was out of the question. So they didn't come down. One exception was a young BBC TV producer called Paul Jackson.

It took us almost a year just to get back the cost of the opening party! One of the biggest start-up expenses had been the enormous perspex signs I had had made up bearing the club's logo – a huge laughing mouth. Before each show we would hang the signs over the strip club ones. Occasionally the strip club members would still turn up and find themselves sitting through two hours of comedy, waiting for the girls to come on. This usually led to demands for a refund of their £4 entry fee.

At the pre-opening press conference a year earlier I had been asked whether there would be any censorship. I had replied that 'anything went' – as long as it wasn't racist or sexist! Of course almost immediately the audiences decided for themselves what they wanted to hear and the gong became the ultimate censor. Heckling was a phenomenon of the Store from the start, veering wildly between being funnier than the comic on stage or just drunken abuse of the 'Why don't you Fuck Off?' variety. 'It's the kind of place where even the bouncers heckle,' read one article. Actually we never needed any bouncers, but we did have Joe, our seventy-two-year-old doorman. A forty-year Soho veteran, Joe was both immaculate in dinner jacket and bow tie, and unfailingly courteous to the queues waiting to get into our tiny lift.

We only once had a fight and that was when Andy de la Tour decided to explore the doubtful comic potential to be found in a discussion of a TV programme on Auschwitz. A group of National Front-type skinheads who had found their way in suggested, 'They should have gassed more of them.' They were standing next to a large group of North London Jewish kids and a tremendous punch-up followed. The police arrived and broke it up but seemed mainly interested in warning me about a 'sweet sickly smell' they had observed in the club atmosphere!

11

At the end of the first year I decided to do an act myself, liberally 'borrowing' a few lines from American comics I'd seen in the New York comedy clubs. I attempted to talk about premature ejaculation for ten minutes. It wasn't possible and I was gonged off in record time. I kept trying and finally beat the gong. But the general consensus amongst the comics was, 'Don't give up the daytime job, Peter.'

After about a year, Peter Richardson wanted to do an early evening show five times a week featuring the best of the Store's acts, but it would have interfered with the operation of the Nell Gwynne, and Don turned him down. Richardson went round the corner to Paul Raymond – who had been along to the Store – and started the Comic Strip shows at the Boulevard Theatre, which gave them a whole new audience at 8 pm of people who didn't want to come to Soho at midnight on a Saturday.

Within a few months of opening the Comedy Store I'd felt that we were doing for comedy what the Sex Pistols had done for rock 'n' roll. Now nearly ten years later I think that perhaps for six months in 1980 it was true. It certainly beat selling life assurance! Being a stand-up comedian is one of the world's toughest jobs. Before I'd opened in May 1979 I had a poster printed that I stuck up on walls all over Soho. It read, 'What's the difference between Sky Diving and appearing at the Comedy Store?' Answer: 'In Sky Diving you can only die once.'

When I was a teenager whichever Saturday night party I was at, I always felt there must be a better party going on somewhere else. For a period of about a year in 1979 to 1980 for a lot of people the Comedy Store was that somewhere else.

Part Two

'HEAVE!!'

by Roger Wilmut

'It's shifted the mainstream a little bit –
but to move the mainstream just a little bit
you have to get over there and go *HEAVE*!!,
and I think that's what we did.'

Tony Allen

B.C. (before Comedy Store); early Comedy Store

1

Although the Comedy Store was the most important springboard for so much later comedy, there was indeed a certain amount of life before Rosengard . . . a small handful of performers were pioneering the return of live comedy on stage, despite the absence of suitable venues or any form of organization.

The most influential of them all was, of course, Billy Connolly, although in many ways he belongs to a different stream of comedy and has never really been associated with the alternative comedy movement. Starting as a folk singer on the rudimentary folk circuit – mostly cellars in pubs – he began to introduce monologues into his act and developed a strongly personal style in which, because he was not dependent on television or the now defunct variety circuit (and its family audiences), he could be as outspoken as he wished. In a sense it was his progression into the larger concert venues around the country which paved the way for the later tours of people such as Alexei Sayle, Rik Mayall and Ben Elton, who came out of the Comedy Store.

One of the most intriguing aspects of Connolly's career is how widely known he had become even by the end of the 1970s. The impression remains that he must have done a fair amount of television, but in fact it was just one appearance on Michael Parkinson's chat show that established him in the public eye; the impact of his boisterous personality and relatively outrageous material was stunning in the context of the bland TV production line.

Even without the Parkinson appearance Connolly had built up a large following, which allowed him to play the larger venues which normally handled folk or rock concerts; but for other new comedians in the 1970s there was hardly anywhere at all to perform. The old variety theatres were almost all gone, and the only other organized area of live performance was the northern 'working men's' club circuit – which, though well established and with its own circle of performers, was totally unsuitable for the newer generation of more intelligent and sensitive artists. The club audiences wanted their shows loud and filthy – in the contemptuous words of Dennis Main Wilson, one of radio and TV's most experienced comedy producers, 'tit, bum and wee-wee jokes'. A very small number of club performers had made it on to television, and it was precisely their style – usually racist and sexist (though few performers had yet really begun to think about the implications of this) – against which the leading Comedy Store performers later revolted.

For those trying to start a comic career it was only barely possible to find places to perform – little arts centres, universities, tiny fringe theatres, the Edinburgh Festival fringe – where the audiences were more sympathetic. The two most important people working in solo comedy in this embryonic circuit were both to be influential, but not as part of the main alternative comedy scene. The first, John Dowie, has always dissociated himself from the cabaret circuit which grew up in pubs and fringe theatres in the years following the opening of Comedy Store, dismissing it as 'standing up pretending to be more stupid than you actually are'.

Dowie was born on 8 August 1950. He went to Sparkhill Commercial School, near Birmingham, which did mainly secretarial courses; however he did take part in school dramas and, more importantly, was able to write comic material – in French. He remembers: 'I used to try and write things that were funny instead of writing essays – depending on the teacher, obviously. My French teacher said I could write about anything I liked; he didn't mind if it was funny, as long as it was in French.'

After leaving school he worked in the paperback department of W. H. Smith, and then in an office job. 'I wasn't quite sure what I wanted to do, but I knew it had something to do with writing and something to do with performing, and I could only think of writing as writing, or of being an actor. Then I saw Spike Milligan in *The Bed-Sitting Room* when I was sixteen or seventeen – that was very exciting.'

He took a part-time job and started writing, eventually putting on small shows with friends in a Birmingham arts centre, moving gradually into doing one-man shows: 'I used to do them very sporadically – write one, do it, not like it very much, write another one, and three or four months later do that ... until about 1972, then I went up to Edinburgh, and started doing it more or less full time after that.'

Performing in smaller venues – church halls and the like – on the so-called 'fringe' of the Edinburgh Arts Festival each August had long been a tradition with revue groups especially from the universities. In the sixties and seventies many alternative comedians would also play at Edinburgh solo or in groups. Dowie's Edinburgh show was about an hour, made up of the best of his material up to that time – the first time he had ever performed for three weeks continuously. Putting together an act of such a length is always a difficult undertaking, and the more so at this early period when there were no other performers to compare notes with: 'When I decided I was going to be a stand-up comedian the only alternatives were either going to Oxford or Cambridge and going into revues – which was obviously beyond me – or else being Jasper Carrott [then coming up, like Connolly before him, in the folk circuit], which I didn't particularly want to be. And I couldn't play the guitar anyway – although that's never stopped *him*. And I knew I didn't want to be silly – it's not in my nature to be deliberately silly, though it does happen against my will from time to time. My only contemporaries were those touring as theatre groups. I was going round the same sorts of places they were playing, but as a "one-man show" – a very raw attempt at stand-up comedy. Nowadays it's very obviously me speaking – me saying "This happened to me the other day and I thought this about it. . . ." Then, it was "Wouldn't it be funny if . . . such and such a thing." It was all very light fantasy stuff.'

Dowie's material included parodies of folk singers, sketches which were half in French and half in English, fantasies: 'The Shakespearean School of Speech Defects and Dramatic Art used to get big laughs, which was all about actors with various speech impediments – and then I had a review in *Time Out* which pointed out that a lot of the laughs came from mocking people with speech impediments – which wasn't intentional, but I thought it was a valid point so I had to elbow that piece, which was a real drag because it was a very strong one.'

As the 1970s went on he developed his style, working in the unsatisfactory venues available – the worst being cabaret spots at student balls, when he would be booked to go on at two in the morning to a half-drunken audience who only wanted him to stop so that they could have the disco back on. In 1976 – around the time of the explosion of punk rock – he started working with a small band under the name of John Dowie and the Big Girl's Blouse: 'I used to – I wouldn't say "sing", but just do vocal things – it was only a three-piece rock band. I used to write a song and then the band would play it in the idiom of somebody; and then I started going into more issues. ... The band broke up because of a song I wrote called "Abortion" which used to depress the hell out of everybody. Especially the band. But it was like saying, just because it's funny doesn't mean to say it can't be heavy ... some of the stuff was a real slap in the face for the audience but you could still make them laugh. I started getting bored with the idea that comedy has to be kept within a framework of niceness.'

From this standpoint Dowie began to develop a style which was more a matter of his own observations on things – in the manner of much alternative comedy, putting his own personality in front of the audience. Although he would tend to deny it, many of the performers who came up in the following few years would regard him as influential. (His later style will be examined in Chapter 15.)

In 1978 Dowie did a short tour with another performer who was then in an early stage of her career, and would later become a major figure – Victoria Wood. She was acting as support to him, but he doubts if he influenced her in any way: 'I think she probably made up her mind to be rich and successful and famous and to get well away from people like me who have no audience.'

The audiences' response was varied. Sometimes one would go well, sometimes the other; but on one occasion when they both 'died' they developed a theory: 'When comedians die, they start sweating, and their eyes get bigger, and they start to talk faster and faster ... and they swear to make it funnier. None of these routines works – they make it worse. When you see a sweating bug-eyed lunatic screaming abuse at you from the stage, it doesn't endear him to the audience.'

Victoria Wood herself is dubious whether she should be regarded as 'alternative'; but she does apply many of the precepts of alternative comedy even though she has never worked the Comedy Store and, by the time the cabaret circuit was expanding, was already touring her own one-woman show.

She was born on 19 May 1953; after going to grammar school in Manchester she studied drama and theatre arts at Birmingham University, graduating in 1974. Having decided that she wanted to be an actress, she tried to get into drama school, but failed. However, she had been with a youth theatre for a time when she was at school, and had also taken up writing plays from an early age – and songs, which she never performed for anyone. She remembers: 'I had written several plays by the time I went to Birmingham – all nicks of Joe Orton, who was about the only person I'd ever read at the time. And then at university whenever they asked me to write an essay I always used to write a play instead. So I got a very bad degree, because I wasn't getting any marks for them. I didn't really take to the course very much because it was very academic, and I wanted to be doing things. There was a lot going on but I never got the parts – I wasn't considered to be very good, so I did a lot of stage management. I think they thought I didn't fit in – there were a lot of tall good-looking blonde girls and that was supposed to be the norm for an actress, and that put me off the idea of acting because I don't look like that. It was a good thing but at the time it was rather depressing.'

However, what was to turn out a more important career development for her had already taken place before she gained her degree. She had begun performing her songs occasionally and was spotted at a party by a BBC producer, after which she was asked to do an audition at the Birmingham Pebble Mill studios. This led to her being asked to write odd songs for various magazine programmes (seen only in the Midland region): 'It would be the reporter "going into" something or other, and I would write the song – about money, or food, or whatever – and they used to say it had to be two minutes ten seconds because that was the "perfect length". I found it very difficult to write a longer song than that for years. I don't think I was copying anybody's style at the time because I was very conceited – I never thought anyone else was worth bothering with. I never thought, "He's good, I want to be like him"; I thought, "He's dreadful, I'm not going to do that!" Which is why I was so hopeless for so many years, because I wouldn't copy anybody.'

She is scathing about her early work, feeling that she was pushed ahead too quickly; shortly after graduating she went on the TV talent show *New Faces* and won the first heat. She signed up with an agent – 'a mad band leader from Hove' – who turned down everything except TV work: 'So whenever I did work live, which was very rarely, I was diabolical because I'd had no experience. My idea of an act was to put together every song I'd written – about twelve songs, each two minutes ten seconds – and just sit there and play them. I didn't know how to walk on, how to say hello – I couldn't play the piano and look at the audience at the same time. I thought I was doing terribly well because I was in a TV show with Marti Caine and Lenny Henry – *The Summer Show* on ATV. It was dire, but I thought it was great because it was £120 a week. You don't learn anything in television – you only learn how to do television. Whereas the theatre teaches you everything. It wasn't until I started to do live work later that I ever got any better.'

17

From 1974 to 1978 she did mostly these odd TV appearances – including some on *That's Life*, which at least got her a wider audience than the Midlands – and then, while she was working with John Dowie, she was asked to be in a revue called *In At The Death* at the Bush Theatre (in London's Shepherd's Bush area), which was topical, being based on each week's news. The show got good reviews – and also enabled her to work with Julie Walters, whom she had met briefly some years earlier and who would later appear regularly in Wood's TV series. She then went on to write a play called *Talent*, about a girl and her fat friend who go in for a talent contest, which was bought by Granada Television. This was also staged at the Crucible Theatre, Sheffield, in November 1978, and she appeared in a late-night show there with her husband, a magician working as 'The Great Soprendo'; both shows later came to London – *Talent* in February 1979 at the ICA (Institute of Contemporary Arts) Theatre, and the late-night show, under the title *Funny Turns*, in October 1980 at the King's Head Theatre Club.

In 1979 she wrote a musical play, *Good Fun*, which featured a song that she used in her act for years – 'I've Had It Up To Here With Men'. 'It was about sex, and everybody used to think I was being really daring, and saying I didn't like sex, and so on – I couldn't be bothered to explain that it was just a song from a musical':

> ... No more nights of drinking
> Nodding, smiling, thinking,
> 'Jesus, when can I go home?'
> No more struggling in taxis
> In Vauxhalls, Imps and Maxis
> With stupid little bleeders
> With all the charming manners
> Of the average garden gnome.
>
> And when they're down to socks and grin
> You know it's time to get stuck in
> Full of self-congratulation
> They expect a combination
> Of Olga Korbut, Raquel Welch and Rin Tin Tin.
>
> I've not had an encounter yet
> That didn't leave me cold and wet
> I'd be happier, I know
> If we could only go
> From the foreplay
> Straight to the cigarette.

Victoria Wood's later career developed from her increased ability to handle stage appearances, and to fill out the songs with stand-up patter; we shall return to her in Chapter 8.

When Peter Rosengard's rush of blood to the head produced the Comedy Store in 1979, many of the performers who established themselves there came not from the small comedy circuit then struggling into life, but from the more established world of fringe theatre which had been going for some years, presenting plays whose range included the surrealistically fantastic and the radically political. The watershed for its development had come in 1968; perhaps the primary event of that year for political theatre – which made it possible at all – was the abolition of theatrical censorship. Up until then (and since 1843) the Lord Chamberlain's office had operated tight censorship on all public theatrical performances; originally intended to protect God and the Monarch from subversion, the censorship was applied firmly to 'smut', bad language, vulgarity, etc. – and political expression – even direct reference to political figures – was discouraged if not totally forbidden. After 1968 the only controls were the danger of prosecution for obscenity, so that political theatre could speak with a much freer voice. There was much in 1968 to speak about: the Soviet invasion of Czechoslovakia, the student revolts in Paris and elsewhere, the Vietnam War, the assassinations of Martin Luther King and Robert Kennedy, Enoch Powell's notorious 'rivers of blood' speech ... and in the following year British troops were ordered into Northern Ireland.

The range (and quality) of political theatre was very wide. At its worst it could be unsubtle, boring and – if trying to be funny – flat in the extreme. However, established authors such as John Arden also made their mark in the field. Arden, best known for his play *Serjeant Musgrave's Dance* – studied in universities and performed on television even while Arden's developing political stance in work written jointly with Margaretta D'Arcy estranged him from the theatrical establishment – wrote a number of strongly political fringe theatre plays, including one stormy collaboration with the company which is perhaps most significant in terms of the development of alternative comedy – CAST.

Standing for Cartoon Archetypical Slogan Theatre, CAST was formed in 1965 by Roland and Claire Muldoon as a breakaway from the long-established left-wing Unity Theatre. Muldoon trained as a technician at the Bristol Old Vic but didn't want to work in the mainstream theatre 'because of the bullshit'. He worked at the Unity Theatre, and was impressed by shows they did in an old-time music-hall format. Developing from this starting point, CAST toured folk clubs and small fringe theatres with a series of plays featuring various characters who were usually called Muggins – Harold Muggins, Hilda Muggins, Horatio Muggins, etc. – and which made their political points by the use of variety techniques. (The collaboration with John Arden and Margaretta D'Arcy produced *Harold Muggins is a Martyr* in 1968.) Roland Muldoon: 'What made us unique was that we had that variety attitude – we would play off the audience; we played directly, we kept in character but looked at the audience, and we made a deliberate attempt to adopt all the variety techniques in relation to the audience. This could mean we had to change the play when the audience didn't appreciate what was going on – improvising and changing and adapting was our most important thing.'

CAST got an Arts Council grant for ten years and started to build up a circuit. Realizing that they couldn't rely on arts centres (which were often unconcerned about getting audiences in), they began to work in small theatres and large pubs up and down the country: 'Travelling in the North we began to realize that they're not necessarily into theatre – you would be playing in a trade union centre for example and you could see there was going to be bingo another night; we could see that the real culture of the North was this bland type of northern entertainment, that increasingly shows like ours had to adapt more and more to comedy. If you were "fronting" a play in the North, and they didn't necessarily want to see it, the link character – playing directly to the audience – was like a cabaret or a comedian; you had to take them with you. So increasingly the Alexei Sayles and the Tony Allens and the Andy de la Tours, all those people learnt to front off Arts Council-funded type plays to audiences in order to be the link between the audience and the production. That's where the training came for Left comedy.'

It was from this sort of left-wing theatre that the first group of influential performers at the Comedy Store came, including Alexei Sayle, the first to give Peter Rosengard some real hope for his venture. Sayle was born in Liverpool on 7 August 1952; his father was a railway guard and his mother a pools clerk, but more significantly they were both members of the Communist Party. He remembers: 'It was a sort of a literate household – and also widely travelled; because my dad worked on the railway we got free travel and we used to go all over the place before people really went abroad. We went to Eastern Europe before anybody bothered going there. I used to swank about having been to Czechoslovakia.'

He went to grammar school, got expelled halfway through sixth form, did two years at Southport Art School and then studied painting at Chelsea Art School for three years. When he left, in 1974, he did a number of odd jobs for a time, including being a DHSS clerk for nine months. He also worked occasionally as a freelance illustrator – 'one of London's bottom ten'.

Then around 1976 a friend called Cliff Cocker wanted to start a theatrical troupe doing Brechtian cabaret. He and Sayle had been in a school play together, and Cocker asked Sayle to join the troupe, which was called Threepenny Theatre – in Sayle's opinion 'a terrible name. We had endless rehearsals – and terrible rows.... I played Brecht – I sat by the piano looking Brechtian, smoking a cigar and drinking whisky, wore a green leather jacket and did one poem. And joined in some of the ensembles. The thing that's often ignored about Brecht is that he was a very solid member of the Communist Party and took a very didactic party line in many ways – this is something that people try to gloss over. The thing about this production was that it was very Communist Party orientated, which in that sense was right.'

The show ran at The Factory, a fringe theatre in Paddington, for two weeks to very small audiences; they toured round colleges and Communist Party benefits – and then split up after a major row. Feeling that there were possibilities in comedy, Sayle and a couple of others put together a one-hour show with sketches and toured round the same places Threepenny Theatre had been. 'We used to start off by giving out bingo cards – which were all the same – and have this bingo game with surreal bingo calls, then a load of people would win at the same time and I'd get them on stage and humiliate them. It was incredibly dangerous – I think out of the first five gigs, one ended in a riot, several ended in fighting ... one of them ended with me throttling somebody on stage, with several hundred punks and skinheads just howling with anger. Nobody understood what the fuck I was attempting – it seems quite easy now, but there was no tradition of rock stand-up comedy in Britain, no one like Richard Pryor or Lenny Bruce, so people didn't understand what you were doing and things could get out of hand fairly easily.'

They toured in this show for a couple of years – still using the name Threepenny Theatre – never really feeling a part of the theatrical world, and working in community centres, Communist Party events, the odd university – once at the Woolwich Tram Shed, a tram depot converted into a fringe theatre; this gig ended in yet another fight. Sayle was developing some stand-up comedy material during this show – very much in his own style. Because they are both loud and dominant performers it is possible to make false connections between Billy Connolly and Sayle, but in fact Sayle never saw him – though he does feel that in a sense Connolly made his kind of comedy more possible simply by not being 'a jacketed buffoon' like so many mainstream comics.

When Sayle's wife spotted the advertisement for the forthcoming

Comedy Store it seemed like an ideal opportunity. Sayle remembers his audition for Peter Rosengard: 'He was completely unlike anybody I'd ever met before, because all I knew were ordinary people ... and he's not an ordinary person – and completely from another world ... so I did this monologue out of the show, about a Liverpool docker coming to London, going to exhibitions at the Hayward Gallery, and getting into arguments with people about the nature of futurist art, and then hitting them ... and having a row with a barman about structuralist poetry.'

Being asked to compère the Comedy Store turned out to be a tremendous break both for the club and for Sayle himself: 'Because I'd had a fairly good grounding in crowd control I was ideally suited for that job – I was physically intimidating, confident, I had a lot of material and a quick mind. If an act had stiffed I'd take the piss out of them *afterwards* – I'd give them a good build-up but afterwards be fairly merciless – if they're shitty you might as well acknowledge it.'

The Comedy Store was of course noted for its heckling – something which never much bothered Sayle: 'I didn't rely on prepared put-downs too much – it was more interesting to use whatever they were saying. Being a comic when things are like they were at the Comedy Store – it's a bit like drowning – if you're in danger your mind works astonishingly fast and you're constantly scanning for things to refer to, going through your material to see if there's anything appropriate, looking at the person to see if there's anything you can use. I think my mind just worked faster than anybody else's in that context.'

What made Sayle's act stand out was his sheer presence – the ranting, the speed of attack, the willingness to say anything he wanted to say – and the amount of swearing (not that he was alone in that; indeed it was rapidly becoming *de rigueur*). In this sequence (which developed in his later acts into a demonstration of the relative paucity of swear words if your conversation consists of nothing else), he presented a portrait of an all too familiar type of Londoner:

> Turn it up, knock it on the 'ead, bollocks, there you go, all right, do what, as it 'appens, turn it up, all right, shit-piss-cunt-fuck-bollocks as-it-'appens, leave-it-out, all-right wanker, give-it-a-portion, knock-it-on-the-'ead do-what leave-it-out wanker ... stereo – wanker, wanker, wanker ... (etc. etc. ...)
> Wally! ... Cortina! Millwall – fuckin' Millwall! ...
> Jean-Paul Sartre – what a fucking cunt, eh? What a fucking cunt old Jean-Paul Sartre is, you know what I mean? We fuckin' *hate* him round our way – you know why? 'Cos he knows fuck-all about the Cortina, that's why.

There was a good deal more in the same vein — the same handful of words and expressions frequently repeated. He also made digs at various targets in his own Liverpudlian persona:

> They fucking love me down the Arts Council, you know ... down Piccadilly with the ponchos and the Lapsang Suchong, you know ... and the trousers tucked into the boots ... they say, 'Here's a working-class half-wit ... *let's patronize him!*' I live in Fulham, right? I fucking love going down the Riverside studios, y'know what I mean? — seeing an avant-garde Polish mime troupe ... doing all that, all the old bollocks ... that's a man milking a goat, that is (*mimes it*) ... frighteningly fucking precise.... Then for the community they have a bit of alternative bingo — you don't shout 'house', you shout '*squat!*' ... Lenin's Party card, number ones ... over-subsidized left-wing theatre group, 7–84 ... right?

His material was more carefully thought out than a first hearing of it might suggest; and he was not afraid to attack targets which up to then had been avoided by the socially and politically conscious:

> This gig is actually in aid of a charity — called 'Help a London child — kill a social worker' ... a very good cause, I think you'll agree ... Although I am very alternative and do have my own roller-skates and everything, there's one thing about the whole scene I can't get behind — and that is all the people taking drugs ... and not giving *me* any, the bastards! I think, if you want to get out of your head, what's wrong with going out and having ninety-three pints of real ale, you know — Scruttock's Old Dirigible, with the twigs and the bits of beak still in it....

Sayle's targets also included the trendification of Stoke Newington, his own childhood, street theatre ... and, inevitably, the (then) new Conservative Government. However, although he did make politically flavoured jokes, he did not make the political message the *raison d'être* of his act. One of the most important of those who did was Jim Barclay, who first appeared at the Comedy Store in its fairly early days with an act that managed to be politically direct and completely wacky at the same time.

Barclay was born on 23 May 1947; he went to a comprehensive school in South-East London, and then did various jobs — the civil service for a time (allocating disposable syringes to the NHS), cleaning a pub, driving, working on a building site.... He was also with the National Youth Theatre for a while, then at the New College of Speech and Drama. Finally he got a job in repertory theatre at Stoke-on-Trent in 1970, and the following year started a three-year stint at the Cockpit Theatre, London, working with children of

fourteen and fifteen (mostly doing O-level material and projects on, for example, trade unionism).

Feeling that this was a bit too comfortable, he left and joined the 7-84 theatre company (so called because 84 per cent of the wealth is owned by 7 per cent of the population). He comments: 'This was changed by the alternative comedians to mean that 7 per cent of the theatre companies get 84 per cent of the Arts Council grants. In fact 7-84 don't get any at all, now. I played the giant in a thing called *The Trembling Giant* by John McGrath, which was the story of capitalism from the medieval merchants to what was then Jim Callaghan and the "social contract" thing. It was a very send-uppable play, full of mid-seventies political zeal, but not completely thought through. It had all the faults of political theatre of the period, and I thought, I can't go on doing this – there must a more honest, less patronizing way of talking to people and getting ideas across.'

About this time Barclay met Tony Allen, and they got involved in a pub theatre company called Mayday, doing a cabaret about sexism which Allen had written and which involved Barclay being a stand-up comic. This put into Barclay's head the idea of doing a political stand-up routine.

Jim Barclay's early appearances at the Comedy Store were, like most people's, drawn from the work he had already been doing; but gradually he put together his own style. Most notable was his eccentric appearance; unlike the others, most of whom appeared in their normal clothes, Barclay kitted himself out with yellow tights, a Union Jack T-shirt, a black jacket, and a hat with two metal balls on long springs (like antennae) and an eighteen-inch nail apparently through his head. He took the idea for the opening of his act from the thick Chilean accent of an acquaintance:

> *Audienceros ... rastafanarias – homosexuales – lesbianes – e los wegetenarios – e pensionistes – marxistos, socialistes, liberales, anarchosyndicales partasistos, namby-pamby itsy-bitsy milky-watery wastytimey sociales democraticos – e Pakistaneros – Indianes – Cyprianes – feministes radicales – los masculinistes contra-machismo e braggadacio* ... (*normal voice*). Now, is that everybody? Good evening, ladies and gentlemen. My name is Jim Barclay, and I'm the wacky and zany Marxist-Leninist comedian; and it's my job to come on here and tell you jokes which precipitate the downfall of capitalism and bring an end to tyranny and injustice wherever it rears its ugly head, so 'ere we go with a starter for ten.

His material managed to be serious in intent without losing the 'wacky and zany' approach – delivered in a fairly strong cockney accent, and with a general good humour that belied the underlying message:

What I'm going to do now is a joke that, I'll be quite honest with you, I've plagiarized from that great American comedian Mr Caspar Weinberger.... Here we go, a starter for ten, a lovely quote this – 'Even an inaccurate missile is an effective deterrent'! Ha ha ha! Even an inaccurate missile is an effective deterrent! ... to which side, that's what I'd like to know. 'Cos these Cruise missiles are very clever things, you know. They tell you they're piloted by computers – they're *not* piloted by computers, they're piloted by members of the under-21 section of the Millwall FC Supporters Club – on a job creation scheme. 'S what you might call a dead-end job! They go up 100 metres above the ground, and then for thousands of miles they go along, reading the terrain. Very clever. What they don't tell you is, these Cruise missiles that go along, reading the terrain, are dyslexic! So they're going along, looking for Leningrad ... (*imitates motor noise*) 'Mmmmmm ... where's that Leningrad? I'll give that Leningrad some stick when I see it.' Because they're dyslexic they land up in Leamington Spa.

This is what we find, eh? Ha ha ha! Look at it, it's all in here ... (*reads from pamphlet*): 'The US Airforce officers have arrived in Greenham Common. To fire a Cruise missile, two officers – both Americans – will simultaneously press separate buttons. The two officers sit in chairs twelve feet apart, and their arms are measured periodically, to ensure that they cannot extend further than 11 foot 6 inches.' Very reassuring, ain't it, eh? But one of 'em, one of 'em could get a twelve-foot-wide garden rake! Boom! 'They are an elite squad'! Ha ha ha ... that's very reassuring.... I'd hate to think that the destruction of civilization as we know it was brought about by a set of wallies!

While Barclay's straightforward political stance was influential in the forming of the new alternative comedy standpoint, one of the most respected of all the performers, Tony Allen, claimed no political allegiance – he disliked the Socialists as much as the Conservatives. He was responsible for introducing a sense of morality into the proceedings – perhaps ethics would be a better word, in the sense of individually responsible behaviour – and indeed promoting the whole attitude, which came to be the hallmark of alternative comedy, of being non-sexist and non-racist.

Allen was born on 4 March 1945 in Hayes. Of his background, he says: 'I didn't get on well at school, got into gambling – spent my teens running bets, not working properly, playing snooker – got out of that, got married – got out of that in '67, I suppose – then moved to Ladbroke Grove [near Paddington] and got into the whole hippy-squatting-free-love ... and became a political activist – squatting, anti-nukes, all that sort of stuff – and got into street theatre.'

He wrote a number of sketches and plays – none of which was published, although in the end he did sell a few sketches to BBC

Radio – and worked with a street theatre group called Rough Theatre. One of his plays was about a character who wanted to be a stand-up comic; realizing the potential of stand-up comedy, he adapted the material and began to move into this field: 'By 1978 I'd been compèring the odd gig with bands – and I still do that – and I decided to re-write all the stand-up material I'd been writing for other people for myself. My first gig was at the Oval Theatre [Kennington] – it was mainly folk artists, and I did about forty minutes. It was my writing but very much in the style of Lenny Bruce. That was May 1979 – I was very excited.'

The Comedy Store had just opened at the time, and there were few other places to try out his act: 'The only places to play were talent contests in working men's clubs or pubs – all run by agencies; and the reason I wanted to do it was because it was all mother-in-law jokes and Irish jokes, and totally politically against everything that I believed in. So I did all this stuff against that style of comedy. And when I went to the Comedy Store, the audience was full of these people who had been running the talent contests – seedy showbiz – and Peter Rosengard was hanging round with a slightly up-market version of people who did the same thing. Alexei was there – I'd met him earlier – and we immediately connected ... so the Comedy Store was a platform and for about a year there was this sort of civil war between us and people like Les Dawson and Lenny Bennett who were occasionally there – and their clones doing this old-fashioned stuff.'

The staple diet of the club comic had been the sort of joke that many people found offensive – jokes that perpetuated the old and rather unpleasant myths (every woman is just dying for it, every woman really wants to be raped, all Irishmen are dead stupid, etc. etc. etc.). Allen in particular mounted an attack on this sort of attitude, joined by Sayle, Barclay and others whom they encouraged to come to the Comedy Store. Allen combined these attacks with his own deft and deliberately anarchistic observations of life:

> OK, stand-up comedy, I know what you want. ... There was this drunk homosexual Pakistani squatter trade unionist takes my mother-in-law to an Irish restaurant ... says to the West Indian waiter, 'Waiter, waiter, there's a racial stereotype in my soup ...' No, no, no. ... That's not to say that I haven't got prejudices, 'cos I have. There's one minority group that I *loathe* ... the Metropolitan Police Force. And in particular the drug squad. You can always recognize the drug squad where I live, on Portobello Road, Saturday afternoon – they're the only people in plain clothes ... khaki anoraks, C&A denims, short but unfashionable hair, and sensible boots, right? They look like lapsed Mormons. And they're sidling up to

Rastafarians saying things like, 'Hi, man – where can a cat score some, er, reefers?' . . . And they're offering 1965 prices as well. . . . As it happens, that's all bollocks, that's just a joke. They don't look like that at all. They look just like me and you. In fact they look more like me and you than me and you . . .

What I want to know is, where is the cop on the beat when it comes to arresting the *real* criminals . . . you know, the *real* criminals – the multinational corporations . . . that move the economy of one part of the world to another part of the world and blitz whole communities. . . . Where's the cop on the beat when it comes to arresting *them?* 'Well, I was walking in a north-easterly direction in the boardroom of Amalgamated Conglomerates, when I noticed the accused and several other persons unknown, making a dubious decision as to the economic future of Latin America. Well, I cautioned him, arrested him, and bunged him in the back of the Transit. That's when he must have hit his head. . . .'

Certainly many of the people in the Comedy Store audience didn't care whether the performers took a moral standpoint or not, as long as they were funny (and loud); but it was largely due to Allen, Sayle and their colleagues that the place built up its reputation for the birth of the New Comedy. Tony Allen: 'The Comedy Store wasn't an alternative venue and it wasn't a venue set up for the New Comedy – I suppose Rosengard wanted the sort of American-style comedy which in a way I was influenced by; but people were doing really racist and sexist sort of stuff and the rest of the acts were what we called the mother-in-law comedians. What Alexei and I did was get all the actors we knew – like Andy de la Tour, Jim Barclay; I got hold of Keith Allen [no relation], who was squatting up the road from me, and as soon as Keith walked on the stage it started to work for me – that's when we took it over, really, and that must have been the end of 1979.'

Many people would cite Keith Allen's tremendous influence on the new direction comedy was taking – although his participation in it was short-lived, lasting only about fourteen months, at least in terms of his stand-up work. He was born on 2 June 1953 in Llanelly, North Wales. He went to various schools, including Hampshire's first ever comprehensive, from which he won a scholarship to a public school at Brentwood in Essex. He comments: 'I was there for two years and then got expelled, and went back to the comprehensive school – and of course, you take two years out, I suddenly noticed that my language had slightly changed. I remember people's behaviour quite shocking me that would never have shocked me two years earlier – swearing in the classroom, stuff like that. So I had to work doubly hard to exert myself over my schoolmates, and of course that

Tony Allen

31

meant that I ended up in a lot of trouble with the police and got expelled, and then went to detention centres and borstal – and I got O-levels in borstal, then went to a college of further education in Swansea.'

From this uneven start he went on to the Welsh College of Music and Drama in Cardiff, more out of a feeling that it would offer him an easy time than from any desire to be an actor. He came to London around 1975 and worked as a stage manager for two years at the Institute of Contemporary Arts, eventually appearing in *All Along The Watchtowers* by Colin Bennett, which led to a part in an all-male production of *Macbeth* in Glasgow (as Lady Macduff and the First Witch) – an experience which decided him against being an actor.

He then came back to London and formed a small rock band: 'The idea was that we'd just go and do talent contests – this was in the days before talent contests were chic – the terrible thing was we kept winning . . . I was obsessed with Max Bygraves because he was symbolic of everything I didn't like about entertainment, and I'd walked on stage during his show – I was a stagehand at the Victoria Palace, and I'd got so pissed off with his act that one night I just walked out with no clothes on – of course I was sacked . . . and I did this song with the band called "Max Bygraves Killed My Mother" – and for some reason we got this following of National Front skinheads. We won two of the heats of the talent contest and got into the final, and there was a riot because we only came fourth and all these NF fans went ape-shit . . . that was when we thought, hullo, give it up.'

When Tony Allen suggested that Keith Allen try the Comedy Store, he drew on his experience with a surrealist theatre troupe in Bristol – called Crystal Theatre of the Saint – with whom he had worked from time to time; he had acted in a play called *Radio Beelzebub* in which he played a very bad music-hall-style comedian. In the play the character started off doing an act cobbled together from tatty joke books, but then went into the country and changed his style completely, describing what he saw around him in a surrealist style. Since the character was a comedian, it provided a starting point: 'So I got up this first night at the Comedy Store and started doing that – and of course there wasn't a critical audience at that time, so anything that was racist or sexist didn't mean anything anyway. So when I got past that journey into the country, I suddenly found there was this freedom – it wouldn't have made sense to that audience since they hadn't seen the context, so I just used to make it up – and this act developed out of that aspect of it.'

In the end the idea of the journey into the country simply provided the springboard for that part of the act:

> I've read a lot of books, you see, I've read a lot of books – I have to, because I'm a performer; I've got to have knowledge, access to knowledge, to communicate with people. And I've read these books, and these books tell me that all revolutionary movements start out in the countryside – see? China – all the peasants uprising, out in the countryside, moving towards the city. Cambodia – Chile – (it's only an act, settle down) – and I learned that all revolutionary movements start out in the countryside, so I thought, right, get out of town, and get out in the country – and I did, I went down to Dorset. And there's fuck all happening in Dorset of a revolutionary nature, nothing at all. I was a bit upset, obviously, because I'd just paid for a ticket on the train . . .

Keith Allen

33

However, he starts to explore the countryside:

> ... and suddenly I saw what was quite possibly the most moving thing I've ever seen in my life ... I was in this field – and I saw a load of horses without policemen on. I couldn't believe it – herds of horses and not a bank robber in sight! (What am I talking about – you idiot! ...) No policemen, but bank robbers everywhere! Bank robbers all over the place! And they're not like the city bank robbers, the ones out in the country, they're truly revolutionary by nature, because they wander around – they've got no fear – they don't wear stockings over their heads, they wear these funny hats, with peaks on – you can see their faces – and they've got these shotguns with extra bits welded on 'em. And anything that moves, shoot it.

Keith Allen comments: 'I suppose it was surreal – but surreal in a very un-surreal way. It was very approachable – the language wasn't too difficult – it was the imagery that was powerful and worked; and I had this ability to convince people that I was telling them a funny story, whereas in fact I wasn't at all. I had a great advantage over the others because I really did know about performance techniques, and a lot of the others didn't, and it showed. I did have an ability to stop, and not be funny, but keep an audience – and that was because I actually knew about holding an audience.'

He experimented with his material, often taking a rise out of the audience: 'I would tell them I found it very difficult to do an act, and be very serious and tell them my father had died that Tuesday – tell them all the details, how we buried him on Thursday, and I had to look after my mother – and I know I shouldn't be here doing this ... and by this time the audience is really quiet ... and then I'd hold it and hold it ... and then say something like I was really tired because we'd been celebrating at a disco – because we hated him! And sometimes I would get really serious, not funny – you mustn't get the idea of me planning to do something – sometimes I would just not be funny at all.'

He never planned his performances in detail. Usually he just walked from his home in Notting Hill, calling at one or two pubs, and roughed something out in his mind: 'I never had an "act" – and I used to get really fucked off that people would just come to see this "dangerous" comedian – which seemed to me absolutely ludicrous, because I know that one person in an audience who's not with a gang, who heckles, on their own, is far more dangerous and far braver than the person standing on stage doing an act. Comedians think they're brave, but they're not – all they're doing is joining that gang, which is the audience. Whereas my idea was always to *not* be one of them.

'That's what I didn't like about any of these other acts – because none of them were themselves. I would always go up as Keith Allen, not something else ... and they would all do it – some in obvious ways, like put on funny voices; and Tony Allen would have a personality change when he went on stage from this old hippy that I knew, with his flared loons and all the rest of it – Tony had a dreadful problem with culture – and he would try and become this streetwise guy; and some people in the audience would believe it, but I would think, what the fuck is that? Who *is* it? And that was where I scored a lot of points in a way, because there was no difference when I walked on that stage ... you just have to have confidence bordering on arrogance to go out there and not be afraid. And of course I also knew I was being made to look a lot better than I was by the quality of the other acts.'

It was Allen's refusal to join any movement, and his distaste for everyone else's material, that gave his appearances much of their edge – though inevitably he got fed up with the whole scene in a relatively short time and refused to do any more stand-up work. As he admits, he could misfire badly – and also audiences would come to expect him to be 'dangerous', and would heckle and attempt to provoke him, which was one of the factors contributing to his withdrawal; but at his best he could spin a strange and individual chain of logic which held his audiences spellbound. In this example he started from the sudden public appearance of the SAS when – in full view of the television cameras – they stormed the Iranian Embassy to break a siege there in May 1980:

> The SAS – the Squatters' Advisory Service – I don't know if you've
> noticed, but the SAS are extremely adept at keeping a low profile.
> I know why: their heads unscrew. It's true – they actually come off
> their bodies. Now I don't know if many of you people have been to
> Wales, in your second cottages or whatever – what's left of 'em –
> but if you have you've probably seen some very odd sights. Namely,
> a bunch of nutters running around the Welsh hills ... with no heads.
> This is the SAS out on manoeuvres – getting fit and strong, you
> see. And while they're out on manoeuvres, all the heads are back at
> secret HQ ... and it's not a very big secret ... and what they do,
> they keep the heads in these buckets of cool dog's piss – just to keep
> them in the right condition, see. And what they do, they've got the
> most marvellous educational techniques – it's not enough to be a
> fucking hatchet-man – you've got to have the brains to do it
> nowadays. They've got lecture theatres on camp – but they're a bit
> different from the ones we come across – because there are no seats.
> Instead, what they've got is rows and rows of poles – with screw
> threads. And what they do is, they take the heads out of stores, and
> they march them over to the theatre in the buckets of cool dog's piss,

then screw them on the poles like that ... and then they play them old Roy Rogers movies. Just to make sure they're getting the right training, you see. Now, I don't know if you saw the show – marvellous little show – on the TV for us, about the storming of the Iranian Embassy; now, I'm an ordinary punter, much like yourselves, and what I don't understand is, how these blokes – who can save us from every known crisis in the world today – can't get over a two-foot gap on a balcony without fucking ropes and ladders.

Keith Allen found the change in the Comedy Store over its first year annoying. He could see a certain bravery in the acts which were absolutely no good but kept going week after week; but the audience became more demanding of a professional standard, and the whole atmosphere began to change: 'I didn't think *any* of this was alternative comedy at all – just thought it was all old hat that I'd seen before – and it really did annoy me that it had changed into a chi-chi place where "things were happening" – and I thought, it's old tat. When it started it defied that sort of criticism – it wasn't about that, and it was a joy to see the audiences be affected, because nobody knew what was going to happen. But then it just became a circus with all the attendant media bollocks ... and all these middle-class people who were going to make a career out of comedy. The audiences became a lot younger, and a lot more straight, and a lot more team-handed – they would ask for people's routines ... and it just seemed like it was all over then.'

At the time the Comedy Store opened in May 1979 there were a number of fringe theatre venues in London, but none of them was presenting anything resembling cabaret or comedy. The nearest would be the occasional revue – for example, the *Lesbian Left Review* (spelt that way in *Time Out* at least), which was on at Oval House, Kennington, in March and consisted of songs and sketches. Many fringe companies presented agit-prop plays, with occasional forays into less polemical material such as *The Hitch-Hiker's Guide to the Galaxy*. One or two of the venues which a few years later would be presenting cabaret – such as Jackson's Lane Community Centre – were already open, but presenting plays. CAST were doing their political plays; and, apart from a few imitation Victorian music-halls, the nearest thing to a comedy gig was the team presenting *Fundation* at the Woolwich Tramshed – topical sketches based on that week's events.

Concurrently with the opening of the Comedy Store, Tony Allen and a few associates were attempting to set up a loose sort of organization in which performers could operate, finding gigs in pubs and arts centres. The Elgin pub – on the corner of Westbourne Park Road and Ladbroke Grove in Notting Hill – provided their first venue. Tony Allen: 'The area's bohemia, so the average person in the Elgin is a sort of would-be poet/anarchist/nutter or whatever. We used to do it every fortnight on the Thursday – Alexei and I would do it with a jazz band called Combo Passé; and we'd get everybody we liked down from the Comedy Store.'

They got together to try to decide how to operate. Tony Allen had strong views about their standpoint: 'I was really against Arts Council funding, because I thought the economics should determine the style, and I couldn't understand how you could get these large amounts of money from the Arts Council and then put on something with thirty people in the audience – if you were good and it worked, you should fill the place and be able to make a living out of it. So we formed "Alternative Cabaret", which is what I called the thing – and then we became "alternative comedians", although I called myself a "cathartic comedian" at the beginning, and thought we'd open up lots of pub rooms in London, get ourselves a circuit and then just do it.'

The principal members of this loose organization were Tony Allen, Alexei Sayle, actors Andy de la Tour and Pauline Melville, a comedy/folk double act called Gasmask and Hopkins – one of whom was Oscar McLennan, who later worked as a solo comedian – Jim Barclay, and the Combo Passé band. Keith Allen wouldn't join anything, much less an even mildly institutionalized comedy circuit, but he did make a number of appearances with them. He also attended part of their first meeting. He remembers: 'Tony called a meeting in the West London Media Workshop. The idea was to give it some sort of generic title that could be bookable . . . and they called it Alternative Cabaret, at which point I walked out . . . it was against all my arguments, which were that you're not an alternative, you just *are*, you're *it*. I predicted that all these people were going to be was just part of the cyclical nature of things – like the Goons, TW3, Monty Python . . . I said, you lot are going to be the next thing, and I didn't want anything to do with that cyclical thing.'

One of the people brought into Alternative Cabaret was Andy de la Tour, an actor who had, like Barclay and Sayle, been working in fringe theatre in ways which made stand-up comedy a logical next step. He was born on 24 April 1948, and studied English at Sussex University, where he also got involved in a number of plays. When he left he spent several years doing various jobs before going back into theatre at the age of about twenty-six. He appeared with the Belt and Braces political theatre company, in plays including Dario Fo's *The Accidental Death of an Anarchist*, which they later performed in the West End at Wyndham's Theatre in April 1980.

However, his first taste of stand-up work came when he was touring with a band. 'We took this band show to community centres and working men's clubs; but I can't play a musical instrument, so I volunteered to drive the van . . . Then I thought, I've always been interested in stand-up comedy, so why don't I try some. I didn't know anyone who was a stand-up comic; all I knew was what I saw on the television – this is before the Comedy Store opened. I was an actor but I hadn't ever actually done any gag-telling in front of a microphone. I just wrote the jokes myself, because I wasn't going to do other people's jokes, and it went down well, so I got the taste for it. By coincidence the Comedy Store opened shortly afterwards. I went down there pretty quickly, and there were a lot of like-minded people . . . a lot of people from fringe theatre – it's the classic case of something responding to a need – there were all these people who wanted to be comedians.'

At about the same time he appeared in the comedy cabaret show at the Half Moon Theatre in London's East End – then at its old venue where it held only about 150 people: 'We did it up to make it look like a club – fairy lights round the walls, and we borrowed some tables and chairs and put candles on the tables ... there was no alcohol, but there was a pub next door and people would bring their drinks in and sit round tables in groups, so it actually did feel like a club. It was just a crude variety bill – there was no attempt to "concept" the evening.'

He joined Alternative Cabaret early in 1980 and found that it provided the ideal opportunity for his developing style. Some of his material articulated his own experiences and thoughts in a way that few people before had attempted:

> I'm walking past this shop, and it sells pornographic magazines. I'm looking at this picture – woman, black leather and all the business – and I'm looking at it ... critically ... denouncing to myself this particular aspect of women's oppression ... and to my surprise, I find I'm getting an erection at the same time. And I suddenly thought, well, actually, that's not a surprise, because the picture, the image, that I was looking at on the back of the magazine was very familiar. And the reason it's familiar is because I think I've been carrying an image like that around in my head for the past fifteen years. It's in the little mental library that we all keep at the back of the brain. And I whip this picture out – mentally – every time I need it to get out of a jam – sexual impotence, problems like that. I've used images like that – in my early twenties sexual impotence was a regular occurrence for me.... Jesus, the excuses I used to make ... 'I'm sorry, I've got a lot on my mind, love, actually ... the invasion of Czechoslovakia....' That's amazing, isn't it? – you're in bed with a girl, and your prick's just lying there like a limp mole with a mind of its own ... 'Not tonight, Andrew, ha ha ... I'm going to sleep! (snore) ...' Can you imagine if other parts of the body exercised the same degree of autonomy? ... You're running for a bus, one of your feet stops.... 'Come on, there's a bus coming!' – 'Fuck off! I'm tired! If you want to catch the bus, hop.' – The other foot goes, 'Oh, fuck off ...' ... I wonder if the Yorkshire Ripper carried the same image round in his head?

He also did a good deal of directly political material; he comments: 'I did quite a lot of stuff about Northern Ireland – and it was good satire and the audience used to appreciate it – but sometimes people would respond badly, simply on the grounds of its politics, no matter how funny other people in the audience had found it. One of the most exciting experiences I've ever had was a series of gigs in some Republican clubs in Belfast in 1981 – it was very unusual for them to see an English comic making jokes about Northern Ireland that were basically pro-Republican and anti the army presence.'

His best-remembered routine imagines the Northern Irish conflict in terms of a film script:

> If it had been generally acknowledged that there has been this war going on in Northern Ireland for the last ten years, think of the war film they could have made in that fine old tradition of British war movies. Scene one – a battleship cruises down the Falls Road, Belfast. Sitting on top, Kenneth More in a duffle coat. He says quietly under his lips to Number One, 'Paddy's being damned quiet tonight.' Number One doesn't hear – he's dead. He's been dead for a week, but he doesn't fall over – he's British. A faint smile crosses More's lips as he recalls the sunny days filming *Genevieve*. Poor Kay Kendall – she died of leukemia – and he thought of all those red corpuscles eating the white corpuscles, a bit like this war, really.

Meanwhile the British Army feels trapped:

> ... Over at Long Kesh, looking for a sixteen-foot bed to jump over – Steve McQueen on his motorbike ... and John Mills before he went senile rushing inconspicuously fast across the compound, pausing only slightly by the garden to empty his trouser-leg. Down below, fourteen feet, tunnel Harry's being dug, and tunnel George – when they meet up with tunnel Edward they'll form one tunnel and become the Jubilee line (but only after Baker Street). The escape committee's worrying – some infidel has graffiti'd all over the escape tunnel, 'Revlon kills rabbits'. John Mills bursts into Hut 14 where the escape committee are meeting. . . . 'I'm sorry to interrupt, sir, but we can't escape, the escape's off, dammit, we *can't escape*!' – 'Why not, man, pull yourself together, why can't we escape?' – 'We can't escape, sir – we're the fucking guards!'

In more recent times de la Tour has done little stand-up, being more occupied with straight acting and with play-writing – the plays he has written include *Viva*, performed at the Theatre Royal, Stratford East, in 1985; *Here We Go*, set in the miners' strike and performed at the Sheffield Crucible in 1987; and, for television, *Clem*, transmitted in 1987.

It is noticeable that most of the performers in the early days of Alternative Cabaret were men; there is perhaps something inherently masculine in stand-up comedy, particularly with a potentially aggressive audience. However, there were a small number of women appearing in the early days, most of them actresses doing what were in effect character monologues. The earliest was probably Pauline Melville, who was in Alternative Cabaret from the beginning and did appear at the Comedy Store.

41

She was born in London; her mother was a Londoner and her father a West Indian from Guyana, but although she can put on a West Indian accent and characterization, she does not look as if she has mixed blood and normally sticks to English characters. She was brought up in Brixton, and after leaving school went into straight theatre, including a period with the 7–84 company. She then worked for a time with the Sadista Sisters, a rock cabaret group, and it was here that she first developed her stand-up style: 'I had a very vague idea . . . I wanted to mock a certain sort of mysticism that was going round then – there was enough of communes and gurus and things for me to want to take the mickey out of them. So I developed a character called Edie, who is a standard housewife, very conservatively dressed and in a great big green velvet hat. She's an innocent, really, but she's very enthusiastic and ambitious to get into the latest cults.'

She played this character with tremendous success in the Sadista Sisters' show, and was asked to repeat it as they played in the various fringe theatres – 'diving in and out of little black holes like a pit pony'. Edie's gullibility provided an excellent vehicle for some sharp digs at the ersatz Eastern religions which were still lurking on from their 1960s heyday:

> I was really studying Zen Buddhism . . . you know Zen Buddhists? – the thin ones with anorexia nirvana . . . to be a Zen Buddhist you have to study for years just to reach the state of mind that you had before you started studying. Then I took up existentialism – because they ask those profound questions that you really want to know the answer to. Especially in Hampstead. Am I here or aren't I here? Are you there or aren't you there? If I leave the room will you disappear? (It happens.) If *you* leave the room will *I* disappear? If we all leave the room will the room disappear? Well, you see, it worries you at night. One night I popped right out of my body – floating above myself attached by a little blue thread. I looked down and I thought – 'Edie, you must take that nightie to the launderette.'

She did play the Comedy Store: 'But I didn't have this great thing that it was a place where you should test yourself. I wouldn't go there for a long time for one simple reason – they didn't pay any money. The first night they started paying I was there! – I wasn't going to work for no money!' She didn't have the sort of problems with the audience that might have been expected, possibly because by the time she started working there the audience had calmed down a little from their first most boisterous days.

Alternative Cabaret provided a better opportunity for her to develop, although she did mostly work as Edie – to an extent hiding

behind the characterization. Later on, after encouragement from the others, she did some stand-up material as herself, but Edie remained as a successful vehicle for indirect comment. By now Edie's interests had expanded to take in the political scene:

> I'm in the Women's Movement, you know. I am. I mean, I'm not in the most militant branch – I'm just in the branch that pulls faces behind men's backs. Yes, you can laugh, but there's a lot of us. And I'm the new BBC woman's sort-of-roving reporter – I just talk about world affairs as they pop into my head. No, I do – I mean, wasn't it funny, did you notice that terrible fuss they kicked up about those two Labour MPs going to Afghanistan? I thought that was very strange – they only went just to have an unbiased look – just wanted to see the situation for themselves, that's all. They went all that way just to see all those women in peasant clothes, and earthenware pots and things – and they could have come up to Hampstead. Anyway, I heard that there were two Afghanistani MPs come over here because they wanted to look at *our* system. They wanted to have a look at it for themselves, to see what actually happens. Mind you, of course their skin's a bit darker than ours, so they actually got stopped at the airport, didn't they? They're actually in the detention compound at Heathrow. I think that's a shame, really because now they'll never know what our system's like.
>
> Look at my friend Eileen. She's had a horrible Christmas. Actually, Eileen's had a horrible year. Actually, she's a horrible *person*. I felt sorry for her the other day, though, because she came in – you'll never guess what – I mean, you sit there, quiet as toast, and you'll never guess that Eileen came into my kitchen in absolute floods the other day – thirty years of marriage and she found out her husband is a monetarist. I said, 'Listen, Eileen,' I said, 'sit down – I think all this monetarism's just a cry for help, you know.'

In general the Alternative Cabaret performers got good reactions from their audiences; but their lack of any experience in arranging gigs did lead to some odd happenings. One of the oddest was set up by Jim Barclay: 'None of us knew how to get gigs, but we all wanted to perform; I actually just walked into the art college which was at the bottom of the road where I was living then – it was part of Goldsmith's Art College, and it was full of punks – which was *de rigueur* in art college in 1979.' He explained who he and his colleagues were, and asked for a gig; he was asked how much he charged, and, not having any idea what he should ask, said £100.

'Because there was nothing formalized, I went to the Comedy Store on the Saturday before the gig, and I booked everybody that was there – Tony, Keith, Alexei, Gareth Williams, a singing group, a violin and guitar duo, myself – about eight acts for about £100! I thought, some of them probably won't turn up – and they all went on to complete indifference, including Alexei. They were very punky, aggressive sort of art students – Johnny Rotten had just finished then, I think – and, complete indifference and "make us laugh". Then at the end of the evening I introduced Keith Allen.'

Keith Allen went on with a wooden box containing forty-eight fruit-juice bottles. He remembers: 'I said, "some comedians have ad-libs called put-downs when the audience is being lippy ... well, here's mine, I've got forty-eight of them" – and broke one on the stage to make his point.' The next time someone heckled, he up-ended the entire box on stage: 'And I'd taken the fire extinguisher on with me – and this woman in the front tempted me with this fire extinguisher.... "You wouldn't fucking dare" ... then she came up to the stage.... I was a bit stupid, really, because I thought it was water – it wasn't, it was gas – I let it off in her face ... she just disappeared – and it's freezing, that stuff. (I did apologize afterwards.)' Barclay remembers the fire alarms going off at that point and security men bundling everyone into the corridors.

However, most gigs were less alarming than that, and sometimes their act would stimulate the audience into thinking harder than usual about the subjects. Jim Barclay: 'There was one terrific night when Tony Allen and I and a musician called Timon Dogg played the Huddersfield Polytechnic; it was when the Falklands war had just started, and the audience was divided absolutely down the middle between your day students, who were lefty Yorkshire students, and Mr and Mrs Huddersfield, who were evening institute people.'

A lot of the jokes in the show were about the Falklands, for example, Jim Barclay's gag – 'What cost £120,000,000 and lies at the bottom of the South Atlantic?' – or his marines recruitment poster – 'Excitement, adventure ... it don't say nothing about dying, does it?' He remembers: 'At the end of the show there was this debate, pockets of debate all over the audience – "They shouldn't have been allowed to say those things" – and that evening did more in terms of polemic than all the 7–84 shows with bands and so on. We disappeared down the M1 and they were still arguing – we don't know what time they finished. That happens just very occasionally, and for me that's part of what it's all about – my catchphrase for it is "challenging and denting the audience's prejudices" – not laying on them my own, but just challenging theirs.'

This sort of comedy is sometimes known as 'dangerous' comedy – the main danger being that of not getting a laugh; but on occasion Keith Allen brought a new concept to the expression. At one gig he threw darts at an audience who were being difficult (fortunately they didn't think to throw them back); at another he made a joke about the IRA bomb which blew up an RAF band in Hyde Park (he said it was because they were playing out of tune) and was knocked cold by an irate soldier. He is also credited with one of the most on-the-edge jokes – Bobby Sands (the IRA hunger striker) saying to Peter Sutcliffe (the 'Yorkshire Ripper'), 'I bet I've had more hot dinners than you've had women.'

Alternative Cabaret lasted for about two years, during which time it created the beginnings of what later became a thriving circuit of upstairs and back rooms in pubs all over London, as well as university campuses and other gigs outside London. At first the university gigs were difficult because no one really knew what to expect and organizers would lay the hall out as for a dance, with seating round the edge and a huge space in the middle – no help to a comic trying to communicate with his audience – and extremely poor PA (public address) equipment, if any; in later years things improved as the idea of a comedy evening became established. The main effort was, however, concentrated in London, where the original small handful of pubs gradually expanded as the idea caught on. Here again conditions were extremely variable, ranging from reasonably good rooms to awkward-sized and uncomfortable ones with, again, terrible PA – and sometimes performers were located in the bar area, where most of the audience were not paying attention anyway.

There were also some other venues opening. One, the Earth Exchange, has become the longest continuously running cabaret venue. It uses part of a sparsely furnished vegetarian restaurant in a basement in Hampstead, with three rows of chairs plus a few more at tables; it seats about forty people – placed at very close quarters to the performers – and can scarcely be called comfortable, but the friendly wholefood atmosphere somehow seems to typify the small beginnings of what was to become a driving force in the development of comedy.

Most of the people involved in Alternative Cabaret eventually moved back into acting, or on into their own solo careers; but for Tony Allen it never really finished: 'I kept the name and started working with another generation that were coming up – people like Sharon Landau and Roy Hutchins. ... Meanwhile John Dowie seemed to be going on a parallel course and not having anything to do with it – it needs to be said that he was there; while we were struggling to get twenty minutes together he was going round the colleges and arts centres doing an hour. I knocked "Alternative Cabaret" on the head when the name got too naff.'

Dowie had already worked at the Edinburgh Festival in a fringe venue, but Tony Allen and Alexei Sayle were the first of the Comedy

Store generation to get there. They did three weeks together in August 1980, doing half an hour each. Tony Allen: 'In the end I had to go on first because Alexei was scaring people away – he'd got that mod character together and he was just standing there swearing at the top of his voice – it wasn't always good but the cognoscenti liked it, and if you didn't mind swearing you could see that there was something happening.'

From that jumping off point Sayle and Allen established themselves as solo comedians, and the remainder of this chapter will examine their careers in this field. (Sayle's contributions to *The Comic Strip* and *The Young Ones* will be examined in later chapters.) There are parallels between them, although Sayle has been by far the more spectacularly successful. However, Allen's work, though less well known, is important because of his commitment to the meaning behind (and sometimes in front of) the comedy.

In 1981 he started working as a compère and support comic with bands such as Poison Girls, working in what he describes as the 'anarcho-punk sub-culture': 'I would go down in the audience with the follow-spot and a microphone and just argue with all these young anarchists, and have great big political arguments with them and take the piss out of them. Obviously when you're improvising you're learning answers to the same questions and put-downs for the same heckles – "you're queer", "you're a poofter" and all that sort of thing – and you get to talk about all that. Standing in some pub in Hampstead in front of thirty people is hardly alternative – if you're talking to two hundred kids in some cellar in Walthamstow that's far more alternative.'

Some of these events were like something out of *Mad Max 2*, with the band in a cage with punk kids climbing up it, and Tony Allen covered in saliva because the audience were spitting at him. He would argue with them, repeating their heckles and coming up with answers – and constantly risking a punch-up. He had methods for defusing this situation: 'I got this thing going with the sound guy – if I got into a sticky situation I used to take the energy away from myself by banging the microphone and saying, "What's the matter with this thing?", then I'd walk through the audience, grabbing the sound guy out of his box and we'd start fighting . . . then in the end we'd start dancing and kissing. In the end he was really getting into this – he was only a young punk guy – and he got really carried away and threw me across the stage. I ended up in Exeter hospital.'

The important thing to Allen is the message he is trying to convey – he is prepared to regard being funny as secondary to getting the message over – and for him, proof that he has succeeded is as important as laughter: 'At the Fridge in Brixton somebody said this bloke was a fascist – he had tattoos and union jacks – and he says, "I'm not a fascist, I'll bring my brother out here", and he went on about his brother. . . . There was lots of tension, no one was quite sure whether he was going to get up on stage and knock me out. . . . Eventually he stormed out of the room because everybody was against him, and he gets hold of this young black kid and brings him on stage – "This is my brother", and puts his arms round him and kisses him . . . in front of all these punks. Well, fair enough . . . and afterwards, another guy, young, beautiful looking guy, comes into my dressing room and shakes my hand, and says, "That wasn't his brother – *I'm* his brother. The bloke he brought on stage is my lover, and he's not spoken to me or any of the family since I started having a scene with him. And whatever happened out there tonight, thank you." So this guy with the tattoos has finally recognized that his brother's gay, and his brother's having a scene with a black guy – and it all happened in my gig!'

This last was said with pride. The serious side of Tony Allen's performances is most noticeable in a sequence he did about rape, in which he paralleled the reaction of a woman to a rapist to the reaction to the whining approach of someone trying to get laid . . . a resigned 'All right, get it over with' – leading to the conclusion that the sort of pressure applied to women by men who expect sex is in its own way just as much rape as the more obvious physical attack.

He also tries to make audiences aware of manipulation: 'Rock shows are great – you go "Let me hear you say Yeah!" and they all go "Yeah!" . . . "Let me hear you say Ye-*eah!*" and they go "Ye-*eah!*" . . . "Let me hear you say Ba-aa-aa" . . . and I said, "Don't let me catch you out again. . . ." That's the sort of politics I've got – that you shouldn't be taking any notice of people who stand on stage and try to rabble-rouse you. Me included.'

However, despite the serious intent behind much of his material (and he has lightened his touch since the early 1980s, from which period the rape sequence mentioned above dates), Tony Allen is quite prepared to send himself up, as in this routine where he talks about having done a bad gig:

> And then I look on the bright side – I think, Tony – Lenny Bruce finished his career out of his head on drugs, hassled by the police, dying in a toilet. And that's the way you're starting off! I got really optimistic – I thought, yes, there's people pissing away fortunes going to India, spending months in ashrams for this much ego loss.

The similarities between Tony Allen and Alexei Sayle are largely concerned with their willingness to perform at punk gigs like the ones described above; but their reasoning and methods are different. For one thing, Sayle is unusual among comics in that he makes no attempt to woo the audience. As he comments: 'Every comic there's ever been wants to be liked by the audience, except me. I'm not interested in their approbation – not that I necessarily dislike them, although I did at the Comedy Store – but what I have added is a genuine disdain for the audience, there's no hint of "please like me". Even when I was at school – you know Dudley Moore used to say he did comedy to get out of trouble because people used to pick on him – I used to do comedy to *make* trouble, because I was big anyway, I could look after myself, and I used to do comedy just to be irritating. So there's a genuine take it or leave it – although I'm still concerned with giving a good show, I insist the tickets are cheap and I'd be upset if the show didn't go well – but I would never do a gig where people hadn't paid to get in. People say, will I come and do their firm's party – I say no; because what I am doing is avantgarde, people have to come on to my territory – I have to dominate them, not vice versa. If I'm on their territory, they're dominating me ... I'm forcing them to laugh at stuff which is completely stupid sometimes – the best comedy is when you're getting a laugh out of something which isn't really funny.'

The usual standpoint of alternative comedy is held to be 'non-racist and non-sexist'. Sayle takes a slightly different view of this: 'The important thing about racism is oppression – I won't do stuff about the Irish or women or blacks or Pakistanis because they are oppressed, and I don't want to make that oppression any greater. I think that in many ways *we* are oppressed by the Japanese, and therefore I would be perfectly happy to do stuff about the Japanese. People don't really think it through, they just babble this thing about "non-sexist, non-racist".'

Like Tony Allen, Sayle moved away from the small venues of Alternative Cabaret – though rather than working as a support to bands, he built up an act lasting over an hour and toured that. Because the old music-halls have mostly been pulled down, the only large venues left are those which normally put on rock bands; so inevitably anyone performing at these halls tends to inherit the same type of audience as for the bands.

With his tremendous appeal Sayle was able to work in the remaining large theatres like the Sunderland Empire or the Dominion in London, as well as more modern civic venues like the Fairfield Hall, Croydon – 'a bit of a barn' – and, because many of these venues were known by rock fans, he could pull in a much wider range of audience than any of the other comics: 'I got a fantastically mixed audience when I toured – like bikers, skinheads, a lot of gangs, soldiers, schoolteachers, college lecturers – a mixture I don't think anybody has ever got before or since ... people with their name tattooed on the inside of their lip. ... A lot of them are fascists, even though I talk about Communism and being anti-racist; I got a whole front row in Southend – cross of St George and swastikas on their heads ... I didn't tone down anything that I said. I said afterwards, "You're all fucking Nazis" ... they said "Yes." Ordinary theatre doesn't speak to them, it doesn't have anything to offer. ... Because I understand about youth tribes and actually do look like a skinhead they could see I was saying something they might conceivably find interesting – and funny.'

By the time he came to tour these larger venues he had adopted a skinhead haircut, and he identifies himself quite firmly with the working class – an expression which Sayle uses in the scientific sense, as Marx did: 'Those people who work for a living and have surplus value extracted from them – as opposed to those people who own their own means of production, who are petit bourgeois. It's a term which refers to the mass of humanity in Britain, who are sorely under-represented in any fields except pop music and football. They're certainly under-represented in comedy – we live in a society where everything is done to stop the working class doing anything the least bit interesting. (When you start getting to white-collar workers, their subjective allegiances are to the ruling class rather than the working class – with the employ*ers* rather than the employ*ees*; those are subjective notions – what they feel rather than what they are. But if economic conditions ever get really bad, as far as the employers are concerned, those white-collar people are going to be with the employ*ees*.)'

Sayle sees his audience as being largely working-class (or unemployed); but it is interesting that he refuses to do what many people would and moderate his vocabulary to their supposed level of understanding: 'One of the attitudes the working class adopt in this country is to limit their vocabulary – polysyllabic words have been appropriated in a way into a kind of ruling class argot. I'm "bilingual" – I can talk working-class, or I can talk posh; but working class tend not to use long words – which doesn't mean that they don't know what they mean – they do, but they just refuse, for various sociological reasons, to actually use them. A lot of what my comedy has been about is saying that you can speak working-class dialect and express complex ideas. ... If I'm about anything at the core I'm about vaunting working-class culture. The reason I adopted the guise of a skinhead is because it's the one working-class tribal form that posh people will never rip off, because it's too ugly.'

Alexei Sayle

By the time of his 1985 tour Sayle had blended the pick of his earlier material into long performances – co-written with David Stafford – having a very loose construction, which he could vary as necessary. Some of it was rather weird, but mostly seemed to go down well with the audience, and he switched rapidly from subject to subject, using different accents at times, to produce a complex impact:

> I'm not a virgin, you know – I've done it . . . well, I've done it once. . . . I'm not doing it again, I got me fuckin' head stuck. Recently, actually, it was kind of sad for me because recently I had to get married . . . 'cos I got me girl friend into trouble – I got her involved in the civil war in Angola. I'm actually sorry that I'm spouting this filth, ladies and gentlemen, I really shouldn't be doing it because I have an announcement to make – ladies and gentlemen, I have become a born-again Christian. It made enough fuckin' money for Cliff Richard, why shouldn't I fuckin' do it? No, I have become a

born-again Christian – for did not the Lord appear to me outside the Norwegian Ex-Servicemen's Club – for yea, verily, spaketh not in the town, was it not half-price Bailey's Irish Cream night? And did I thence not after quaffing of my fill, yea, verily, go down to Chan's Takeaway, smiting about mine enemies with the bumper off a 1963 Hillman Minx ... and did I not at Chan's Takeaway have double fishcake, curry sauce, chips and peas ... and was there not a blinding explosion – and a voice spaketh unto me, saying 'Tubby, you gobbed on me fuckin' jeans!'? And then the Lord appeared to me, right, and in his hands he had all the separate bits of an MFI wardrobe ... and the Lord spaketh unto me, right, the Lord spaketh unto me, and he said, 'How the fuck do you get these fucking things to fit together?' ...

(*American accent*): Yes, so I've come to preach to you tonight my friends, yay-us ... yayus, fuck off, yes yes, fuck off ... come on, come on to meet Saint Vuvuvu, the patron saint of drunks ... Saint Cacky-trousers, yayus. ... I had a dream, my friends, yayus, I had a dream. ... I dreamt, my friends, of a land where everybody had turned to God ... and then in my dream (*normal voice*) I was standing completely naked in a car park in Walton-on-Thames with me dick covered in Marmite ... you don't have those sort of dreams?. ... oh, fuck ... fuck me, the last thing I remember is sitting down to do me fucking O-levels ... I must have failed. ... Wasn't it Dr Johnson who once said (*mumbles*) ... It was either him or me. I've just got a pet, actually, just got a pet ... I've got a lemming. You know most animals leave shit all over the house – this leaves fucking suicide notes.

It was after this tour that Sayle gave up live comedy – partly because of his increasing distaste for the audiences. He has since largely concentrated on writing – including a novel (*Train To Hell*), columns in the *Sunday Mirror* and *Time Out* (the latter leading to a book, *Alexei Sayle's Great Bus Journeys of the World*) and an illustrated not-a-children's book (*Geoffrey the Tube Train and the Fat Comedian*) – and on straight acting in films and the theatre, including *Gorky Park* and *The Tempest*. However, his reputation in alternative comedy still remains – most of the others speak of him almost with awe – and it was the impact of his work that gave the new comedy a good deal of its initial impetus; in 1988 he made his own television series, *Alexei Sayle's Stuff*, and a strikingly effective contribution to the 'Comic Strip' series of television films, and these will be covered in Chapter 18.

20th-Century Coyote
(Rik Mayall and Adrian Edmondson);
The Outer Limits
(Peter Richardson and Nigel Planer)

Those who were at the Comedy Store from its opening tend to regard the next batch of people to attract attention as a 'second generation' – a generation in this case being about ten months. Even in this short time there was a noticeable change in approach; whereas most of the important performers at the beginning had definite political motivations, the 'second generation' – though on the whole holding left-wing beliefs – tended not to regard themselves as political performers, but simply as comics. (In saying this, it should not be forgotten that we are talking about the ones who made an impact, and survived. All through this period there were still plenty of hopeless amateurs doing acts ranging from the merely weird to the merely bad.)

Of this new group, the one who was to make the most obvious public impact was Rik Mayall. He was born on 7 March 1958 and from early on was interested in drama – his father ran the drama department in a teacher training college. Mayall went to King's School, Worcester; starting at nine rather than the more usual eleven, he was at university by the early age of seventeen. King's School did not have a drama department as such, but Mayall did manage a fair amount of dramatic activity: 'I used to do shows after school with mates – it was also a way of getting off games. We used to do absurdist drama, mainly – *Waiting for Godot*, a bit of Pinter, *Rosencrantz and Guildenstern Are Dead*, *Endgame*, *The Real Inspector Hound* – good fun to perform, and would have a bit of an impact on the teachers and the parents. Those plays are quite significant because you can be very serious by being funny . . . that was mainly where I developed my distaste for being serious.'

Mayall went to Manchester University, leaving in 1978 at the age of twenty with a 2–2 degree in drama. While he was there he met and started working with Adrian Edmondson, who would become his partner in much of his professional work. Edmondson was born on 24 January 1957; his father taught abroad for the Forces, so he lived abroad until he was twelve, then went to a boarding school in Britain.

He remembers his early involvement with drama at school: 'I

was always the arty-Mr-Farty-who-organizes-the-school-arts-festival type – directs and produces and paints the set and stars in it – that was my sort of rôle. I was a very obnoxious child ... truly, I was. I was horrible. Some people say I haven't changed, but I think I have.'

He was at Manchester University in the same year as Mayall, also reading straight drama; he got a 2–1 degree: 'It is pathetically simple to get a drama degree – it's just a name-dropping course, really. As long as you can name four Expressionist German playwrights, you're in. And all it fits you for is to teach degrees in drama.'

However, he and Mayall did get a lot of useful experience. Edmondson: 'There was a scam that you could get your Equity cards down at this club [in fact you couldn't], and we used to do lunchtime theatre there – it was improvised, mostly – and mostly rubbish. I don't think we actually did anything of note until we started doing things like the Comedy Store.'

Edmondson and Mayall worked with three others – Mike Redfern, Mark Dewison and Lloyd Peters (who was the mastermind behind it, according to Mayall) – under the title 20th-Century Coyote. The shows were largely improvised, as Edmondson remembers: 'For example, one week we thought we'd be God's testicles – so we went down to Brentford Nylons and bought a couple of pink duvet covers and tried to string them up from the studio roof. We discovered that you can't string them up from the roof and sit in them with safety, so we did it on the floor, and it was called *How To Get A Man Out Of A Bag* in the end.'

Mayall remembers: 'We were very inspired by the *commedia dell'arte*, which we were studying, where everybody had particular rôles that they took, depending on what they were doing on stage. We didn't have time to write and learn – we had time to write a bit, but not learn, really – we were doing a half- to three-quarter hour show every two weeks. So we had personas that we would do best – I was best at being angry and petulant and selfish and a nuisance and ugly and unpopular. Adrian generally played either heavies or women, and the others had things that they played appropriately as well. There were titles like *Dead Funny*, which is about two guys waking up in a flat and finding a dead body there, and this man was trying to construct the perfect woman, and all he needed was a pair of breasts; and this body had an enormous pair of breasts on it, so this man kept trying to get into the house in various disguises ... and finally he managed to trick his way in and it turned out that the body was a policeman in disguise waiting for him, so he got caught. That was the plot, which we'd improvise our way through.' Other plays included *Who Is Dick Treacle?* and *King Ron and his Nubile Daughter*, and there were many others.

They played in pubs, then moved gradually to touring various university venues; but as the others were in different years the group eventually split up as they left Manchester and in the end Mayall and Edmondson were left as a double-act, still under the same title. Mayall then toured America for six months with the Oxford and Cambridge Shakespeare Company playing parts such as Dromio of Syracuse in *The Comedy of Errors*. When he got back he had to try to pay off his university debts: 'I was living in Droitwich with my parents and working in a foundry during the whole of 1979. Adrian and I did a show every month or two; we put together a show called *Death on the Toilet* – I played God and Death, and Adrian played a character called Edwin.'

They took this to Edinburgh in 1979. Edmondson: 'We did very well, for us – we didn't get much in terms of critical response, but we actually made money, which we thought was fantastic – and which enabled us to get drunker than usual, which was our main pastime.'

After this they came to London, in late 1979, to find themselves involved in a strange incident at the Woolwich Tramshed. This venue had been running a weekly show by a group called the Fundation, which included Joe Griffith and the double-act of Hale and Pace. Edmondson describes the show as 'a very raucous, very light entertainment – Benny Hill type show – very funny, not quite my taste, but a good evening out'. The venue was taken over by a man described by Edmondson as 'a mad Welshman', who removed Fundation and put 20th-Century Coyote, plus one or two other acts, on instead.

Mayall: 'We didn't know this was going on, except suddenly we were doing this cabaret on our own in front of four hundred people who wanted to see the Fundation. We stuck at it for a couple of months – because we thought our Equity cards would be in it; and then he mounted this appalling production of *Macbeth*. This is in early 1980 and he was saying, "I want to make it really relevant, I want to make it really punk" ... four years after that had happened ... "I'll set it in Vietnam" ... so there are these green-haired people in boiler suits in Vietnam smoking dope through shotguns ... dreadful. So I walked out. And as I walked out he said, "I'll make sure you never ever work in the business again." I'd like to see him again, some day.'

Apart from punk *Macbeth*s, Edmondson describes the mainstay of their own material: 'The Samuel Beckett skits were jokes about being old and deaf and blind – anyone who'd read Beckett would find them hysterically funny, but anyone who hadn't wouldn't know what the fuck was going on. There were jokes like – this isn't actually one of them – "What's the time?" – "Yes, it is." It was as bad as that. We tried to write an awful lot of topical stuff, but that didn't work out; we did the odd song – lifted an old tune and wrote different words to it ... we were desperate men, trying to come out with an awful lot of material each week.'

The best part of their act at this time was Mayall's impersonation of an 'angry' young poet. He remembers: 'Richard Turner, who I'd been on the tour of America with, and I wrote some poems which I used to do on stage at a fringe club, and became the basis of my act and the "Rik" character ... I saw a lot of poets down at this fringe club, and I thought, that's stupid, look at them entertaining people with these shit poems; and Richard and I got drunk one day and wrote these poems and I just got up the next night and did them. And every time people sniggered at me I'd shout at them, so they'd snigger even more – they didn't know who I was – they thought there was this genuine mad appalling poet.'

> Theatre ... are you theatre?
> Whenever I carry my spear-ter
> The theatre
> To do Hamlet
> I ask it this question
> It says nothing, except
> 'I don't know – Ask Vanessa Redgrave!'
> But I don't know Vanessa Redgrave!
> And neither do you, theatre.
> ... Or do you?

... It's easy to clap, isn't it? (*Bitterly*) I'm sure it's very funny. It's easy to laugh as well, isn't it? They laughed at Lenny Bruce. Right, the last one I'm going to do now ... I was going to do fourteen of these ... Ha ha ha! Very funny! The last one I'm going to do, OK? ... It's because of people like you that they build airports ... The last one I'm going to do is an angry love poem I've written ... and it's called 'Vanessa'. (*Over the laughter*) It's called Vanessa, right? *Shut up!*

> Do I love you, Vanessa, Vanessa, Vanessa, Vanessa ...
> Vanessa ...

Shut up! ...

> Vanessa, do I love me?
> You made a mess-a-

f my life, Vanessa
Where do I find the key? . . .
It's a metaphor . . . you open doors with . . . tut . . .

Against mounting audience hysteria he would force the poem
through to its dramatic conclusion:

Vanessa, I shall go to my grave with a bleeding heart
But at least it will be a red grave.

Mayall and Edmondson auditioned for Don Ward at the Comedy
Store, and were playing there concurrently with their difficult stay
at the Tramshed – which latter almost closed the venue; the mad
Welshman was slung out and Fundation returned 'by popular
demand' in May 1980.

Another double-act was making its mark at the Comedy Store at
around the same time – The Outer Limits, consisting of Nigel Planer
and Peter Richardson. Planer was born on 22 February 1955 in
Fulham, and went to Westminster School. He went on to Sussex
University – which he hated – reading African and Asian studies.
After leaving there he did various jobs, eventually going to drama
school. He explains: 'Since the age of about eight I'd been doing any
kind of dramatics I could lay my hands on. At Westminster I was a
colleague of Stephen Poliakoff – we wrote a play together and I
directed, and then he directed me in plays – I was never allowed in
school plays, but we were putting on "alternative" productions –
we'd just write what we wanted and then tender a budget to any
teacher who we thought had a tenner for costumes and put on a
production in lecture rooms. So we didn't do much work.'

When he went to Sussex he didn't do any drama but got interested
in music instead; but his early interest revived when he was doing
odd jobs, and he decided to go to drama school. 'The first year there
was good – really good training, which was just what I needed; but
the second year started to get a bit silly – and I re-encountered Peter
Richardson, who I'd worked with at a summer camp school his
parents ran, so we started writing together, and were joined by Pete
Richens, who writes now with Peter.'

Peter Richardson was born in Devon on 15 October 1951. He
came to London when he was seventeen, having decided that he
wanted to be an actor. He was one of the schoolboys in Alan Bennett's
Forty Years On; he got an agent and did a few TV plays as an extra;
he also worked as a lifeguard at a swimming pool for a time. He then
went to the same drama school as Nigel Planer, but didn't really
enjoy it: 'I wasn't really interested in the established forms of enter-

57

tainment like television and theatre. The most exciting thing was music – people our age were interested in going to see rock groups and things like that; so the fringe theatre side was quite attractive, though it never seemed as exciting as I would have liked.'

When he met up with Planer he found that they both had similar ideas of what they would like to do. Richardson: 'We felt we'd like to try something like Frank Zappa had been doing on records, which was being funny but using music as well. There were two guys I saw in 1974 or '5 who were very influential, called Sal's Meat Market, who I think were the funniest pair I've seen on stage – they were Americans, called Ray Hassett and John Ratzenberger. They used to do shows like *Trouble On The Night Shift*, which was an hour and a half long; just the two of them, and between them they'd play about thirty or forty characters – they'd even play crowds: one of them would be the crowd and the other would be the guy talking to it. It was very funny – slightly Cheech and Chong, but not the drug humour. Nigel and I decided to try something like that; one summer we worked in Devon with lots of kids, and we started developing lots of characters. And there was another group called Alberto y los Trios Paranoios; they were a parody rock band, so we thought we'd try to do what Sal's Meat Market were doing, but do it with music and a band – fuse the two things together and make a rock comedy show.'

This idea developed into a show which Planer and Richardson, assisted by Caroline Jay, put on at the Round House Downstairs in August 1976. Inspired by the 1974 Windsor Rock Festival (which had been raided by the police), it was called *Rank*. Planer: 'We got great reviews – and an Arts Council grant. So I left drama school and off we went on tour, with a different band ... we blew the grant on a PA. Peter played the Chief of Thames Valley Police, and I played Neil and a character called Paul, who's a sort of pioneer of drug abuse – he has a three-year-old daughter he keeps losing and a wife he forgets exists ... he's thick-skinned and optimistic, and everybody round him's having a bad time because of him.'

Planer's character Neil was the terminally depressed hippy who later became one of the four characters in *The Young Ones* – he was based on the sort of long-haired guitar-playing incompetent folk-singer which was all too common at this time. Richardson played, among other characters, a police chief who has his own TV show and whose men break up the festival in the manner of traffic cops ('Going a bit *fast*, aren't you, son? Didn't you see the three-bar change? ... That A-string's a bit worn ...').

The show itself was insanely ambitious. Planer: 'On the stage we

had what was going on on the festival stage, and the fantasy sequences – it was an incredibly complicated show to do, I was painting and decorating to pay for it all – and we also had the band; and below the stage we had fake grass, which was meant to be where the punters were, and we played all those characters as well. We played about forty characters between us – with a lot of quick changing. It was the most amazingly expensive complicated show to do – it had back projection as well – and to take it on tour! Typical Peter, really – that's how we wanted it to be, and we didn't compromise. We got national press reviews … it gave me a sense of achievement to have done something so ridiculously ambitious.'

Richardson comments: 'It was bit naïve the whole thing, looking back on it, but our enthusiasm – and I think we had a kind of panache – carried it through. We didn't make any money out of it – I was squatting at the time.'

After *Rank* finished, Planer worked with a street theatre company, got a job as an actor at the Leeds Playhouse, started a harmony band gigging round wine bars, and then got a part in the chorus of *Evita* – despite not being a dancer and still having no Equity card (which he didn't admit to them): he also understudied the David Essex part (Ché Guevara). 'I did that for a year – because I'd signed a year's contract – which was really good because it consolidated in my mind that I wanted to do comedy.'

Richardson meanwhile toured with a band in Italy for a period, and then helped to run drama courses for children at his parents' farmhouse in Devon: 'With another friend of mine, who's an actor, we'd put on small plays which I'd write and direct during the course. One of these became a show called *The Wild Boys*, based on William Burroughs' book – which I put on at the ICA in London and toured around, with a band called Furious Pig – it was quite a visual sort of show. That's how I met Michael White, through that; it was supposed to be going into the West End, but it never happened. While Michael was trying to find a theatre, Nigel and I started going down to the Comedy Store.'

Michael White, a theatrical producer of long standing, had presented the first West End appearance of some members of the Monty Python and *Goodies* teams in *Cambridge Circus* in 1963. Although this particular venture with Richardson came to nothing, the association was to lead to the development of one of the most important strands of the new comedy, in the form of the Comic Strip.

Appearing as The Outer Limits, Richardson and Planer did well at the Comedy Store on their first appearance, so they went away and prepared some material; they became regular performers there for a time. One of the most effective parts of the act was a solo by Planer, using the character of Neil from *Rank*. He remembers: 'It's rather like Rik's act with the poet; I'd walk on as a hippy, with a guitar – this is what I used to do in *Rank* – and say, "I'm going to do a couple of numbers for you ... I've lost my plectrum" ... and spend ages getting to be able to do the number. In the right situation, people really think that this absolutely shit folk singer's coming on – there are plenty of them – then they start to laugh because he's so bad – then they realize that you're actually in control and you know what you're doing. There's a lot of acts since then that play ineptitude with great professionalism ... but I don't think we had the professionalism, I think we were just inept!'

As time went on, Planer added to and refined the character of Neil, still keeping the basic idea:

> Hullo ... um, I'm going to do a couple of numbers off my latest ... um, demo tape ... Never mind, they're both pretty bad, so I'm going to do the worst one first so the second one won't seem so bad. OK ... right, the first number's sort of about this really heavy scene that I had, OK ... with this chick, right ... (*sighs*) Yeah ... In the whole two years that we were together, OK, she never had an orgasm ... so like I wrote this song ... OK, about how she never had an orgasm ... it's called ... 'How She Never Had An Orgasm' ... It was really bad, actually ... really bad ... we tried everything ... we tried all sorts of new positions ... like me lying on top ... nothing worked.
>
> (*sings*):   She said
>   You're as good in bed
>   As you are (*searches for chord*)
>   At playing the guitar (*Pete Townsend leap*).

Planer and Richardson had swiped the name 'The Outer Limits' from the American TV fantasy series of the early 1960s, and wrote several sketches with each of them playing a number of parts. Accepting the limits of the Comedy Store, they avoided props and costumes, and kept the approach lively and frequently violent – miming spurting blood and severed limbs in *Are You Being Severed* as the characters commit mass murders in the style of an American TV situation comedy; and in the airline-disaster-porno-movie *AC-DC 10* they added to this an attempted airline hijack. This sequence takes place in the control tower:

> **Nigel:** OK, OK, You want the DC-10, right. (*Phone*) Hello, this is, er, Dayglo Danny to Jasmin Johnny, request Panzer Divisioney Policey car car quickety quick.
> **Peter:** Hey, what is all that codey code stuff?

Nigel: No, that's not codey code, that's just normal procedure. I'm just getting your plane. Be here any minute.

Peter: You called the cops, didn't you?

Nigel: No, I'm just getting your plane, mister, normal procedure, don't shoot, buddy, we're friends.

Peter: Oh God, I'm so frightened and nervous and paranoid I might do something stupid ... BLAM! ...

Nigel: Choom, choom, choom (*mimes neck spurting blood*).

Peter: Oh my God, I shot him, he's going to die, ha ha ha, die, can't you, die? BLAM! ...

Nigel: Choom, choom, blerp blerp (*neck and eye*).

Peter: BLAM BLAM!

Nigel: Choom choom, blerp blerp, splud splud. You put my brains on the ceiling mister, I'll get you for this you mother-fucker.

Peter: Oh my God, he's still not dead ... BLAM! ...

Nigel: That's my guts ... you bastard ... yech!

Peter: Maybe this spade will do ... KLANG!

Nigel: Dujung dujung dujung.

Peter: KLANG!

Nigel: Bchaadung!

Peter: KLANG!

Nigel: Yaaa, you mother-fucker.

Peter: Oh God, he's still not dead, where's my knife?

Nigel: Ah, that's my leg, look at that, it's sticking right through my leg, I'll get you, you bastard.

Peter: Oh no ... I know, the microwave oven.

Nigel: Not the microwave oven!

Peter: Zee ... SLAM ... how would you like to be cooked?

Nigel: Er ... well ...

Peter: Well done it is.

Nigel: Hey, mister, can you do me a favour?

Peter: What?

Nigel: When I'm done ... the oven cleaner is under the sink.

Nigel Planer: 'We did space invaders ... "Sarky and Bitch" ... it was all very media, and very fast. We used to vie for the right place on the bill with Rik and Ade, because they were the only other energetic double-act ... we really had to fight, because both wanted the end of the first half; because once you got into the second half at the Comedy Store it just turned into a throwing match.'

Mayall and Edmondson were still working at the Tramshed during most of their Comedy Store period – they would come on after the Tramshed show. They hardly varied their material at all, doing mostly the poet solo and a routine worked up from a section in one of their earlier plays. This was 'The Dangerous Brothers', with Mayall as Richard Dangerous, who was played in the style of someone presenting a stunt act in a circus; and Edmondson as Adrian Danger-ous, the nervous stuntee. Later, on television, they were able to give

the idea of the dangerous stunts full rein; in the Comedy Store they spent most of the act arguing with each other:

> **Rik** (*to Ade*): Stand up straight.
> **Ade:** I'm *standing* up straight.
> **Rik:** Stand up *straighter* ... Ready?
> **Ade:** OK.
> **Rik:** Right ... three ...
> **Ade:** Three ...
> **Rik:** Four ...
> **Ade:** Four ...
> (*They both start doing the introduction at once.*)
> **Rik:** Shut up! Shut up! *Shut up!* I'll do the talking, right? Face the wall. *Face the wall!* (*To audience.*) Shan't keep you a moment. (*Squeezes Ade's testicles sharply*) Ready?
> **Ade** (*in some pain*): OK.
> **Rik:** Stand up straight!
> **Ade** (*in agony*): I'm standing ... (*starts to fall over*).
> **Rik:** (*catching him*): Steady, steady ... Now, I'll do the talking, all right? Three ...
> **Ade:** Three ...
> **Rik:** Four ...
> **Ade:** Four ...
> **Rik** (*rapidly*): Good evening ladies and gentlemen, we are the Dangerous Brothers ...
> **Ade:** Ha hah! ... Dangerous Brothers!
> **Rik:** I've told them.
> **Ade:** Oh, good.
> **Rik:** My name's Richard Dangerous, and this is Adrian Dangerous. (*Ade head-butts the microphone.*) Thank you very much, ladies and gentlemen – unusually dangerous, I think you'll agree. We'd like to start this evening with a little joke. (*To Ade.*) Joke!
> **Ade:** Joke. Er ... Knock knock.
> **Rik:** Who's there?
> **Ade:** Open the door.
> **Rik:** Open the door who?
> **Ade:** Open the door please, I want to come in.
> **Rik:** Open the door please I want to come in who?
> **Ade** (*by now shouting*): Look just open the fucking door!!
> **Rik** (*also shouting*): Just open the fucking door who?!!

They abandon this and launch upon another joke which, through their arguments and explanations, gets completely garbled. The idea of people who argue – or even talk in a monologue – without achieving anything other than a complete waste of time seems to be one of Mayall and Edmondson's major obsessions, which has surfaced frequently in the course of their careers.

Although they did occasionally try doing the Beckett sketches at the Comedy Store, they never met with much success; so Mayall and Edmondson tended to stick to the same two routines every week, which got honed to a fine edge. Edmondson: 'We were never stand-up comedians.... I think we seemed to be, and we sort of half became it with that particular act; but before it we were doing sketches and plays. We kept trying to bung in a new act, and it would go down so abysmally that we knew it would take three months to work it in – and we were too scared of failure to try it. Occasionally when we got too drunk we would try something new. And because we were drunk it would fail anyway.'

Mayall comments on the Comedy Store audiences: 'In the first year, when I think it was at its best, the audiences were as experimental as the performers were. What it subsequently became was middle-class people pretending they knew what cabaret was about ... they thought cabaret was all about going to rough clubs where people throw beer glasses and punch each other. It was a much more artistically experimental place ... if anyone did anything boring they got gonged, so people would come down with great ideas and try them out, and the audience were supportive. You have to remember, it came out of punk as well ... this punk thing of, it doesn't matter what you're doing as long as you mean it. So if you were lying, or a hypocrite, you got gonged. That first year was the best in the Comedy Store ... when they took the gong away it was a terrrible mistake.'

However, the next stage in the careers of the two double-acts was about to happen. There were to be two causes; one was Peter Richardson's determination to run his own show; and the other was the presence in the Comedy Store audience – though in a private capacity – of a fledgling BBC Television producer.

A legend of the Comedy Store is that it was full of television producers scouting for talent. If it was, most of them did precious little about it; the first step into TV came as a result of the presence of Paul Jackson, who at the time was a production manager for the BBC. He had joined the BBC in late 1972 or early 1973, having abandoned his original plans to be an actor. He started as a call-boy and slowly worked his way up the system – assistant floor manager, floor manager, vision mixer, production manager, later becoming a director, a producer, then a senior producer.

He worked on the standard Light Entertainment programmes – *Top of the Pops*, *The Generation Game*, *Blankety Blank*; and in particular on *The Two Ronnies* at every level of production. Whatever one may think of the humour in *The Two Ronnies*, it is an extremely professionally produced programme incorporating outside filming, sketches, monologues, musical numbers . . . and so provides an excellent grounding in most of the techniques of television.

(At this time the distinction between director and producer in Light Entertainment was largely a matter of promotion, with the producer overseeing the whole programme and the director handling the more artistic and technical side; in the Drama Department the producer would handle finance and hire the director, who would often be a freelance – the relationship being very similar to that in the making of cinema films.)

Jackson went to the Comedy Store – purely for his own pleasure, not in any talent-spotting capacity – and was excited by what he saw: 'A good thing about the BBC is that you do feel it's worthwhile putting in programme proposals, because they do actually read them, and they do occasionally get done; so I wrote this completely unrealistic programme proposal which was that there was such a good cabaret circuit in London – in every sense, music, comedy . . . the off-West-End circuit was getting quite important – that we would be able to do a weekly programme for twenty-six weeks based on that kind of music and comedy. They quite rightly said, we won't do that, but if you would like to try a quick pilot. . . . The Head of Variety was Robin Nash, and he'd seen a show called *George* at a café theatre, which was performed by five girls from the cast of *Angels* [a TV hospital soap opera]. It was a very funny and likeable musical show.'

Nash booked a studio for two days, mounting *George* on the first day and letting Jackson have it for the second day: 'I then went out, flushed with success – I'd never directed anything in my life, and here I was going to produce and direct this thing – and I approached the people I had liked; most of them I vaguely knew – and I knew Peter Rosengard and I spoke to him about it, and I bought *Time Out* and went and saw all the other places that were listed. The first discovery was that it was very sensible of the BBC not to go for twenty-six weeks, because it was mostly the same few people doing the same acts.'

He hired Alexei Sayle, Keith Allen, Tony Allen, Mayall and Edmondson, and Planer and Richardson; but in the end decided against using the double-acts as such and settled for Mayall's poems and Planer as Neil. Peter Richardson was upset at being left out and there was a major row between him and Jackson, which was more important for its later effect than at the time. American comic actress Ruby Wax and a feminist theatre group called Bloomers did some material which didn't make the final version; and the music was provided by the Blues Band.

The title – *Boom Boom, Out Go The Lights* – was chosen because Jackson couldn't afford a special signature tune on the show's tight budget, and so he looked through the Blues Band's repertoire and chose a song with that title to open the programme.

Jackson had a set built in the style of a cabaret, with a small stage and some of the audience at tables in front of it, the rest being in the usual tiered rows at the sides and back: 'It was appropriate for both shows; all of them had only ever performed in very small club venues to a very committed audience – a lot of them got their Equity cards out of that show, they still hadn't got them – and I thought it would be destructive to put the fourteen-foot gap of technical robotics between them and the audience. (A lot of people said, why didn't we just go to the nightclub, but it would have cost a lot more to do it that way.) When you're as raw as some of them were then, it's very difficult to be suddenly removed from your audience, and the problem of whether to play to camera or not becomes very apparent when that's all you can see in front of you.'

The show was recorded on 16 May 1980. The performers worked without scripts or tight rehearsals, for the most part doing excerpts from their existing acts (although Tony Allen and Keith Allen added a few remarks suitable to the occasion). Alexei Sayle rather worried the technical crew by saying 'fuck' – which was bleeped out in the transmission version – and the whole thing was a bit rough at the edges; but it edited down into an interesting half hour.

On looking at the show now, all of the performers come over well, but the most assured is Mayall. He does 'Theatre' and 'Vanessa' with complete confidence, using the camera effectively (even managing to follow a camera change made in the middle of a remark to camera) as a rapid succession of expressions passes across his face while he apparently struggles to keep his audience serious. Interestingly, compared with much of his later television work which is deliberately overplayed, he is quite subtle, obviously aware of the camera's tendency to exaggerate performances.

Paul Jackson

The transmission was on 14 October 1980. Paul Jackson: 'The BBC never showed *George*, although I still think it's a good show, and they showed *Boom Boom* to the worst audience response in the history of the department – it went out to a very small audience, and an "Appreciation Index" of 46 [out of 100] – one expects not to drop into the 50s – but the BBC did see something in it and commissioned another one a year later.'

Though *Boom Boom* did attract a small amount of critical attention, the next career step for the two double-acts arose largely because of the lack of anywhere much to perform – there were a few pubs and a couple of fringe venues, but not nearly enough to provide a living. They performed at a small venue called Pentameters – at the Three Horseshoes pub in Hampstead – on 18–21 and 25–27 September 1980, together with another Comedy Store regular, Arnold Brown (who had been there on the first night and had stuck with it despite little success – 'I usually get gonged off in the lift'; more about him later in the chapter).

69

They discussed the possibility of a permanent venue. Adrian Edmondson: 'It might have been called the New Depression Club – dreadful title. Everyone it was offered to leapt at the chance, and everyone it wasn't offered to got very bitter – that seems to have been where the split between the obvious two camps of supposed alternative comedians arose, I think.'

The new venue arose from Peter Richardson's production of *The Wild Boys*, for which Michael White was still trying to find a theatre. For Richardson the whole Comedy Store business was a bit unexpected, since he was still intending to put his play on. However, he threw his energies into the new venue – to be called the Comic Strip: 'My idea initially was to find a theatre to put *The Wild Boys* on at, and run the Comic Strip late-night, after it. Then I found the Boulevard Theatre in the Raymond Revue Bar; it wasn't possible to do *The Wild Boys* because it was too small and it was too expensive ... and the enthusiasm had run out. So the Comic Strip took over, in a way. I guess that from it, all the things I originally thought that I wanted to do when I was seventeen started to happen in an unexpected way ... though I did a lot of comedy with Nigel I never really thought of myself as a comedian, and I still don't – I just like doing comedy and acting it.'

Just as the Comedy Store had opened in a strip club, the Comic Strip opened in October 1980 in premises run by the king of the spectacular strip show, Paul Raymond. Unlike the Comedy Store – which required its audience to be club members because of the licensing laws – the Comic Strip was a theatrical presentation, with the more usual audience seats and a proper stage with lighting. This had an effect on the style of their performances. Nigel Planer: 'Suddenly the whole thing moved up a gear, and it became a show – which we didn't really realize at the time. It was an exciting show, well structured ... but we all childishly thought we were in an experimental club, and it took me ages to realize that that was not what we were doing. We were saying, why can't we be like the Comedy Store and write new material every week, but it became not like that because you've got audiences coming three or four times and saying, "What happened to the Vanessa routine?" It became silly to do new material which was inferior – it was better just to run the material which was good, and tailor it. Alexei quickly realized this was happening and refused to change his material.'

Sayle attracted most of the media attention because of the ferocity of his act – for the Comic Strip rapidly became an 'in' place to be seen at, and got a number of write-ups in the press. (It was also the subject of a TV film by Julian Temple, which was very oddly made, was hated by everybody in it, and was never transmitted.)

Alexei Sayle comments: 'People talk about what an exciting groove the Comic Strip was – but it was nothing compared with the Comedy Store. By then it was quite a calculated move for us to enhance our careers – there was never that much danger at the Comic Strip. It took a time to get its final form – we messed about with the set and the band a bit ... When everybody had finished their act they went home, so I used to be left there by myself, which was a really weird feeling – nobody backstage, just me doing my final number – so I invented this finale number we all did, just to make sure that everybody stayed.'

Though Sayle more or less took charge of the running order for the show, and compèred it, the behind-the-scenes control was very much Peter Richardson's. After its initial period the show settled into a format consisting of Sayle, Mayall and Edmondson, Planer and Richardson, a guest, and two other regulars – Arnold Brown and the female double-act of French and Saunders.

Arnold Brown was born in Glasgow on 27 December 1936 – it is his proud claim to be the oldest alternative comedian in the world. He describes his family as not quite working-class, not quite middle-class: 'Culturally we were slightly working-class, I felt – no books in the house syndrome and all that – but no poverty. And I was Jewish, which added to the ghetto-izing of my mind. Glasgow was very sort of dark and grey in these days ... I had a very conventional life; we didn't go abroad ... sex was for other people. I had vague longings to write ... I also sometimes scribbled bits and pieces of short stories which I didn't show to anyone. A sociologist would say that I was irredeemably being sucked into the vortex of being an accountant because this would meet the sociological need of getting away from the class I was born into ... and so it was. My real name is Abraham Arnold Lizerbram ... people don't become comedians by accident, there's a force of apartness ... and I changed it to Brown when I was going into accountancy at the age of seventeen.'

He qualified as an accountant, staying in Glasgow for about three years, then coming to London in 1963. He worked as an advertising copywriter for a time, then went back into accounting, working for the same firm for fifteen years.

As an antidote to accountancy he used to go to a coffee bar in Swiss Cottage, meeting with a regular group every Saturday: 'I always wanted to be hip, like Kenneth Tynan. ... I saw myself as a Finchley Road version of Lenny Bruce. ... I would take the *New Yorker* and be equated with humour – talk about Woody Allen films ... only now I recognize that I learnt that there's a kind of timing,

to come in with a joke – you have to wait until that certain moment. I didn't do it consciously – I remember on one occasion a couple at the next table, before they left they said to me, "Thank you very much, we've enjoyed it ..." as if it was a performance! I didn't realize I was performing.'

He became involved in a comedy writers' course, run by Brad Ashton (the brother of stand-up comic Warren Ashton), and from there got into writing one-line gags for BBC Radio programmes such as *Week Ending*. By the time the Comedy Store opened he had been improvising sketches with friends on a private basis and was wondering about the possibility of opening a club for improvisational comics; so the Comedy Store was the natural next step.

He was there for the opening, and became sucked into the brief media attention it received: 'Because I was an accountant, and the media are always into labelling and stereotypes, *Nationwide* did a little piece on me ... and on the night, I naïvely thought you could go up with a couple of half-sketched ideas ... and when I went on, I couldn't believe it because all these people were drinking – and the guy with the gong was half pissed, too – it was like Dante's Inferno. My opening joke was supposed to be, "I'm an accountant, I check things – can you hear me at the back?" ... how funny that is, eh? ... and before I could say this, someone said, "We can't hear you at the back." I was about to think of something when someone said, "Put him out of his misery." And it was my first involvement with the media – I thought it was incredibly glamorous then. I remember seeing someone from Radio 4 interviewing someone from LBC. ....'

Despite the difficult beginning, he kept going back – usually getting off quickly before he was gonged – until one night, quite suddenly, it all clicked and he did a forty-minute set which is still spoken about by those who were there.

By the time Peter Richardson asked him to be in the Comic Strip show he had honed his material and was much more successful. He describes his approach as an antidote to the others in the show: 'I was laid back and nervous, they were up-front and confident – I was old, they were young. ... You couldn't have a whole evening of Rik and Ade doing the Dangerous Brothers, and Alexei ... so I was the difference in pace. My lines were more quotable than the others', because they were more honed – they were into performance, I was into observation.'

Brown's jokes often take a moment or two to sink in – the audience can be heard thinking before they laugh – and combine clever observation and exaggeration of reality with a refreshing touch of pure madness:

I must reveal myself – I'm Scottish ... why not? ... and Jewish ... not sure how to react, are you? Liberals, eh? Still worried, eh? Two racial stereotypes for the price of one – perhaps the best value in the West End today – perhaps not. People ask me about being Jewish – no they don't – but at the end of 1980, I noticed with a smile the death of Oswald Mosley, the Busby Berkeley of British fascism ... or was he the Roman Polanski? – we'll never know. Anyway, it got me thinking, and I questioned myself: Arnold – yes? – being Jewish must mean more than this inner compulsion you have to buy all Barry Manilow's records ... or see *The Jazz Singer* seven times in the one week. And I thought, proudly – Freud, Marx, Einstein, wonderful people, they're Jewish, I'm Jewish ... I drop their names at cocktail parties – why not? Sir Keith Joseph and Milton Friedman, they're not Jewish – I have categorical proof to the contrary.

I told you I was Scottish – I went back to my home town of Glasgow recently – you know Glasgow at the moment under the Tories, the deprivation, the two-year waiting list for people who want to vandalize telephone kiosks. ... On the building the plaque still hangs in the wind – '1936–1956 Arnold Brown was socially deprived here'. I remember my father working long hours in his second-hand fruit shop ... the sign in the window – 'Melons, guaranteed only one previous owner.' It was no picnic in Glasgow being Jewish – he's on at that again – no football team to support ... I remember the schizophrenia of the annual Scotland versus Israel match – what should I do, rabbi? I also remember the difficulty in Glasgow of my father being a ... teetotaller – and the shame on Saturday nights of him being constantly thrown *into* pubs. ...

The other new members of the Comic Strip team, Dawn French and Jennifer Saunders, joined only after it had been running for a few months. Neither had made plans to become comedians; in fact both had trained as teachers.

Their lives ran strangely parallel, even before they met: both had fathers in the RAF and consequently travelled about a lot; and they both shared the same best friend – consecutively. Dawn French was born on 11 October 1957; after taking her A-levels she went to America to study in New York for a year on a scholarship from the English Speaking Union.

Jennifer Saunders was born on 6 July 1958; after leaving school she spent a year in Italy; and then the two of them met in 1977 on a teaching course at the Central School of Speech and Drama. Jennifer Saunders: 'It was just something that happened to be vacant at the time I had to go to college – I thought, I'll go to London, that's good. I actually had to pretend that I'd seen plays, whereas all I'd ever seen was *Charlie's Aunt* in Worthing when I was about seven. They did teach me something, because you *have* to stand up in front of people, and you *have* to speak a poem, which was completely hideous as far as I was concerned – so it gave me a little bit of confidence.'

They came into close contact by pure accident, as Dawn French remembers: 'We happened to move into the same flat – we were both looking for somewhere to live, and a mutual friend had a flat to share but she needed seven people – so we signed up, but not together. Jennifer very quickly became in charge of the flat – and I was her right-hand person who gave all the orders to everybody else.'

They started writing together only in the last term or so. Dawn French: 'We never wrote anything down for a long time – we used to improvise stuff and just remember the best bits.' Jennifer Saunders: 'It was never *for* anything, we started doing it as a joke in the flat, then we did it at the end-of-term cabaret; then when I was unemployed for a while and Dawn was teaching, we thought, we'll do it as a joke in the evenings at the Comic Strip. It wasn't until Peter Richardson decided we could make some money at it ... complete innocence was what got us through. And ignorance, probably.'

They started as guests, fortnightly, but soon joined the regular team – working five nights a week until Sayle and the others rebelled and the show came down to two nights a week. Dawn French was still teaching through all this: 'We made the mistake of thinking we had to change our material regularly, so Jennifer would come into my school sometimes and we'd work out new material – dreadful, dreadful material – and go and perform it that night. Gradually we realized the boys weren't changing their acts – and of course it was the audience that changed every night. So we stuck with the characters that we knew best ... but it was hard to fit in because it wasn't really stand-up material.' Jennifer Saunders adds: 'We didn't really have a double-act then; all we did was sketches, and then we'd stop and be slightly embarrassed and bow and say "Thank you".'

The sketch that they first performed at the Comic Strip, and which was their mainstay throughout the show's run, was called 'Psychodrama'; Jennifer Saunders played an American woman supposedly running a course, who is interrupted by a friend from back home. As with most of their material, there are few actual joke lines, the humour being more in the performance, which they honed into detailed character studies:

Jennifer: Do you know what I really miss in London, Muriel?
Dawn: No – what do you miss?
Jennifer: My analyst.
Dawn: Do *I* miss *my* analyst?
Jennifer: Do you?

> **Dawn:** Yes, I miss my analyst. You go to Shmuckermeyer, right?
> **Jennifer:** Yes ... how do you know I go to Shmuckermeyer?
> **Dawn:** Oh, he told me, you know. I mean, like, he figures I'm your friend ...
> **Jennifer:** I *am* your friend, sure ...
> **Dawn:** Well, like, you know, I can help you with your problem.
> **Jennifer** (*slightly tense*): My problem?
> **Dawn:** Oh, you know about your problem ... I mean, although externally you are a truly *truly* beautiful person, Diana – you are, you are – inside you, you have a kind of ... negative void?
> **Jennifer:** The abyss?
> **Dawn:** The abyss, yeah ... have you noticed you're not being invited to dinner-parties at home any more?
> **Jennifer:** Well, really John and I don't go out much, you know ...
> **Dawn:** No, it's actually because you are a totally, totally boring person ... But it's nothing we can't fight, right, Diana?

'Diana' retaliates by suggesting that though Muriel is 'physically a really disgusting person' she has a warmth of personality. Muriel comments that sharing the problems like this is 'relieving a lot of tension':

> **Dawn** (*sweetly*): Could I ask you a personal question, Diana?
> **Jennifer:** Sure, go ahead ...
> **Dawn:** Are you having, like, really *good* sex with your husband?
> **Jennifer:** OK ... yeah ...
> **Dawn:** Honestly?
> **Jennifer:** No ... no, I'm not having sex with my husband at the moment ...
> **Dawn:** Yeah, I know that.
> **Jennifer:** Really – how do you know?
> **Dawn:** Oh, because *I* am having really good sex with your husband.
> **Jennifer:** Oh, my husband John?
> **Dawn:** John, right ... well, he came to me, OK, he told me about your ... well, I don't like to say ...
> **Jennifer:** No, about what, about what?
> **Dawn:** You're sure?
> **Jennifer:** Sure.
> **Dawn:** OK ... about your clitoral frigidity. Let's share it, right? And I figure like, you know, I can help him – boy, can I help him – and he can help you with your anti-orgasm – we can help each other, right, Diana?

As French and Saunders had gone straight to the Comic Strip, the others used to kid them that they hadn't done an 'apprenticeship' at the Comedy Store. Dawn French: 'The first night we went down to the Comedy Store to perform, Andy de la Tour made a joke about that programme about Auschwitz with Vanessa Redgrave – and somebody shouted out some racist comment, and before you knew, chairs and bottles were flying ... and we were on next ... and the police arrived.... We did another night there to the Thames Valley River Police who were out on a stag night – "Get 'em off, show us your tits"....' Jennifer Saunders remembers: 'Dawn stood up to them quite well ... "Why don't you show us your knob, sir?"'

There was nothing of this sort at the Comic Strip. Dawn French: 'It became the fashionable place to be in London. It was the time when the "New Romantics" were around, and you'd look out on a sea of fluffy shirts; and it was full of minor London celebs and hip people who'd come to be seen there. It was crummy then – but because it had some kind of prestige it meant some people would come to see you when you did the little pub gigs ... well, about ten, if you were lucky.'

The Comic Strip ran until July 1981, after which the show went on tour. A record was made during one evening's performance, but they seem to have used an alternative recording engineer, because the quality is poor and the whole thing gives little idea of the atmosphere of the place – particularly the Outer Limits, who were quite visual, and the Dangerous Brothers act, which is almost unintelligible. It is a pity that no better souvenir remains, because the Comic Strip show was important both in bringing the performers to a wider audience, and for creating the team that would later make the *Comic Strip Presents* ... programmes for Channel Four.

Shortly before they ended, another edition of *Boom Boom, Out Go The Lights* was broadcast, on 5 May 1981 (recorded on 25 January). The same performers appeared again, with the exception of Keith Allen, plus Edmondson and Richardson working in their double-acts; Andy de la Tour and Pauline Melville also did monologues.

The audience figures were about the same as for the first edition – tiny in TV terms; but Paul Jackson was quite pleased with it: 'It was a slicker piece of work; by that time they'd become cult figures even though they hadn't done much TV ... so from the first one, which was real novice time for everyone, we were a year later on – it happened, and one was quite happy with it. It was more interesting for what came after – by that time we were beginning to have signs that *The Young Ones* was going to be taken up.' *The Young Ones* – the real break-through into television – will be covered in Chapter 6.

CABARET
COMEDY AND VARIETY

Please send all cabaret information, including details of times, prices, nearest tube and enquiries phone number, to Peter Nichols. Deadline is Wednesday, seven days before publication.
*Where map references are given, these are to the map in the Visitors' Guide section. A map reference marked with * indicates the place is not actually featured on the map; the reference is only given to indicate general location.*

THURSDAY 4

Ain't We Got Fun The Finborough Theatre, Finborough Arms, Finborough Rd, SW10 (373 3842/670 1232) Earls Court tube. Map C12*. Lindsay Holiday, whose career has spanned from lead singer with Chairman of The Board to cabaret performer in 'Y' presents his own show. Set backstage in a vaudeville theatre in New Orleans in the thirties, a janitor reminisces about the great black entertainers of his day. The repertoire of songs ranges from the soulful Stormy Weather to the toe-tapping Lullaby of Broadway. 8pm. £2/£1.50 concs.

Arfington, Arfington Donmar Warehouse, Earlham St, WC2 (enq 379 6565) Covent Garden tube. Map D2. 11pm. £4.90/£3.90/

£2.90. Concs £1 off all prices.
Cambridge Footlights 1984 UCS Theatre, Frognal, Hampstead, NW3. Hampstead tube. 'The Story So Far....'. Usual stuff. 7.45pm. £3.
Cirque de Barbarie The Albany Empire, Douglas Way, Deptford, SE8 (enq 691 3333) Deptford/New Cross BR. New Cross tube. All female circus company from Paris. **See Caption.** 8pm. Doors open 7pm. £4/£3 concs.
Denise Black Blenheims Basement, 12 Blenheim Terrace, NW8 (624 5313) St John's Wood tube. The powerful vocalist and her accompanist Paul Sand provide the music for this café venue. There's no charge for entrance and no minimum charge should you want to eat, or you can just have a drink. 9pm.
The Crack Club South Bank Poly, Rotary St, SE1 (enq 261 1525) Elephant & Castle/Borough/Lambeth North tubes. Impressionist Rory Bremner and comics Mark Steel and Skint Video 8pm. £2.

FRIDAY 5

Ain't We Got Fun See Thursday.
Alternative City of London Tour Steps of the Royal Exchange, Corner of Threadneedle St, Cornhill, EC2 (enq 673 0528) Bank tube. Map 07*. I'm unreliably informed that there's a statue of Boy George in the City of London. Arthur Smith guides unsuspecting lunchers and City itinerants around these and other crumbling artefacts, that may or may not exist. 1.10pm-1.45pm. £1.50.
Arfington, Arfington See Thursday.
Bush Fires Cabaret The Bush Hotel, Shepherds Bush Green, W12 (enq 740 8223) Shepherds Bush tube. Ian Saville, a magician with strong affinity to Marx, Maria Tollys sings and The Fabulous Rhino Sisters, who sing swing. 8.30pm. £2.50/£1 concs.
Cast at The Old White Horse 261 Brixton Rd, SW9 (enq 487 3440) Brixton/Oval tubes. Femal musical duo, The Moonlighters, Bradford poet Joolz, and TO Street Entertainers of the Year, The Vicious Boys, who've had a dream summer playing the pavements and piazzas, and not a bad one on the boards either. They packed out the Masonic Lodge in Edinburgh where they shared with Kafka's The Trial (another rip-roaring, side-splitting little number) in just about the most incongruous double billing imaginable, and though their act may be its strongest on the streets, they should still be worth a viewing indoors. 8.30pm. £2.50/£1.50 concs.
Cast at The Diorama 14 Peto Place, NW1 (enq 487 3440) Gt Portland St/Regents Pk tubes. Map H5*. Crowded stage for the first full week of the new Cast circuit. Fatima the Fantastic fire-eats, Porky is the Poet, Topo may mime, although he had a one-man show in Edinburgh that wasn't and fell well short of his cabaret work, Mark Miwurdz regales with stories of his native Sheffield, and Tooth,

The First Friday The Approach Tavern, Approach Rd, Bethnal Green, EC2 (enq 247 0216) Bethnal Green tube. New regular venue initiated by the Tower Hamlets Arts Project and happening, as the name suggests, on the first Friday of every month. They're hoping to keep a local feel to the bill and the first weeks line-up certainly does that. Screaming Abdabs, Mick Jackson and John Say from Dancing With The Dog, provide the eccentric acappella, comic pair Dusty and Dick do a spot, as does Bob Boyton. Woof, perform their comedy/drama and there will be poems and songs from the Tower Hamlet Writers Group and music from Sam Spades Pocket Trio. A full night indeed. 8.30pm. £2/£1.25 concs.

SATURDAY 6

Ain't We Got Fun See Thursday.
Apples & Snakes The Captain's Cabin, Norris St, Haymarket, SW1 (enq 699 5265). Piccadilly tube. Map B4*. Jamaican poet Valerie Bloom heads this weeks billing; further poetry from the very Irish Ian McPherson with, one would suspect considerable comic content; puns and songs from Dave Reeves and Mr Phipps; and songs only from Penny Wood. 8.30pm. £2.50/£1.50 concs.

Arfington, Arfington See Thursday.
Banana Cabaret The Bedford Hotel, SW12 (672 3129) Balham tube. 9pm. Doors open 8.30pm. £2/£1 concs.

Cast at The Cricklewood Hotel Mora Rd, Cricklewood, NW2 (enq 487 3440) Cricklewood Lane BR. Line-up as Friday (see Cast at The Old White Horse) with the addition of comic Oscar McLennan, the egregious Glaswegian with plenty of front. Doors open 7.30. £2/£1 concs.

audience is altho ... with ... re-adjustment — before it carried ... there was an hiatus, perhaps a re-adjustment ... till one of them played so much a part that he action, pulling the audience in and in, ... an evocative and bewailing tempo accompanies all: took a curtain call. The music ... defying them and who could not love a magi- the trapeze ... doubts ... the illusions, defying them ... 'Why are you laughing? It is not easy to cian that responds to her audience thus: 'Why are you laughing?' But it was the clowning speak English with a Russian accent when you are French.' But it was ... a diverting and digressing that excelled and the char, who was the chief clown, ... extending the expected into the hilarious. It spindle of energy, all eyes and duster, ... and there can be no higher praise than that. (Peter Nichols) *Circus* was pure kids stuff ... *de Barbarie* at The Albany (Thur-Sat). See Listings.

music with this weeks bands Happy ..., and Carol who play Brechtian oom-pah-pah. Topo is the Grimes, with great blues/rock accompanying cabaret act. 10.30pm. £2.50/£1.00 concs. 50p first time membership.

Cirque de Barbarie See Thursday.
Crown & Castle Cabaret 600 Kingsland Rd, E8 (enq 254 3678) Dalston Jct/Kingsland BR. Comedy with a poetic slant on offering with Clive Benson and Alan Gilbey plus comedy, without poetry, from Simon Fanshawe. 9.30pm. Doors open 9pm. £2/£1.30 UB40s. Late bar.
Finborough Cabaret Finborough Arms, Finborough Rd, SW10 (373 3842/670 1232) Earls Court tube. Map C12*. This week three male comics of one style or another, Jeremy Hardy, John Sparkes and Clive Benson. 9.30pm. £2/£1 UB40s.
Fundation at The Tramshed See Friday.
Not the Camden Palace Oxford Arms, 265 Camden High St, NW1 (enq: 267 9724) Camden Town tube. Map H1*. A mixture of music and comedy from Ronnie Golden, Mac McDonald, Lizzie Shirley and special guests. The cabaret is in a small room above the pub, reached by going through the saloon bar, and has the reputation of filling up quickly, so it's advisable to go early. 9pm. £2/£1.50.
Saturday Night at the Fez Club The Albany Empire, Douglas Way, SE8 (enq 691 3333) Deptford/New Cross BR, New Cross

Tooth, Tooth are also listed although they will probably front-up as Ra Ra Zoo (which is Tooth, Tooth, Tooth + Dave from Amazing Mendezies), expect a mixture of juggling, clowning and acrobatics. 8pm. £2.50/£1 concs.

Cirque de Barbarie See Thursday.
Fundation at The Tramshed Woolwich New Rd, SE18 (855 3371) Woolwich Arsenal BR. 8.30pm. £3.50/£3 members.
Jessica Martin The Palace Bar, The Palace Theatre. Lunchtime spot for the singer/impressionist. No entrance charge and well priced food and drinks. 1pm.
Jongleurs at The Cornet Lavender Gdns, SW11 (enq 582 6622 day, 627 3266 eves) Theatre de Complicité, a mime troupe of some repute, The Brothers Bleak, who are Comedians, Lee Cornes, Steve Dixon and Mark Elliott, Dave Cohen who plays guitar and parodies folk, and Denise Black whose striking voice is accompanied by Paul Sand's piano. 9pm. £3.50/£2.50 concs. Late bar. Disco till 1.30am.

From the beginnings of the London cabaret circuit in the performances by Alternative Cabaret, there was a very slow expansion as various pubs and other venues caught on to the idea; even by the end of 1982 there were still only a handful of gigs each week. It was not until November 1982 that the listings magazine *City Limits* separated the cabaret from the fringe theatre shows and gave it its own section.

Not all the venues were run with the same ideals as those started by Alternative Cabaret. Some pubs caught on to the idea and cashed in, providing totally unsuitable surroundings for the performers. Dawn French remembers working with Jennifer Saunders at a pub gig in North London: 'It became very obvious that this was another one of those gigs that was just one end of the bar ... people were chatting, nobody took any notice whatsoever of us. There were two microphones – one didn't work, the other was down so low it was just as well to shout ... and the other acts were going on one after another and just being ignored. We went on and started our act – both using the one mike – we very quickly realized nobody was listening – not one face was looking at us – so I said, "Skip to the end." It was an Irish pub on St Patrick's night – everybody had come because they wanted to see a cabaret – then the local butcher got up and sang "Danny Boy" and everybody went completely quiet....'

There were, however, more responsibly managed venues. The Earth Exchange has already been mentioned; two other venues which, though principally fringe theatres, also did cabaret were the Finborough and the Albany Empire. The Finborough Theatre Club – a large upstairs room over the Finborough Arms in Earl's Court – was doing the occasional cabaret by the end of 1982; it was a more sympathetic venue than the Comedy Store and was welcomed by performers as a chance to work in a more receptive atmosphere. The Albany Empire had been a political fringe theatre venue in Deptford in the 1970s, doing a good deal of anti-racist and left-wing material; it was burnt down in the summer of 1978 (probably by right-wing arsonists, though there was no full investigation into this) and re-opened in December 1978 as a community centre/fringe theatre which presented occasional cabaret shows. In February 1981 it presented Keith Allen's last stage appearance, in his one-man show *Whatever Happened to the AA Man's Salute?* (after which, tired of audiences who expected him to live up to his 'dangerous' image, he concentrated on writing and some film appearances).

Though both venues were welcomed by the performers, they were not as influential in the alternative comedy scene as another pub theatre, at the Crown and Castle in Hackney. Like so many others, it was merely an upstairs room with a rostrum, holding an audience of 120 at a pinch; but it was run specifically as a cabaret venue, with care and thought going into its management.

Jean Nicholson was closely involved in it from the beginning, and later on ran it until it closed in early 1987. Her involvement was purely accidental – she was a social worker by profession – and came about simply because a friend of hers was involved when the venue opened in 1981 and roped her in to help with the early shows.

She remembers: 'The original concept was one of a collective, very politically conscious, venue. About twenty-five people were involved in running it, some of whom had expertise in the theatre, some of whom didn't. Originally it was the early crowd – Tony Allen, Nigel Planer – and a number of small theatre groups who also did a cabaret style of work – this was before cabaret as it's commonly understood now had developed, so there were very few performers within the tradition we now take for granted. There were quite a number of theatre groups who used music and comedy in small-scale shows that they took round community centres and the like; and we used quite a few local poets.'

The audience was mostly young, professional – what Jean Nicholson calls 'begrudging yuppies'. (Hackney itself was about to join the trend in becoming 'upwardly mobile' – which meant that house prices were shortly going to go through the roof.) Unlike some other venues, the Crown and Castle audience retained a general political awareness and sympathy for the performers. They kept ticket prices reasonably low and gave reductions for the unemployed, so a better mix of people came in than was the case in the West End venues.

On the whole the audience tended to agree with the political standpoint of the performers; but, as Jean Nicholson points out: 'It's possible to hit raw nerves, and give people reminders. . . . The fashionable Left are a complacent bunch – I include myself in it – and sometimes it's quite good when prejudices which we don't really acknowledge exist can be prodded a little. You'd get heckling sometimes, depending on who was on and what chums they had in –

Tony Allen is legendary for bringing the anarchists with him. But on the whole people were well behaved – it wasn't anything like the Comedy Store in style.'

At the Comedy Store itself, Don Ward – who by late 1981 had dissolved the partnership with Peter Rosengard – was trying to extend the venue's brief: 'I expanded it to all week – and it wouldn't stand up all week. So I started to promote and advertise it more, but it still wouldn't stand up, so I knocked out the Monday, then the Tuesday ... then the Wednesday ... then I brought Wednesday back and called it "The Gay Comedy Store", with all gay comedians. It didn't work.... In the end I had discothèque Monday to Thursday, and the comedy on Friday and Saturday – and that's the format I found was the winning one. Then in 1982 the lease expired on the Gargoyle, and the terms offered were bad.'

The last performances at the old Comedy Store were in December 1982; in March 1983 Ward re-opened at new premises in Leicester Square, closing again that summer and finally re-opening in 1984 in the premises it still occupies: its latter days will be examined in later chapters.

One of the regulars at the Comedy Store throughout its life has been Lee Cornes; he was there on its mad opening night and in more recent times has frequently compèred the shows. Like so many Comedy Store performers, he was basically an actor who found that comedy gave him a wider outlet for his talents than straight plays.

He was born on 7 October 1954. He went to grammar school in Hastings, and then to university, where he read biology and geography. However, activities in university revues soon convinced him that he would rather be acting; he did take a post-graduate teaching course, so that he could teach as a second string; but got into fringe theatre fairly soon afterwards, working with a university revue group called Strode Jackson and at the Orange Tree in Richmond around the time the Comedy Store opened.

He remembers his early days at the Comedy Store. 'I was doing very dodgy stuff, as I'm continually reminded by Tony Allen.... I did a very racist sketch as a Japanese who couldn't speak English very well ... that sticks in my mind because I'm embarrassed by it now ... and stuff like Hamlet in one minute. I don't use anything from those days now. The big change for me was seeing Keith Allen at the Albany Empire – he was the first person I'd ever seen who said what he thought, did what he thought and was funny.'

Cornes gradually worked his way into a skilled act, rejecting all his earlier material and building on his physical slightness as he developed his own character. He identifies the process that most

comedians go through as they develop: 'There's the egoism to think: I can do it, it is that easy ... followed by the great crash when you realize it's virtually impossible. Followed by the great depression – I will never ever do it ... but you still do it; and that's the dodgy phase, when you're still doing it and you don't know why. Then you slowly claw your way out of it, and stop looking at yourself and start looking at what you're doing.'

For Cornes, an equally important part of his work comes in his periodic teaming, as 'The Wow Show', with another pair of Comedy Store veterans – Mark Arden and Stephen Frost, who work together as The Oblivion Boys.

Mark Arden was born on 31 July 1956. He describes his background as 'middle-class'; because his parents were moving he left school at sixteen, going on to a college of further education where he studied speech and drama, and drama school. (Before this he had a brief spell with The Young Generation, a large teenage dancing team best remembered for its TV appearances on *The Rolf Harris Show*.)

He met Stephen Frost at the drama school auditions: 'We thought he was a lecturer, because he was one of those eighteen-year-olds that look eighteen going on thirty....' Frost was born on 28 December 1955, in Leeds. His father was an artist, who painted and taught there, subsequently moving to St Ives. He then went to school in Banbury, where he got involved in dramatic activities in preference to schoolwork. He insists: 'I did *not* make people laugh to stop them bullying me. I did the bullying, because I was big. I did all the school plays – I played the lead in Arthur Miller's *A View From The Bridge* when I was fifteen.... the accent was based on Groucho Marx, who was the only American I knew.'

While they were at drama school they formed a group with two others, Bob McCully and Malcolm Ward, called The Five Erics and toured round various universities. They managed to get their Equity cards out of this, so that when they left they had the tremendous advantage of being able to do auditions straight away.

They left drama school in 1976 and went their separate ways for a couple of years, working in various rep companies – with interludes selling double-sided window cleaners, clip-on koala bears, polythene aeroplanes and other such useful articles. Frost had been working with Paul Elliott – who later came into The Wow Show with them – in *The News Revue*, a fringe theatre equivalent of radio's *Week Ending* (topical sketches on the week's events), and both he and Arden went to see the Comic Strip show. This gave them the idea of working as a double-act – partly as an antidote to the unemployment caused by

The Oblivion Boys –
Stephen Frost and
Mark Arden

their agents still trying to get them cast as Romeo. Adopting the name 'The Oblivion Boys', they began to work the Comedy Store and other venues. One of their most successful early sketches presented a pair of terrorists trying to hold the audience in a siege – an idea deliberately designed to get them off to a good start in the Comedy Store bear-pit. Mark Arden: 'We used to come in and shout with guns – this was our ploy, to shut them up, then we could shout, then bring it down until they could hear some jokes. It took us several years before we decided we didn't have to start that way.'

Mark: Right, stay exactly where you are OK? Nobody move.

Steve: Have you got the flares?

Mark: I wouldn't be seen dead in them, what the matter with you? You said straight combat gear.

Steve: Didn't you get a phone call this morning?

Mark: No.

Steve: Didn't you get a parcel in the post?

Mark: No.

Steve: You don't know about this? (*Opens jacket to show 'Adidas' sweater.*) ... We got the sponsorship!!
(*They hug each other delightedly.*)

Steve: What we do is three sieges a month, right – we get paid and everything, right – we do small-time sieges, then we get promoted on to embassies.

Mark: How many?

Steve: Twenty a day, or something like that, I don't know. All we got to do is to mention the product once during the siege.

Mark: Just once?

Steve: Just the once ...

Both: Ad .. ad .. i .. di ... das ...

Mark: All right! Now stay exactly where you are, come on ... on the bellies, move ...

Steve: All right, this is a sponsored siege!

Mark: Come on, stop prevaricating, hands on heads ... move! ... all right, you can leave your hands by your sides, then, please.

Steve: Don't say 'please'.

Mark: Sorry.

Steve: Don't say 'sorry' – you don't apologize on a siege.

Mark: Will you stop picking on me, please?

Steve: I'm sorry ... the reason why I'm getting narked is 'cos I'm on the wrong side, you know that, I'm supposed to be on the right-hand side, that's how we rehearsed it – three months in the Oman desert, I was on the right-hand side!
(*They change over with a good deal of shouting and gun-waving.*)

Steve: OK, nobody's going to get hurt as long as you do what I say, simple as that.

Mark: What's that?

Steve: Nobody's going to get hurt as long as they do as I say, simple as that.

Mark: Oh, as long as they do as *you* say? So this is your little siege, is it?

Steve: No, we're in it together, Mark.

Mark: I'm sorry, I didn't realize you'd promoted yourself to leader, that's all.

Steve: Somebody's got to give the orders, I was just . . .

Mark: That's all right – you take that (*Gives him his gun.*) – I'll go and be a hostage.

Steve: Oi! Don't you ever turn your back on me when you walk away like that.

Mark: Would you re-phrase that, please – come on, we're in this together.

Steve: Nobody's going to get hurt. (*To Mark.*) All right so far?

Mark: Fine, fine.

Steve: . . . As long as you do as *we both* say. . . . (*To Mark.*) All right?

Mark: Thank you.

Steve: Pretentious prat.

Mark: I'll pretend I didn't hear that.

Steve: I'll pretend I didn't say it.

It was as a result of both Mark Arden's and Lee Cornes's involvement in *The News Revue* that The Wow Show was formed. There was a disagreement amongst the cast, as a result of which Cornes and Arden left and decided to set up their own team. Lee Cornes: 'In direct reaction to this revue set-up – sketch, sketch, blackout and off . . . which I was never very happy about – I get annoyed at the audience just sitting there, whether they're laughing or not; there's something about the formality of a theatre I don't like . . . so as a reaction to all that sort of thing three of us set up The Wow Show, which was like linked crazy sketches – like a naff talent show, everything we could think of.'

Arden, Frost and Cornes joined forces with the vocal group Johnny Hubcap and the Axles, and the all-women group Cirrus. They put together a show which they did at the Hampstead Theatre, doing sketches and also playing involved practical jokes on the audience. Lee Cornes: 'The vocal group looked really tough; they'd have come in with the audience, and sat there talking amongst themselves – they'd make the audience think there were four yobs there who were going to give us a hard time. Then they throw something at me, walk down and start roughing me up . . . and the audience are stunned, because they believe it . . . and we go and "get the police", and the group go into their act.'

When the Comic Strip stage show finished in 1981 The Wow Show tried to get into the Boulevard Theatre where the Comic Strip had been playing, but this fell through (largely because of the anarchy of their material) and in the end Cornes and The Oblivion Boys were asked to go to the Gate Theatre, Notting Hill, without the other acts. It was there that The Wow Show took its more familiar form which they have repeated off and on over the years, Mark Elliott joining them later.

They continued in their tradition of confusing the audience. Lee Cornes: 'For instance, when we were at the Latchmere [in Battersea], the audience came back after the interval and they were taken through the kitchen on the way into the auditorium, where one of us was dressed up in a bloodstained apron, chopping meat and spitting into the soup ... then in the auditorium we'd put a sheet right across it, and left them to see whether they'd sit in their own seats where they couldn't see ... some of them sat behind it, and we'd argue with them.'

Because Arden and Frost continued their careers as actors, The Wow Show's appearances were erratic, depending upon everyone's availability; but, because they could play it in smaller fringe theatres perfectly well, they were able to do it at relatively short notice whenever circumstances permitted.

One straight acting job which was particularly interesting teamed Arden and Frost in the title roles in Tom Stoppard's *Rosencrantz and Guildenstern Are Dead*, performed at the Piccadilly Theatre in autumn 1987. Though billed as The Oblivion Boys, they did not impose their established characters on the parts; but because of their long-standing teaming they did convey the impression that Rosencrantz and Guildenstern had known each other for some time. Their own off-beat approach suited the play's slight surrealism well.

The actual Oblivion Boys teaming also continued, between the interruptions for straight acting jobs – they both emphasize that The Oblivion Boys act is only part of their careers, and that the acting is still important. However, it is for that teaming they are best known, largely as a result of the series of Carling 'Black Label' television advertisements. The best of these is well in their tradition of jokes on the audience, since it begins like a jeans advertisement, with a young man entering a launderette, stripping down to his briefs (to strange looks from the other customers) and putting his clothing, jeans included, in the washing machine. Arden and Frost, seen at the end to be sitting decorously naked, comment: 'I bet he drinks Carling Black Label' – 'Nah ... he doesn't wash his underpants.' With this – and a series of *The Wow Show* for Radio 4, using the potential of the medium in the tradition of the Goons – The Oblivion Boys have made themselves a staple part of the alternative comedy scene.

Another performer who has become a regular part of the cabaret circuit is Ronnie Golden, who mostly does musical parodies. His real name is Tony de Meur – he adopted the name Ronnie Golden when he started doing comedy, and since it is by this name he has become known it will be used in this book – and he was born on 2 April 1948 in Enfield. He describes his background as 'very average lower middle-class': 'I went to Enfield Grammar School, I left when I was sixteen and had a whole series of really boring jobs – I never took my education any further, I wish I had. I got into music when I was about fifteen, and I was making a living out of playing music on really odd tours with Engelbert Humperdinck and people like that when I was eighteen. We had a spot opening these shows in this weird band wearing cream flares, hipsters and paisley shirts and sunglasses ... and backing up these middle-aged girl singers.'

Around 1975 he started the comedy rock band, The Fabulous Poodles, which lasted for five years: 'We were sort of compared with Alberto y Los Trios Paranoios, and then we got sucked in with the punk thing, and everyone thought we were a punk band even though we were taking the piss out of *everything*. We got an American record deal, and did two three-month tours over there.'

It was on the last UK tour of the Poodles before the band broke up in 1981 that he started doing comedy: 'We were talking about having an opening act, and I said, "Let's get Ronnie Golden" – they said, "Who's he?" – I said, "He's brilliant, he does music and comedy, a stand-up act ... it's me." I did about thirty-five minutes as Ronnie Golden and then came on and did an hour and a half with the band. A lot of people who booked me didn't realize I was the same person. Then the band folded, and I thought, I might just develop this and keep it going. I lost interest in the music scene – I left it because I got ripped off by a bent manager – then I saw Alexei Sayle at the Comic Strip, and I thought, this is for me, it's great.'

He developed an act which has continued since then, based largely on musical parody – for example, the 'waiter, there's a fly in my soup' joke done as a blues holler – together with some stand-up jokes and character sketches – in particular the Texan redneck 'Roy', who has a pronounced Southern accent, a gee-tar, and a peaked cap with a plastic dog-turd on it: 'He was based on characters I'd bumped into when we were touring the South in America – I really like Texas, it's a great place, and the people there are very loyal and patriotic to their home state to a bizarre degree.'

Although he has had no formal musical training he plays the harmonica and guitar, and has made three- and four-part vocal arrangements for the group he works with as The Dialtones, with

Mac MacDonald (who also does stand-up comedy on the circuit), Phil Nice (from comedy team Fiasco Job Job) and sometimes Andrew Bailey.

He comments: 'What I like to do with comedy and music is to take two totally disparate things and put them together. I don't like the easy parodies – I don't see the sense in just rewriting a song mentioning current political things, it's just not interesting. I did a thing like Ewan McColl singing a James Brown song – singing "Sex Machine" as a stand-up folk singer – and it still works because it's such a ridiculous idea. And the doo-wopera thing, where you take a trash fifties song and do it as an opera – all this is funny because you're stretching things a bit, and it works in a bizarre sort of way.'

By the time Golden started working the circuit, another performer was establishing himself at the Comedy Store – one who, though a late starter whose early appearances made little impact, was to become the biggest crowd-puller in the stand-up scene: Ben Elton. In terms of the Comedy Store's accelerated history he would be 'third generation' – anyone who had been there for six months was a grand old man – and his subsequent rapid rise to stardom is something of a phenomenon in alternative comedy. He has also established himself as an influential writer, collaborating on *The Young Ones* and *Blackadder 2*, as well as solo writing on *Happy Families*, and as host on Channel Four's foray into live late-night alternative comedy, *Saturday Live*.

Elton was born on 3 May 1959: 'I was born in London, in Catford; middle-class, no question there. My dad's an academic, my mother's a teacher, so I suppose I had quite an academic background, but I went to ordinary schools. We went to Guildford when I was ten. I was always grateful I was brought up in a liberal household – I always felt I learned a great deal more at home than I did at school. I was very lucky, I was introduced to a lot of reading.'

He was obsessed with comedy when he was a teenager, and developed a desire to write and perform it. His parents were anxious that he should get his A-levels, so when he left school at sixteen he went on a course at Stratford-on-Avon studying English, history and drama to A-level at the college of further education. He says: 'I feel very strongly that higher education is a process of self-learning – that probably sounds very wanky, but I feel deeply that it should be available to all if we're not going to turn into a nation of barbarians. I wouldn't have wanted to be out facing the world at sixteen – or eighteen; I was pretty ill-equipped at twenty-one – but at least I had quite a lot of time to meet people, to think – no pressure, and I'm grateful for that. I think that's why I'm so political now, because

I'm so aware of the privileges I had. It's made me aware of what it's like to have a start in life, which is sure as hell what I had.'

He went on to Manchester University to read drama – he also wrote thirteen or fourteen comic plays which were put on by students, demonstrating even this early his compulsion to write. Rik Mayall and Adrian Edmondson were there at the time, though a couple of years ahead of him: 'I didn't really know them; Rik and I were sort of pally – he used to take the piss out of me, basically – and I never really knew Ade. But Rik came to see one of my plays, and he must have thought it was funny because two or three years later when he and Lise Mayer were starting to write *The Young Ones* and they felt they needed another element, they thought of me.'

When he left university in the autumn of 1980 he came to London. Still seeing himself primarily as a writer, he was trying to get his plays accepted, without success; visiting the Comedy Store and the Comic Strip, he began to think of performing. He had done a small amount of stand-up when he was sixteen – using gags stolen from established comics, the way most people start – but until he went to the clubs had never thought of doing it professionally.

He comments: 'My actual reason for becoming a comedian was because I wanted to get my writing around. I knew there were TV producers going down to these clubs; I never thought they would look at *me* – and they didn't for some years – but I thought, if I can write some nice stuff and people see me, they may not want me but they might want me to write. I must say, of all the things I've done in my life, that decision was the most astute and the luckiest – I decided to become a comedian; it has to be said that everybody said "don't".'

His early appearances at the Comic Strip and the Comedy Store were, he admits, poor – a stereotype northern comic who wasn't funny, a Ronald Reagan impression, a story based on the Grecian 2000 advert (which he describes as 'utter crap'). After about a month of this sort of thing he hit on the beginnings of his style: 'I wrote a set about jogging, and that was the first time I'd ever done the ranty cockney bit. People said at first I was a bit like Alexei Sayle, but my material was always very different – I've never done surreal material, I do stuff which is more observational and specific. I never did anything after that but be like the Ben Elton you know now, but not so good at it.'

The comparisons that some people made between Elton and Sayle have irritated Sayle, who dislikes Elton's style, commenting that 'he preaches'. Elton's response to this accusation is quite firm: 'I don't use comedy to make a point, under any circumstances – the most

important thing is, I use comedy to be funny. If I did preach, I would be ashamed of myself – I wouldn't listen to a bore in a pub, and I wouldn't expect anyone to listen to me if I preached; for example, I never ever say which way to vote. I look for things to make comic routines about. Why is it that most comics can only do half an hour, and they have to fill up with singing and dancing and booking two vent acts and a dog? – because material comes from the heart. Irishmen are not stupid and it's not funny to say they are – you can pretend for ten minutes and after that your cover's blown. Women's tits are not funny and it's not funny to say they are. So where do you look? You look around you, inside your heart and in what you're doing – that's where the comedy is. And inevitably that becomes social – you have to take a line, and my line is socially committed; but it's not because I want to be political, it wouldn't be funny. For example, I'm not preaching about the little squirrels who don't have a home because MacDonalds have cut the trees down to grow the grain to feed the cows to make the hamburgers – it's *funny* that this organization that has a clown giving blind children money as a logo is in danger of unbalancing the entire eco-structure of the planet! That's funny – it's also true – and let's face it, a good deal of modern comedy is just silliness. If you want to do anything properly, you must have passion – you can't just do it cynically. I think the thing I hate most is cynicism, because it's the easiest pose in the world. I think it's better to be excited, to be enthusiastic, to want to be a part of things.'

From his early gigs Elton went on to compère the Comedy Store for a time before the original venue closed at the end of 1982. He built up his act to the point where he was eventually able to sustain a complete solo evening on tour; these later tours and his involvement in TV writing will be examined in subsequent chapters. His stand-up material has always been perceived as heavily political; but although he does do jokes about the Thatcher government and the politics of the society it has created, most of his material is based on the observation of everyday life – the prevalence of dog-shit in the streets (especially when you're wearing expensive shoes), the travelling public's unstated preference for a double train-seat to itself, and, in this sample, the problems of sunning oneself on the fashionable beaches of Ibiza:

> What I don't like is nudie-sunbathing! It is pure exhibitionism! Who wants to sit on a beach all day watching a pale knob turn pink? Now – a lot more women nudie-sunbathe than men – this is true – now, there's two reasons for this: the first is, your average dick – and believe me, lads, they're all average . . . well, mine's not, mine's

fucking enormous.... (*big laugh from audience*) Oh! and suddenly the alternative pose drops for a moment, and the little bit of Benny Hill in us all jumps out on to the stage! Recognize the devil within you and conquer it! ... your average dick does not look good. Be honest lads – it's not the most attractive part of the anatomy. It might feel very nice but it looks fucking horrible. Could you honestly stare yours in its one eye and think, 'Oh, you're a lovely little knob, you really are ... you're a pretty little thing, you're my best feature, you are, you're lovely, you ...?' Bad design, you see, bad design, we've been stitched up.

I mean, down Lamborghini, down the sports-car factory when they unveil the new designs, do they say, 'Oh, lovely looking sleek beautiful lines, but where's the bulbous veins, eh?' – no, they don't. When they've got a new tower block, do they say to the architect, 'Well, it's lovely so far, but when are you going to put the purple helmet on, tomorrow, or what?' ... And when nudie-sunbathing, the naked dick is seldom at its ease. It don't know where to put itself, does it? It flops this way, it lolls that way ... lies down, stands up, shrinks ... 'Well, I've been fucking swimming, haven't I.'

And the other reason that men don't do much nude-bathing:

... is the terror, the absolute mind-numbing, ball-crunching, spine-tingling terror of the *unwanted erection*! That total fear, that total paranoia that the little bugger's going to pop up just when you don't want it to – 'cos we're not used to it, are we, lads? Topless beach – fuck me, I'm surrounded by tits – boing! I'm a lefty, I'm trying to hang on to my politics, I'm thinking I will not ogle, I will not look, I'm not going to stare, it's oppressive, it's invading her environment, I will not look, I'm a lefty, I will not stare, I will not ogle ... *but the dick is not a hypocrite*!! It's going, 'Go on, have a little look, you bastard, go on ... have a little look – put a book on me or something ... come on!' All the little blokes stretched out face-down, drilling little holes in the sands. I'm there, I'm trying to get the sand out from under my foreskin and not look like I'm having a wank! The bloke next door to me is trying to have a wank and make it look like he's trying to get the sand out from under his foreskin.... 'Honest, officer, I was just cleaning it and it went off.'

In his early days Elton's rapid delivery – born of nerves and the desire not to allow hecklers a foothold – earned him the nickname 'Motormouth'; he says it was three years before he got the courage to slow down. However, his ability to build on the experiences and observations of ordinary people gained him a wide following, making him one of the small handful of widely recognized stars to emerge from the alternative comedy scene.

The first edition of *Boom Boom, Out Go The Lights* was transmitted only a couple of weeks after the Comic Strip opened at the Boulevard Theatre in October 1980; although it was hardly a success by TV standards, it, and the second edition the following May, did seem to improve audience attendances – the team's first contact with the power of television. The team had little outward patience for the more established manifestations of television. Rik Mayall: 'We were very anti *Not The Nine O'Clock News* – we reckoned that we were the best because we were doing cabaret and not revue. Revue was a dirty word, and so was Oxbridge, we had a down on the Pythons – although we secretly all thought that the Pythons were great, and half of us were redbrick and university anyway. Also the fact that everyone in the BBC seemed to be Oxbridge.'

During 1981 Mayall was asked by BBC TV producer Colin Gilbert to appear in a projected series of sketch programmes, each built round a particular subject, called *A Kick Up The Eighties*. In effect a re-working of *The Frost Report* format of fifteen years earlier, it was linked by Richard Stilgoe. The performers appearing in sketches included the splendid comic actress Tracy Ullman, who brushed the fringe of the alternative comedy field from time to time (and subsequently went to America, where she achieved her own net-worked show).

Mayall was asked to be one of the actors appearing in the sketches, but he had different ideas: 'I wanted to do a character on the telly which would just waste television time, and be incompetent. I had my name taken off the credits because I was addicted to this form of performance where the audience thought it was genuinely happen-ing. So Colin Gilbert and I wrote the monologues, and the credits just said "Kevin Turvey" – and the key to its success was that fifty per cent of the audience thought he really existed. The character of Rik the poet was designed for a cabaret situation, and Kevin was designed specifically for telly.'

The first series of six programmes went out in October and November 1981 on BBC2, with a second series of four in January 1984 and a *Kevin Turvey Special* spoof documentary between them. The monologues were delivered in a flat Birmingham accent; this

one comes from the programme on sex, broadcast on 19 October 1981:

> Do you know how much it costs to go to America? Ninety-six quid, that's how much. Where am I going to get that kind of money? I'm not, that's where. So I'm never ever going to America. Anyway, good evening, my name's Kevin Turvey ... and here's a good one. Why does Mrs Thatcher always wear barbed-wire underwear? She doesn't – it's a joke. I thought, this week's subject is sex, which is slightly embarrassing, so I thought I'd start with a bit of a joke, right. Well, not a *bit* of a joke, the whole of a joke ... a bit of a joke would be no good really ... not unless it was the funny bit ... So this week, I thought, how am I going to find out all about sex? And I thought, I know, I'll become a prostitute. That's what I did, right – I went out and bought myself a handbag – well, it wasn't a real handbag, it was like a plastic bag – but I stretched out the handles so that it looked like a handbag, put it on my shoulder, and hung around outside Tesco's, right, for about a day. And then my first client came along. He was disguised as a policeman. He sidled up next to me, right, and he says, 'Excuse me, have you got the time?' Which is like prostitute's code. And I said, 'Er – about sixteen quid.' And he said, 'Are you trying to be funny?' I said, 'All right, then – ten quid.' And that's when he started punching me, right. It was about the seventh or the eighth punch – it might have been the ninth – anyway, it was about then I thought, 'He doesn't realize I'm a prostitute.' So I started to run, right, and I ran right into Tesco's and tripped over this big basket they've got in there. And I thought, brilliant – of course, a basket – that's what I should do – I'll invite Teresa Kelly over to supper, and have sex with her afterwards. 'Cos I've got all the things at home – I've got sausages, and potatoes ... gravy ... furniture ... I've got loads of things at home – windows, loads of things ... it was just the food that I was thinking about at the time, right ...

During the second half of 1981 the Comic Strip show went on a tour of Britain, a ramshackle arrangement set up by Peter Richardson. Ade Edmondson: 'It was good fun – it was like pretending to be a rock band because it was in a bus. ... I remember most of the Comic Strip history as a social event rather than a professional event – I don't really remember how it went down ... I was a bit of a drinker at the time.'

Dawn French had left teaching to go on the tour, and rather enjoyed the feeling of being 'on the road' in their own bus, though Jennifer Saunders remembers some of the less salubrious venues: 'Some of it was in horrible places – we did a late-night show after a film in a porn cinema, and a guy came out with something like an insecticide and was spraying all the seats before the audience came in ... and there was only one electricity supply so you either had the sound or the lights.' Dawn French remembers the dressing-room of that venue: 'It was full of old chairs that had obviously gone past the insecticide stage – and two inches of water on the floor.'

However, some of the gigs were rather better, and on the whole the show was well received.

It was also in this period that *The Young Ones* began to emerge as an idea. The first germ came in conversations between Mayall and his then girlfriend, Lise Mayer. He remembers: 'We were talking about the character of Rik, and saying, wouldn't it be funny if you lived with him. Because I was trying to broaden him and try to think of more material I could do than just the poems. We were trying to work out what he would be like – like, he'd be the sort of person who labels his stuff in the fridge. And wouldn't it be funny if he was living with the Adrian Dangerous character – especially if that Neil character was there as well. We started to think this would be a good idea for TV – particularly after *Boom Boom, Out Go The Lights*, which wasn't designed for telly, and was all right but didn't really do what we wanted. So Lise and I had a crack at writing it and realized we needed a more experienced playwriter sort of person, so we brought Ben Elton in.'

It was natural for Mayall to approach Paul Jackson with the idea. Jackson: 'For a long time I had lived in a house with seven guys in Exeter, and had often thought this would have clear potential for a sitcom – and indeed had attempted to write one myself, but I notoriously cannot write – but I'd been thinking of very much a stereotyped sitcom. When I read their script I was just knocked out by it – it was the single funniest script I'd ever read. It was so different from what I'd expected it to be, I'd just expected a sitcom. … I was excited, though I also thought it would be impossibly difficult to do, and highly contentious.'

Jackson was concerned about the technical difficulty of many of the special effects called for in the script; although the writers offered to re-write anything that was too difficult, he checked with a friend who was a visual effects designer, who was so impressed by the script that he promised that he could do anything it called for … somehow.

The basic concept was of student digs, with Mayall's 'Rik' character, Planer's 'Neil', Edmondson as a character – eventually called Vivian – based on Adrian Dangerous; and with Peter Richardson as Mike, a vaguely bossy organizer. In the event, Richardson was not used when the show came to be made in 1982, for reasons partly connected with his differences with Jackson at the time of *Boom Boom*.

Richardson was naturally enough disappointed: 'We were quite a close group, and that was a rift in it. I was upset about the rift more than the fact that I wasn't in *The Young Ones*. Looking back, I'm really relieved I wasn't in it – I really like the situation I'm in.' He also feels that, had he been involved, there would have been difficulties with Jackson, whose approach he did not entirely approve of. As it was, he took some ideas of his own to Jeremy Isaacs, the head of the new Channel Four (which had not yet started).

The BBC was meanwhile approaching the proposals for *The Young Ones* with something less than corporate enthusiasm. Indeed, it would probably never have been commissioned had not Channel Four's published intentions on minority programmes – and in particular the news filtering back about Richardson's approach to Isaacs – caused the BBC to fear that it might lose all these bright young comics to its new rival. Jackson was asked to make a pilot at short notice, using a studio booking left vacant by a cancelled pop programme.

In the absence of Richardson, Jackson found himself having to cast the part of Mike at very short notice: 'It was a very difficult part to cast, because the others knew exactly what they were doing, those characters were innate to them. Whoever was going to do it had their work cut out, because they were coming into a situation where they had to adapt to this tone of humour and understand it – and it wasn't by any means the case that a good actor could adapt to this way of working.'

They auditioned many people – some of them from the cabaret circuit; in the end Andy de la Tour suggested Chris Ryan, then appearing with Maggie Steed in *Can't Pay, Won't Pay*. Ryan auditioned, and after some deliberations and a second audition, was chosen. As it turned out, he fitted in well with the others, creating an equally memorable character.

The pilot was made in January 1982. It came off well, getting an enthusiastic response from the invited (and carefully selected) audience. The BBC was still dubious; it commissioned another show, and in the end gave the go-ahead for the full series of six programmes.

Mayall, Mayer and Elton set to to produce the remaining scripts. The result was very much a blending of their own approaches; Rik Mayall: 'It went through the three of us so many times that everybody contributed to everything.... I guess I was in a lucky position, because I was the one who had the final say, because Ben had been brought in new, and because Lise didn't have as much confidence as me ... so I could finally say at the end of a row, "That's funny", or "That's not funny, that's going out" – and it was rare that the two of them would gang up against me. Everything would be filtered and sifted many times – and then it would go to rehearsal, and it would all be changed again by the boys.'

Ben Elton remembers: 'Rik and Lise tended to write together, and I tended to write by myself, so it wasn't as if there were three lots of writing coming in, there were two – on the whole. Then we'd meet and try and squeeze them together – *The Young Ones* is not the most structurally disciplined show on earth. I think that sort of pleasant off-the-wall quality came from the writing method. By the time I arrived Rik and Lise were very much equal partners in the project; he was a good friend but our relationship was considerably more third-year/first-year than it's become since ... so what he said went, and when I tentatively wondered whether I might play Mike, he just said "no" and I never raised the subject again. That's one particular project where I prefer not to remember the tensions, because it turned out so successfully, and I was so desperately lucky to have been in the right place at the right time to be asked to be involved.'

Much of the writing was done during the period when the Comic Strip stage show was on another tour – this time of Australia. This took place in early 1982; the show went much as the package it had been for some time, except that the promoters thought Arnold Brown too old for their ideas of alternative comedy and left him out.

The Australian tour was more fun for those not combining script-writing with it. Nigel Planer: 'Peter had managed to get his contract with Channel Four. I was already doing *The Young Ones* and *Shine On Harvey Moon* and I didn't know what I was committed to – the BBC wanted *The Young Ones*; and off we went to Australia. Poor old Peter brought Pete Richens out with him and they were writing madly for the Comic Strip films; Rik and Lise hardly went out of their hotel room because they were trying to write *Young Ones* scripts ... and the rest of us spent our spare time on the beach.'

The show went down well – sometimes. Dawn French: 'The problem with Australia was that we had been heralded as the guerillas of New Wave humour; we were labelled as the Alternative Comedy group, and you couldn't have had a group of people more offended by being called "Alternative" because we hadn't invented the phrase, we didn't know what it meant – the press had decided this was what we were. And it was the press in the long run that decided that was what we weren't ... that we'd sold out. In Melbourne we were at a club, with a proper stage, just for comedy – they have a history in Melbourne of stand-up comics, and we were no big deal as far as they were concerned. Then they put us in a huge university campus theatre in Sydney – no one had heard of us, they didn't publicize us at all – and we closed after a week.'

The Young Ones was recorded in the autumn of 1982, the six programmes (number one being the pilot) starting on BBC2 on 9 November. From the first the programme established its anarchic style, with the plot – such as it was – frequently interrupted by what we might call 'cutaway sequences' involving, for example, the people next door (a couple of Chekhovian Russians) or the inhabitants of a rat-hole. The characters were also firmly established from the beginning of the show, with Rik composing a poem about his idol Cliff Richard, and Neil having a really heavy time trying to cook dinner (lentils; it was always lentils).

Chris Ryan's performance as Mike the self-styled 'cool person' was neatly at odds with his diminutive stature. Paul Jackson comments: 'Mike has, if anything, the most difficult dialogue – he was a function of what the other three lacked – all the things they didn't have were heaped on to this one character, who always was fairly unrealistic. In the first episode he had this sort of magical quality – you weren't supposed to know whether he was a Mafiosi, whether he did have secret powers – eventually he settled down to a know-all spivvy Fonzie type character who had some strange hold over the others.'

> **Mike:** OK, guys – don't do anything unusual. Did a guy with a lisp phone?
> **Rik:** Er ... no one phoned you, Mike. We haven't got a telephone.
> **Mike:** Yes, I know – but did a guy with a lisp phone?
> **Rik:** No, he didn't.
> **Mike:** Did he say anything about the bananas?
> **Rik:** Er ... no.
> **Mike:** I thought you said he didn't phone!
> **Rik:** He didn't!
> **Mike:** OK, OK, that's good. But it could have been very bad. Anyway, forget you ever even heard the name.
> **Rik:** Er ... what name?
> **Mike:** Hey, you're learning. That's good.
> **Neil:** I've got an uncle called Dustin.
> **Rik** (*accusingly*): Neil – are these lentils South African? (*Neil looks guilty.*) You bastard! You complete and utter bastard! Why don't you just go out and become a policeman? Become a pig? There's no difference, you know ... (*Gets his hand in the food, which is hot.*) Ow! There's no difference, you know – you think there is but there isn't. I suppose you hate gay people too – (*Insultingly.*) hippy!
> **Neil:** Listen, listen, just don't bring me down again, all right, Rik?
> **Rik:** OK, where's my biro? *Where is my biro?*
> **Mike:** Here, here, use mine. (*Passes it over.*)
> **Rik:** This is *my* biro!
> **Mike:** I saw it lying on your desk, I thought you didn't want it any more.

101

Rik: But look at it – it's half empty!

Mike: It was just lying there, Rik – what's a guy supposed to think?

Rik (*composing poetry*): Neil . . . What are you doing, Neil . . . to make a meal . . . Neil . . . from totalitarian vegetables . . . How much does it cost, Neil . . .

Neil: Well, actually, it's about four pounds fifty, each.

Rik & Mike: Four pounds fifty!!!

Rik: I'm not paying you money to eat black men! I could become a pig and do that for free! Right on!

Mike: Neil, when I eat a meal worth four pounds fifty, I'm not paying for it, you got me?

Neil explains that this is his last supper, that he is going to hang himself, and has built a gallows in his bedroom (which plays 'Rock Around The Clock'). Rik is unimpressed:

Rik (*sarcastically*): Oh, far out! Really great – Wood-stock. (*There is a tremendous crash and Vivian enters through the wall, landing on the dinner-table in a shower of plaster.*)

Neil: Oh fine, great, yeah, why don't you sit in the supper, man?

Rik: Vivian, you might have washed your hands. (*Vivian goes over to the sink, kicks it – it falls off the wall – rinses his hands in the water flowing from the pipe where the tap was, and kicks the wall to stop the flow. He sits down again.*)

Vivian (*brandishing a severed human leg*): I been down the morgue!

Neil: Oh fine, yeah, great, let's talk about death, I mean, don't consider my feelings tonight or anything, will you.

Vivian: Cutting up bodies for my course, you know.

Rik: None of you ever gives the slightest consideration to a word I say!!

Vivian: That's because you're very boring.

Rik: Oh, and I suppose you think ideas like peace and freedom and equality are boring, too.

Vivian: Yes, they are.

Rik: Hah! Fallen into my trap! In that case, why isn't Cliff Richard boring, clever-trousers? Tell me that?
(*Vivian considers his response and then slams Rik's head into the dinner.*)

Although Vivian is largely a destructive force – punk hairdo, jacket with studs spelling 'Very Metal' and a tendency to smash things for no reason – Edmondson comments: 'Vivian was the most logical person in that house, really – it's just his logic was strange. If the plug won't reach the wall, you don't just go off into a tizz about it like the other characters would, you make it happen by moving the wall closer to the plug; which is a joke, but is actually more logical than any of the others' responses to it.'

Alexei Sayle appears in each show as various members of their

Adrian Edmondson as Vivian

landlord's family – an excuse for his jolly Eastern-European-émigré impersonation and a number of short excerpts from his stage act. In the first episode the plot revolves round a threat by the council to demolish the quartet's unsavoury lodgings, but cutaways include a would-be with-it TV programme with Ben Elton as a presenter doing his links in disco-style, and a general feeling of format rather than content ('I'm up on the catwalk because shock is what this programme is all about'). In the end the council is saved the bother by a plane crash.

In the second show the lads move into new accommodation and find oil in the basement (as well as two men stranded on a raft in the middle of an imaginary ocean) and Buddy Holly (played by Ronnie Golden) hanging upside down in Mike's bedroom. In other shows they have a party, find a bomb (Neil gets out his copy of *Protect and Survive* and starts covering himself with whitewash to deflect the blast) and get flooded out. Other inhabitants of the house – played by puppets – include Vivian's aggressive hamster (complete with Geordie accent) and, in one show, a fly-on-the-wall TV team (consisting of flies, of course).

One of the most involved cutaways consists of a spoof American TV special featuring two self-congratulatory singers (Mayall and Planer); and there is a musical item by a different rock group in each show – they just appear in the flat, do their piece and disappear again. There are remarks to camera, and jokes at the expense of the TV medium itself – for example, use of the electronic 'flip and zoom' device causes everything in the set to be thrown about and Vivian to suffer from motion sickness (a minor problem, since he has an axe buried in his head at the time).

The characters of Neil and Rik had been expanded from their originals; Neil is consistently down-trodden and hated by the others, and expected to do all the cleaning, cooking and shopping. He is, of course, into all the usual semi-mystic beliefs and health-care fads: 'Listen, man, everybody knows that sleep gives you cancer.' Rik is more aggressive than the slightly introverted poet of the original sketch (who, although he would berate the audience, could look a bit vulnerable); he hates Fascists but behaves like one, hates Neil, thinks he is a right-on radical, and is a complete moral coward.

> **Rik** (*having found nothing on TV except the test card*): Absolutely pathetic! There's nothing on at all! I don't even know why we bother to pay our licence.
> **Mike:** We don't.
> **Rik** (*taken aback*): Haven't we got a licence?
> **Mike:** No.

Rik: But that makes me a criminal! (*Becomes pleased with the idea.*) Right on! This'll shake 'em up at the Anarchists Society! Occupying the refectory – so what? This is the real stuff. I'm a fugitive – a desperado. I'm going to form a new Union Society, right – with me as president – People Who Don't Pay Their TV Licences Against The Nazis! This is only the beginning!

Vivian: What are you going to do, Rik, burn your bra?

Rik (*superior*): Well, someone's got to do it, Vivian. It's very easy to sit on your backside, isn't it?

Vivian: Not if you haven't got a bottom.

(*The doorbell rings.*)

Mike: That'll be the front doorbell ringing.

Neil: I bet I know who's got to answer it.

Mike: But Neil, you like meeting people.

Neil (*getting up: to camera*): If I had a penny for every time I had to answer the door, I'd have five pounds sixty-three. (*Goes off.*)

Vivian: It's probably someone unbelievably boring.

Neil (*off*): Oh no! It's the TV detector van!

Rik (*panic*): Mike, you bastard! Why didn't you buy a licence? I can't go to prison – I'm too pretty! I'll get raped!

Mike: Yes, steady on. We're not beaten yet. The time has come for diplomacy.

Neil (*off*): Oh no – look, he's asked me if we've got a telly. I think I'm going to have to lie. What a bummer!

Mike: Right, the time for diplomacy is over. Viv – chuck the telly out the window.

(Viv does, but misses. So instead he eats the TV – a ploy the man from the licence van has obviously seen before, for he retires to the loo to wait for the evidence to emerge.)

Interestingly, the movement style Mayall uses for Rik seems to owe something to the 'presenting' style of Richard Dangerous – the original stage Rik was rather more spare in his movements.

The series made use of a number of people from the cabaret circuit; Pauline Melville, Andy de la Tour, Dawn French, Jennifer Saunders, Jim Barclay, Arnold Brown and Mark Arden all make appearances, and Arden also appears with Stephen Frost in several shows. Tony Allen turns up at the lads' wild party (appropriately enough as an anarchist) and there is an appearance by actor Robbie Coltrane, who, though not a cabaret performer, was becoming associated with the alternative comedians.

Paul Jackson produced the series, and spurred his technical team to some spectacular special effects; indeed the series stretched the powers of television as nothing since *Monty Python* had done, although its whole aggressive approach was different from the Python's rather detached viewpoint.

Like *Monty Python*, *The Young Ones* did cause internal dissension in the BBC. The major row came over the show where the lads hold a party; one Light Entertainment high-up objected to the scene where Vivian 'fucked the floor'. Jackson was completely at sea over this; it turned out that Vivian was merely doing press-ups to get into shape. Jackson: 'I said, "He's only doing press-ups", and he said, "Don't be stupid, why is there such a huge laugh?" – I said, "It's a character laugh – this unattractive wimp thinks that doing twenty press-ups will turn him into Sylvester Stallone." He accepted that explanation – reluctantly.'

In fairness, Jackson points out that the same meeting passed the sequence in that show where Rik swipes a Tampax from a girl's bag and plays with it as if it were a toy mouse. Jackson: 'That was one where we had decided it would be a matter of principle and names-off-credits time if it *had* been cut; fortunately it wasn't. I think at the time that was a very brave decision; you have to remember who you're dealing with here, which is middle-aged men, who have to answer to older middle-aged men, and I thought that was a very good decision on their part.'

There is a slight legend that *The Young Ones* was a raging success in its first series; but although it did well enough it was not the cult it subsequently became (partly through repeats). Paul Jackson: 'It got a fairly steady two to two and a half million; it got reasonable Appreciation Indexes – up into the 60s; it wasn't reviewed at all until the *Evening Standard* reviewed show 5. But pretty quickly we were aware that we'd done reasonably well because the postbag was immediate and very heavy; the buzz started to go round, the boys started to be recognized in nightclubs, so it clearly got to its target audience, but it didn't expand out and become seen as a cult on the first series at all. What did happen was that people outside London – and kids in London too young to go to the cabaret circuit – became aware of this kind of comedy for the first time.'

There were the usual disgusted-of-Tunbridge-Wells type of complaints, but the only complaint Jackson received that he did find a little upsetting was in reference to an incident where Jim Barclay, wearing dark glasses, rings a doorbell and is mistaken by Rik for a black man – 'Mr Sambo Darkie Coon, you steal white man's electricity.' These remarks were plainly, in the context of the show, meant to work against the person using them; but Jackson had a letter from a teacher who, while sympathetic to the show, had one black child in his school who had been upset to be called Mr Sambo Darkie Coon all morning by his classmates, particularly knowing the reference came from a show he admired.

Apart from this miscalculation, the response from schoolchildren asking for photos and souvenirs was sufficient to indicate that they had hit quite a large, if unexpected, audience. The second series will be dealt with later in the book; the impact of the first was not immediate, but by the time there had been repeats and its reputation had percolated, *The Young Ones* could be seen as a vital step by alternative comedy – an imaginative grasping of the medium and a fanfare for its invasion by the new wave of performers.

Even while the Comic Strip stage show was still running at the Boulevard Theatre, Peter Richardson had hopes of getting the team on to television in some form – preferably using film: 'I was interested in getting into making films – I'd done some 8-mm stuff when I was younger – but I could never see how you could, I never saw myself becoming an assistant trainee director. It was a real chance thing that Channel Four started at that time and that Jeremy Isaacs came to see us, and we were a new name at that time; everything just coincided in a way that I couldn't have planned.'

The six main members of the team – Richardson, Edmondson, Mayall, Planer, French and Saunders (though excluding Alexei Sayle) – had a meeting at which various ideas were thrown up, and then Richardson went with a list of suggested films to Isaacs – most of which were to be made in the first series. Peter Richardson: 'The best way of using the Comic Strip was not in sketches but as good character actors. I didn't want to get into Light Entertainment – I didn't see how the show could ever transfer to film.'

Six films were planned for Channel Four's opening winter season in 1982. Five were shot earlier in the year – three directed by Bob Spiers and two by Sandy Johnson – the remaining one, *An Evening with Eddie Monsoon*, being abandoned because of worries about its subject matter (written by several of them, it presented a chat show host of more than usual repellence, and seemed to Channel Four to be libellous in places).

Bob Spiers, an extremely experienced director of TV comedy, gave the films he did a strong mood and visual style, as did Sandy Johnson (whose two films in this series, however, were designed to rely less on atmosphere). Richardson worked closely on all stages of the production, learning the techniques as he went along and collaborating with Spiers to get the visual style suitable to each story. The choice of film as opposed to video would have been largely dictated by practicality – much of the filming was location work, and in 1982 film, though more expensive than video, was easier to handle away from studio facilities; but there is also something about the technical quality of film which gives a quite different look from video in the same situation.

Rik Mayall had reservations about the quality of film: 'I wasn't confident about doing the Comic Strip films, because they were film but made for television, which is a very odd thing. There's something about the medium of film which works much better in a big cinema than video tape, which is perfect for telly. Film makes the joke look too grand – it makes everything look too beautiful; tape makes everything look horrible, which is better for comedy. But it was really the dislocation between me and the audience – my great strength is playing off an audience, and there's no audience at six o'clock in the morning in the middle of a field.'

The first film to be transmitted, *Five Go Mad In Dorset*, was chosen as one of the programmes for Channel Four's opening night on 2 November 1982. Written by Peter Richardson in collaboration with Pete Richens, it is a none-too-gentle spoof of Enid Blyton's 'Famous Five' books. The four children (the fifth of the 'Five' being the dog, Timmy) are played with the wide-eyed earnestness of an early Children's Film Foundation epic by Dawn French (as George, the girl who really wanted to be a boy), Jennifer Saunders (Anne: sugar and spice), Adrian Edmondson (Dick: introverted earnestness and the grace of a badly manipulated marionette) and Peter Richardson as Julian, the self-appointed leader (everyone keeps remarking how mature he is).

Like many Comic Strip films, *Five Go Mad In Dorset* makes heavy use of external references, in this case the Blyton books; however, the world it presents is strongly enough constructed for it to be enjoyed by those lucky enough to have avoided the originals. Adrian Edmondson: 'I'd never read the books, but when I read the script I thought, I know this world – it's the same world that's portrayed in Victorian children's melodramas, it's the same attitude . . . you can watch a thing with references and just by the pattern of the speech you can tell it's a joke, you laugh at the rhythm . . . you don't really need the references, you could write a whole show that just had rhythmic noises in it!'

The children in the film do not exactly have the liberal outlook of the Comic Strip – early on they have a railway porter arrested on suspicion of being foreign (he's black). They set off on a cycling holiday, free to go 'completely mad'; but they *are* the Famous Five, and adventures are not far away . . .

> **Dick:** I say, this is a jolly wizard lunch, Anne. You really are going to make someone a great little wife some day.
> **Julian:** Ummm. My favourite. Ham and turkey sandwiches, heaps of tomatoes, fresh lettuce and lashings of ginger beer.
> (*In the background two large men are seen carrying a box across a*

'Five Go Mad in Dorset' –
Richardson, Saunders,
Edmondson, French

field. They stop and start digging a pit.)

Anne: This is just the kind of holiday I like, picnicky meals and not too much adventure.

Dick: Hah! Well don't speak too soon, old thing.

(*A black car draws up. A black-gloved hand throws out a piece of meat.*)

Man's voice: Here, Fido.

(*He drives off at speed. Timmy, the dog, gobbles the meat.*)

George: That's strange. Why on earth would somebody want to feed Timmy?

Julian: Yes, that *was* rather odd.

Dick: Shh. I say, look over there.

(*They notice the two men digging.*)

George: What a strange pair!

Julian: Yes, one's got a big nose and thick lips and the other one's got mean, clever little eyes.

Dick: *And* they're unshaven. Just look at the way they're slouching.

Anne: Ugh! Pooh! I hope they don't come anywhere near me. I feel as if I can smell them from here.

George: Shh. I can hear them talking.
First Heavy: What about the sparklers, Punchy?
Second Heavy: Don't you worry about them, I'll take care of that.
First Heavy: Well, now that you're out of gaol you'd better lie low.
George: Do you think they're escaped convicts?
Dick: Yes, or traitors to our country.
Julian: We'd better call the police.
Anne: Look – Timmy's fallen over.
 (*Timmy is lying still in the grass.*)
George: Oh *crikey*, he's been poisoned!
Julian: Never mind, George, we'll get another. Come on, everybody, let's find a telephone!*

They do indeed get another (identical) dog – indeed, they're on their third dog by the end of the film. The plot involves the unmasking of a couple of crooks (as third-rate movie actors) and their Uncle Quentin (a 'raving' homosexual). There is also a young, rich, spoilt boy (played by Danny Peacock) whose friendship they successfully avoid; as Julian says, 'What if *everybody* wanted to be our friend – where would we be then? We don't even know if he goes to a good school.'

Robbie Coltrane also took part – as the proprietress of a sweetshop and a dubious gypsy (both muttering the same warning about secrets and signs and threats) – the first of many appearances with the team. The two heavies were played by Ron Tarr and Nosher Powell (cast because they were established at this sort of part – and both very large), and Ronald Allen played Uncle Quentin; all three, though found in the first place through the normal process of casting, fitted in so well with the Comic Strip's conceptions that they were used in various later films – indeed, Powell would star in their second full-length feature.

The Comic Strip series proper began on 3 January 1983, including a re-run of *Five Go Mad In Dorset*. Defying the normal expectations of a television series, each film (nominally half an hour, but most of them are more like thirty-five minutes) is complete in itself, and each is totally different in atmosphere and approach. The most deliberate use of atmospheric parody is in *The Beat Generation*, filmed in black and white as a parody of trendy early 1960s films – the technical crew caught the slightly washed-out look of that period exactly. There are few actual jokes as such, the humour being very quiet and based in the characterization and atmosphere. Mayall comments that the series shouldn't be called 'Comic Strip' films because it makes the audience expect to laugh; they should be called 'Interesting

* *Five Go Mad in Dorset*, Comic Strip, Channel Four.

Films', then the audience would enjoy themselves more. Certainly, to approach a film like *The Beat Generation* as if it were the usual laugh-a-line television show is to court disappointment. (There is, of course, no studio audience laughter on any of the films.)

Richardson put a lot of work into the locations and props for *The Beat Generation*, having a very strong idea from the beginning of what it should look like; and this attention to detail characterizes all the films. The plots themselves vary in importance; *Summer School*, written by Dawn French, tells in a straightforward manner the story of a university field course in prehistoric village life (the students live under primitive conditions in a prehistoric village ... in the middle of the university buildings), whereas *War*, written by Richardson and Richens, is much more surreal. Its vague story of an invasion of Britain by the Russians takes in a parody of the Russian roulette scenes in *The Deer Hunter* and some characters who think they are in a Clint Eastwood spaghetti western.

In this and the later series the performers' approach to their parts varies from person to person. Jennifer Saunders in particular is an excellent character actress and can submerge herself totally in the role, underplaying to produce a believable result. Dawn French has slightly less range, although her spoilt sixties model in *The Beat Generation* is very convincing, and she always has a good comic presence on the screen. Richardson's characters tend to be either authoritarian or anarchic (the latter often appeared to be on something), but he usually invests them with some sort of unexpected quirk. Mayall and Edmondson are both very funny, but do sometimes overdo things if not firmly controlled.

Adrian Edmondson comments: 'I don't think that any of us are any great shakes at acting – I don't know what there is to acting, either ... I suppose we are believable. Our acting is very tongue-in-cheek, very wooden, a lot of the time. Purposefully so. We try even when we're on film sets to amuse everyone around us when the cameras are running, which is probably not what you're supposed to do. I think that Jennifer is actually a very good actress, and she works really small ... everyone knows that's what you're supposed to do in films, but the rest of us don't seem to be able to do this.'

Edmondson perhaps undervalues Nigel Planer's considerable acting ability – his characters are often quite difficult to recognize as Planer, since he can create a wide range of different types.

Edmondson's own performance in *Five Go Mad* blends in well with the others, but sometimes there does tend to be a mixture of styles going on at once. Edmondson's only foray into writing on the first series produced perhaps the most pointed parody, in *Bad News*

Planer, Mayall,
Edmondson and
Richardson in 'Bad News
Tour'

Tour, which takes the form of a TV documentary (seen in rough-cut) on an extremely bad heavy metal group. Their music is a barbed parody of the rubbish produced by many such bands; and as the camera team (the director of which is played by the real director of the film, Sandy Johnson) follows the group around, Edmondson demonstrates the sort of problems of fly-on-the-wall filming which don't normally survive to the final cut. The group consists of Vim (Edmondson), Den (Nigel Planer), Colin (Mayall) and Spider (Richardson); here their van has broken down and they are arguing with the director:

(*Shot of the group's van on the A1 from a bridge. It suddenly pulls off the road on to a verge.*)

Sandy's voice: What are they doing? Why can't they just do what they're bloody well told? Mark, give me the radio. Hello – why have you stopped?

Den's voice (*on radio*): Hello. We are receiving you loud and clear, over.

Sandy's voice: Cut the jargon and just answer the question, you stupid bastard.

Vim's voice (*on radio*): Look this is Vim. Just watch who you're calling a stupid bastard, OK? And for your information we've broken down, you stupid bastard.

(*The camera has panned slowly round from the van to Sandy standing on the bridge.*)

Sandy (*to camera*): Oliver, I am not the subject of this documentary. Point the camera at the van.

(*Cut to a shot of the group and the camera crew standing in between the broken-down van and the crew's plush Winnebago.*)

Sandy: I fully appreciate your problem, but you can't use our bus.

Vim: But why not?

Sandy: Because it's *your* problem – you've got to handle it. We're just here to point the cameras, OK? That's the whole point of documentaries. Look, don't worry, this is going to look really good in the film, anyway. It's great. It's really interesting, we're lucky it happened, actually.

Den: You're lucky I don't knock your fucking head in.

Sandy: There's no need to get violent, is there? And try not to swear so much, please, for the sake of this film.

Den: You can always put in a fucking bleep, can't you?

Sandy: Yes, yes, that's not the point, though.

Vim: No, no, that's not the point, is it? The point is, how come you think you can interfere with the way we talk, and not interfere when the van's broken down?

Den: Yeah, right.

Vim: Answer that and stay fashionable.

Mark (*the sound man*): Come on boys, let's keep cool.

Vim & Den: Fuck off!!

Mark: Don't talk to me like that.

(*A slight pause. Sandy looks across to the camera.*)

Sandy: Cut it!*

Peter Richardson became fascinated by the process of film-making: 'I really enjoy the whole process, because I find that each stage is a chance to either improve it or wreck it. The script itself is boss – if the script is dodgy there's no way the film is going to be good; and the script is usually as good as the idea – if you can explain in fifteen or twenty words what the idea is, and it's a good idea, it will probably form a good script.'

The success of this first series of films is due not only to the skills of the writers and performers, but to the fact that they got the backing from producer Michael White and from Channel Four to make it in the first place; if Channel Four had not come about there would have been no outlet for them. Peter Richardson: 'For instance, Adrian came up with an idea for a wedding that gets totally out of hand ... you couldn't go to the BBC and say you wanted to make a

* *Bad News Tour*, Comic Strip, Channel Four.

one-off film about a wedding – you'd have to do a series, "The Wedding", for six weeks . . . The criticism people make of the Comic Strip is also its strength – it moves around in a way that's not very good television. If you have a six-part series, by episode two you're involved with the characters, you don't have to start thinking, what's this about – you know the relationship, you've followed the story line. The Comic Strip has done something different each time, and that's kind of disturbing for a lot of people. It also means that the quality can fluctuate hugely . . . in a sense the Comic Strip isn't good television, although I do think people like them more in retrospect than they do at the time of transmission.'

It is certainly a characteristic of many of the films that they can look better with subsequent viewings, being as they are dependent upon carefully built atmosphere rather than straightforward jokes. There were more Comic Strip films to come (which will be dealt with later), all produced by the company set up by Richardson and Michael White; it is perhaps Richardson's greatest achievement that he began with a minor double-act upstairs in a strip-joint and built it into a successful film production company.

The Cabaret Circuit 1983–85; Lucky Bag;
Book 'em and Risk It; French and Saunders;
Stomping on the Cat

8

It can be quite clearly seen in the listings magazines *Time Out* and
City Limits that there was a considerable expansion in the London
cabaret circuit in early 1983. The groundwork laid down three years
earlier by Alternative Cabaret had at last paid off in an upsurge of
interest. Over the next few years the circuit became a steady source
of employment for the performers. Even though venues came and
went, there were always a reasonable number of places to work.
By February 1984 these included among others the Bush Hotel,
Goldhawk Road; the Donmar Warehouse theatre (doing cabaret in
addition to its more usual fringe theatre); the Finborough; the Gate,
Notting Hill; the Old White Horse; the Roebuck, Tottenham Court
Road; the Crown and Castle (now being run by Jean Nicholson); the
Hemingford; the Cricklewood Hotel; the Croydon Warehouse; and
two important new venues, Jongleurs and the Tunnel Palladium
(near the Blackwall Tunnel).

Meanwhile, forced out of his old venue at the Gargoyle, Don
Ward had re-opened the Comedy Store in March 1983 at what had
once been the 400 Club, in the south-east corner of Leicester Square.
He had the ground floor and the basement, using both for a disco
during the week, and the ground floor for the Comedy Store on
Saturdays. He remembers: 'The power of the Comedy Store was
still there, and Wham! – off we went again. Tremendous business,
good shows – French and Saunders, Ben Elton, Chris Barrie, Tony
Allen, Andy de la Tour ... a slicker show; and able to get more
audience in, so I was happier. Eventually the owners of the premises
lost the lease, and I got the lease for the basement – I didn't want
upstairs because it was going to cost a lot in rates and rents; I had
reasonable rent downstairs.'

The Comedy Store finally re-opened at its new premises in July
1985. One could easily miss it – all that can be seen at street level is
the door with a sign above it, crammed between an Angus Steak
House and a large Chinese restaurant; downstairs the layout is rather
odd, being long and thin, with an area of the floor lower than the
rest (where the floorboards had to be removed because of rot).
However, it holds its audience more conveniently (and is certainly

easier to get into) than the old Comedy Store, and has continued its tradition much as before.

The two new venues mentioned above were, over the next few years, to make themselves, if anything, more influential than the Comedy Store. Jongleurs was run by Maria Kempinska (it has since been taken over by her husband, John Davy), who began her career teaching in drama workshops. It was at the Edinburgh Festival in 1982 that she first had the idea; there was a fringe café there where performers could do short turns, and it occurred to her that the London area could use something a bit better than the usual crowded pub venues.

She found a huge upstairs room, above the Cornet, near Clapham Junction, which was being used for roller-skating – it had been built in the 1920s as an elegant restaurant, the Crystal Room, with a high ceiling and plenty of space. She had definite ideas of how she wanted it to go: 'The intention was to make a full evening of it, with meals – I wanted a place that everyone could feel relaxed in – that women could go in by themselves – I thought, if a woman could come in and not feel intimidated, and talk to people without feeling any pressure, then that would be my criterion for a good atmosphere.'

Jongleurs opened on 4 February 1983 to a full house: '*Time Out* really took to it because it was a South London venue; but the acts themselves, if you compare them to nowadays, were absolutely awful ... I suppose it had to start somewhere. I experimented – I wanted to see how modern dance would go down, and we had all sorts of bizarre things happening – there was a whole mixture, until it was honed down to what Jongleurs is today, which is very much variety, but very much comedy-orientated. In those days you had more people who were politically orientated, who would get away with being just political on stage – without any intention of being humorous – but the audience accepted it because they were a fringe audience, and it was fun; nobody knew what was going to happen next.'

It took about two years of running Jongleurs on an overdraft before it became a complete financial success, but since then it has become firmly established, offering a good evening's meal and entertainment. In that period the audience changed, mostly due to the huge increase in house prices in the area as it became fashionable; the dreaded term 'yuppie' has been much bandied about with reference to Jongleurs. John Davy: 'I don't see any advantage to having a "right-on" venue which is basically full of drunks giving brilliant performers a hard time. If you're going to have an audience which will join in and heckle, let them heckle people who are bad; but when it goes right across the board, it begins to destroy it.'

Maria Kempinska adds: 'You do want audience participation; you don't even mind bad hecklers, because a good performer can handle it.' John Davy: 'But when you get twelve guys – or women – just giving someone a hard time because they think, "This is what we're supposed to do" ... the most common reply we get if we ask people to stop is, "No, you misunderstand – they love it!" '

Certainly the audience for Jongleurs tends towards the relatively well-off, and the heckling is mostly genial (though as John Davy says, it can deteriorate). The other important new venue – which opened about a year later – was at the opposite end of the spectrum from Jongleurs, both geographically (within London) and socially. Located near the Blackwall Tunnel in Greenwich (it is in fact on the road leading to the tunnel's southern entrance), it was started by Malcolm Hardee; he had worked in fringe theatre, including working in sketches at the Tramshed in 1980 when Mayall and Edmondson were replacing Fundation. He worked at various venues with Martin Soan, and a succession of other people as the third player, in the comedy team 'The Greatest Show On Legs' – which included a balloon dance sequence parodying Howard Brenton's then notorious play *The Romans In Britain* (whose director was unsuccessfully prosecuted for presenting a simulated but realistic scene of homosexual rape).

He remembers: 'We used to do a pub-crawl every summer and every winter – just go round the pubs and do shows for nothing (which was how we started out); and we did this place called the Tunnel, which no one ever went to. It was packed, because we were popular. Just by coincidence I went back down there the next Sunday, and there were about four people there.' The pub had a large room with a stage behind it, which was sometimes used for rock concerts, and it seemed to Hardee an ideal venue for a cabaret club.

He opened it in January 1984 – to an audience of forty. Three weeks later, when he had begun advertising in *Time Out*, he got a hundred, and since then it has rarely dropped below a hundred and fifty.

The audience is quite different from Jongleurs. Hardee: 'It's quite riotous – there has actually been a riot, not a fight, a riot – there was a period when some rough Herbert types used to turn up from Eltham – the Cortina lot. The audience is the strangest I know – I suppose it's a third trendies, a third just the normal sort of people who believe everything they read in the papers – and you get dockers going there because it's near the river; it's completely odd. They're

Lee Cornes and Raw Sex

mainly between twenty and thirty-five. They know what they like – you can see someone go down well in one of the North London clubs and at the Tunnel they'll die the death. The audience likes quality acts.'

The heckling level can be very high – there was even some heckling in Latin at one stage (just one person showing off, probably) – but as long as an act is good and hasn't been seen there too recently the audience can be very appreciative. Hardee himself usually compères; he also has built up a stand-up act which he has done at various venues.

A special feature of the Tunnel is its open spots – it is not the only venue to do them, but it offers perhaps more of a baptism of fire than most other places. People can phone Hardee to ask for a try-out spot; it's the usual way of starting in the business. Hardee: 'Generally speaking they're dreadful. When they ring up, I ask, "Do you need a sound check?" – and they don't know what a sound check is. [It's trying out the public address system.] If they say they don't use microphones, you know they're straight out of drama school.'

Although London was the main area in which cabaret was developing in the early 1980s, there was a small amount of activity building up in the provinces; but mostly performers touring out of London would still be relying on community centres and university gigs, much as they had at the beginning of the alternative comedy story.

Victoria Wood, much of whose early career had been spent in just such venues, was by 1983 scaling the two peaks which many performers would later be aiming for – television and the one-person show. Following her play *Talent* for Granada and the musical *Good Fun*, she wrote another play for Granada (which she wasn't in) called *Nearly A Happy Ending*; Granada producer Peter Eckersley then asked her to make a pilot comedy programme. She appeared in this with Julie Walters, whom she had first met at drama school and had previously worked with in revue.

The show was called *Wood and Walters*. Victoria Wood remembers: 'It was dire – but got in the last four for the BAFTA award, I don't understand how – and then we did a series; which was a bit sad because Peter Eckersley had died about the week before we started, so we had no producer really – the one we had didn't know what it was all about. It was a sketch show – very like any other show you've ever seen. I didn't realize, because it was the first series I'd written – it was all written by me – quite how much stuff you needed to write in order to be able to throw half of it away; so I only wrote enough for the six half-hours, and it wasn't enough. Some bits of it were good; some were deadly.'

The series was transmitted in January and February 1982; the best of the scripts were included in *Up To You, Porky* (Methuen, 1985) and show her sharp observation and neat construction of sketches developing well.

The show had various guest performers, including Rik Mayall. Victoria Wood: 'I remember him telling me about French and Saunders. I thought, I don't like the sound of them, we don't want any more girls in comedy, thank you.... I thought they sounded really funny, in a grudging sort of way – so I steered well clear of them for years.'

She and her husband, the Great Soprendo, had been touring a

stage show for several years, but in 1982 they decided to work separately; she built up a solo performance running for about an hour and twenty minutes. Solo shows – usually running between fifty minutes and an hour and a quarter – are the natural next step for cabaret artists from the usual twenty-minute acts, and the problems this presents tend to be solved in much the same way by most of them – usually by providing a tenuous framework linking parts of their existing material. (Alexei Sayle was already adding to this his overwhelming force of personality.)

Victoria Wood had the advantage of being able to mix songs and patter, thus avoiding the problems of constructing an hour of continuous speech in such a way as to hold the audience's attention. Her show *Lucky Bag*, which she first performed at the King's Head Theatre Club in Islington in October 1983, had rather more songs than patter; in later years she gradually increased the proportion of speech. In *Lucky Bag* some of the patter is straightforward personal stand-up material, and some of it adopts another useful technique for breaking up the speech – the character monologue, very much in the tradition of mainstream revue performers of the 1950s such as Joyce Grenfell. Most of the cabaret performers of the 1980s who attempted the solo show would step away from their own personalities from time to time and drop into character sketches – even though the characters themselves, or their material, were often more alternative than the basic format.

In *Lucky Bag* Wood did monologues as a guide round the home of the Brontës, and as a schoolgirl making a debate speech in defence of school uniforms – both well observed and crafted character pieces. The more personal monologues were in the individual style she has since extended, combining sharp observation and a wry attitude. This jaundiced look at Morecambe (her home is not far from there) has less references to the fashionable consumables of modern living than much of her material, but shows her ability for personal observation:

> You know they say 'See Naples and die' – see Morecambe and feel as if you already have. . . . No, it's a very jolly place; it's one of the few resorts where you can get a kiss-me-quick hearing-aid. It's full of little old men going paddling – by the time they've got the knots in their handkerchiefs the tide's gone out. Little old ladies walking up and down the prom with those funny hats that say 'Kiss me quick, but wait till I've got my teeth in'. And there's a pier – well, it's like a council house on a stick. It's got a waxworks on it . . . well, it's four shop dummies in demob suits labelled 'Buck's Fizz', but, you know, they're doing their best. There's a fair – well, it's two rides and a liniment stall . . . and it's got this huge big wheel, and it goes round

really slowly ... and there's antimacassars on the back of each seat. And there's a ghost train – it's really fast, and it goes through Tesco's ... and they all go,'Ooooh – have you seen the price of butter – frightening, isn't it?'

I tell you, things are very wild in Morecambe on a Saturday night. You get old men dipping their garibaldis into another woman's Horlicks ... little old ladies grabbing fellows as they come out of the gents, getting them in a dark corner and showing them photographs of their son-in-law in Australia ... and dance – they do the hokey ... that's like the hokey-cokey but you nod off in the middle. But that's the summer – I mean it's much quieter in the winter ... the prom's deserted, littered with torn pages of the *Watchtower* and empty Steradent tins ... even the Gifte Shoppe's shutte. That's the one with the sign up – 'You don't have to be mad to work here, just old, deaf, and incredibly irritating.'

The songs contain the same sort of sharp observation; unusually in the field of comedy, some of them have a sadness about them which sets them off from the more straightforward comedy patter – though this one has a jaunty tune which takes the sting out of the lyrics:

> She married early – it was the thing to do –
> Smiled for the photos – like a dream come true –
> He said he'd love her for ever – as if –
> It's a shame he never promised not to bore her stiff ...
> > Only the lonely would ever dispute what I'm saying ...
> > Take it or leave it, you'd better believe what I'm saying ...
> > It is a crime to be stuck by the side of a person
> > You don't even like, tell me what could be worse than
> > A life full of nothing, it's stupid, it's painful ...
> > Don't do it.

Despite the apparent 'message' of that song, Victoria Wood denies trying to make people think: 'It's just what's funny – and also, your attitudes will come across. If you are writing your own material, then your areas of interest will become apparent. I'm not trying to make them think, but I couldn't say anything I didn't half-believe in.' In later shows the proportion of more serious songs has reduced, but since a good deal of her work is rooted in observation of real life, there is often a serious point underlying the material, even if it is not overtly stated.

Her own highly successful television series will be examined in Chapter 14. Television was the obvious goal for many alternative comedy performers, bringing with it its own traps. The two widely differing shows from the same stable, *The Young Ones* and *The Comic Strip Presents* ... had each managed the difficult trick of using television in their own manner; but for those still working the cabaret circuit with their own acts, the breakthrough was far more difficult. One of the basic problems is the received idea that television cannot take more than about four minutes of stand-up material from any one person; to an extent this is true, since the viewer can lose interest very quickly, unless the performer is of the exceptional standard of, say, Billy Connolly. Stand-up performers have done longer spots occasionally, with some success; but most television appearances by cabaret artists tend to compress their material to three or four minutes – what Peter Richardson calls the 'K-Tel approach to comedy' – and often strain to produce an unusual format, which is more often irritating than stimulating.

A classic case of this is *Book 'em and Risk It*, an independent production transmitted on Channel Four on 11 August 1983. It is interesting because it provides the first major television appearances of Jim Barclay, Arnold Brown and The Oblivion Boys; but as a programme it is a shambles. The show was recorded in the foyer of the Royal Festival Hall, to a desultory audience of a few youngsters and bored commissionaires (plus a few bemused members of the public pressing their noses up against the window from the walkway outside). The other performers included The Chip Shop Show, about whose spoof of space epics the less said the better; Cathy le Creme, a feminist poet whose work was not really suitable for this sort of presentation; Trimmer and Jenkins, a rather amateurish musical act; and, more effectively, The Joeys – four young men who were then successfully working on the cabaret circuit and whose rhythmically chanted poetry came over well – and Martin Beaumont and Nikki, whose sketch about an unintelligible Scotsman doing a magic act was more in the old music-hall tradition and came over tolerably well.

Jim Barclay's 'wacky and zany' approach survived well; Arnold Brown's material was good, but not unnaturally he looked tense and for some reason addressed much of his act to the ceiling (partly because the camera was almost up his nose). The Oblivion Boys did their terrorist siege act with some success, though the audience seemed rather bemused by it – indeed, one of the biggest problems for all the performers was that the small audience did not laugh enough. All in all the programme was made cheaply and looks it, and remains a curiosity.

A rather more successful approach was adopted by Paul Jackson for the series *The Entertainers*, which, having now left the BBC, he made at London Weekend Television for Channel Four (i.e., LWT's technical and production facilities, for transmission on Channel

Four). Some of the performers involved in the shows drawn from the alternative comedy scene had reservations about the results; but, within the framework provided for him by LWT's requirements, Jackson produced a reasonably successful series.

The premise for the series (of six unrelated programmes) was new performers of any kind, and the shows featured Hale and Pace (from Fundation); and a Kim Fuller script called *Inner City Fairy Tales* for The Oblivion Boys, Chris Barrie and Debbie Bishop. The two shows of interest here are *French and Saunders* and *Stomping On The Cat*; the remainder were more mainstream.

Dawn French and Jennifer Saunders had by now built up a stage act, consisting of character sketches with a tenuous linking thread, which they had toured round the usual fringe theatre venues including the King's Head. The TV show, which was recorded on 19 July 1983 and transmitted on 6 October, was based on their stage material; they had reservations about this, feeling that in the different setting the sketches would not survive as well, but their performances came over effectively despite the unfamiliar surroundings.

They had developed a stage relationship in the patter that linked the sketches, and this was used for similar purposes in the television version; Jennifer Saunders was the star, with Dawn French as the downtrodden sidekick.

> **Jennifer:** We are French and Saunders, it's true ... we're a female double-act ... and we're still very good friends ... and I think Dawn has probably got something she'd like to tell you all now.
>
> **Dawn:** What? ... Oh, yes, yes ... Well, really, I'm just delighted to have this opportunity just to tell you what a super person Jenny is.
>
> **Jennifer** (*fake surprise*): Oh, no!
>
> **Dawn:** She's a very warm and giving ... (*To Jennifer.*) What are you so surprised about? You wrote this. (*To audience.*) That's it ... kind and ... loving ...
>
> **Jennifer:** Thank you, thank you ... that goes to show that we're still very good friends, we go round to each other's houses, that kind of thing ...
>
> **Dawn:** That's not *strictly* true, is it? ... No, sorry, you're telling lies, aren't you. Because you've never actually *been* to my house, have you?
>
> **Jennifer:** I don't want to go into that now, it's embarrassing for you.
>
> **Dawn:** I'm not embarrassed! I'd just like to know why you've never been to my house.
>
> **Jennifer:** It's just that Dawn's family are gypsies.
>
> **Dawn:** *What?* I told you my grandmother went to Ireland on a camping trip twenty years ago. I live in a flat in Paddington, actually.

Jennifer: I'll come and see you, then ... all right? Anyway, this is our first big television spectacular ...

Dawn: It's not a very big flat, of course ...

Jennifer: This is our first big television spectacular ...

Dawn: One of the reasons, Jennifer, that it is not a very big flat is because we are quite a poor family, actually.

Jennifer: Is there anything more you'd like to say? You're just digging your own grave, it's frightfully embarrassing.

Dawn: And one of the reasons, Jennifer, that we are a poor family is because you take all the money!

Jennifer: I didn't want to go into that now ... I'm sorry, it's embarrassing ...

Dawn: You take all the money that we get for doing things like this ... you do – two people, one person gets the money – is that democratic?

Jennifer: It's embarrassing for you ... all right then, I'm sorry, it's just when I got Dawn from the job centre, we agreed on two-year training on a low wage until she's really funny. As you can see, it hasn't quite worked yet.

   The actual sketches in the show, like much of their material over the years, rely more on character performances than actual jokes, and so tend to look flat on the page; their ability to create a wide range of characters gives their performances a depth of humour which they were able to develop fully for television in their later TV series.

The show included the 'Psychodrama' sketch that they started with; this caused some difficulty because of the word 'clitoris'. In another show in the *Entertainers* series, one of the performers used the word 'penis'; the show was scheduled for 8.30 pm, but no complaints were raised by the television executives. However, 'clitoris' was another matter, and the *French and Saunders* show was placed at 11.15 pm – thus disrupting the series' placing, and losing most of the audience for that and the subsequent shows. Paul Jackson comments: 'We'd been trundling along quite nicely at two and a half million, and the figures never recovered – *French and Saunders* got about nothing ... it just struck me as interesting that you could say "penis" one week and you couldn't say "clitoris" another week. It just shows the kind of people who make the decisions at the end of the day.'

The other recording session for the series, which brought in thirteen acts from the cabaret circuit, produced so much material that the decision was taken to split it into two half-hour programmes rather than have to edit everybody down to two minutes. The recording was made on 2 March 1983, and the transmissions were on 20 October (within the *Entertainers* series) and 4 January 1984 (as a single show).

Both shows went under the puzzling title *Stomping On The Cat* – taken from a song performed by Ronnie Golden and the Dialtones. Golden explains: 'That really was a real-life incident, when a girl-friend actually did tread on a cat – it was just awful, and the only way to deal with it was for me to write this song and keep singing it at her – it became a joke; then it seemed to work in my solo act, so I kept on doing it.'

This piece of musical psychotherapy became the title song for the programmes, and the Dialtones also performed two unaccompanied numbers. The audience for the transmissions was not particularly good, but the programmes provided a good showcase for the artists – although the usual process of cutting down and then more cutting down went on, to the irritation of some of them. As with *Boom Boom*, Jackson provided a stage and an audience sitting at tables – in a more spacious setting, this time – so that the performers could feel themselves to be in a familiar cabaret situation.

When one looks at the video tapes today, most of the performers come over effectively. Jim Barclay, Arnold Brown, Pauline Melville and Andy de la Tour all make a good impression, though Ben Elton looks rather odd compared with his familiar more recent image – he

The Dialtones in
'Stomping on the Cat'

has short hair, no glasses, and seems rather nervous. Christopher Barrie does some barbed impressions – in particular of Ronnie Corbett and Kenneth Williams – and Paul Martin, then new on the circuit, comes over well. (He has since established himself firmly on the cabaret scene, under the name Paul Merton.) The Oblivion Boys appear as a couple of heavies complaining about the quality of the preceding acts; their experience in acting shows in their ability to project their characters firmly on to the screen.

The programmes also introduced four relatively new performers, who will be examined in the next chapter: Simon Fanshawe, Jenny Lecoat, Helen Lederer and John Hegley. They had been establishing themselves on the comedy circuit, and *Stomping On The Cat* gave them their first chance to try their hands at television. The shows opened no magic doors for anybody – of all of them, only Ben Elton has really made it to the top outside the cabaret circuit, though the others have all established themselves as firm favourites in live performance – but the video recordings show that on the whole the programmes provided a successful showcase for the performers.

9

Simon Fanshawe; Jenny Lecoat;
Helen Lederer; John Hegley; Interference;
Four Minutes To Midnight

Stomping On The Cat suffered few censorship problems, even though
one of the participants promoted homosexuality – a subject which
would have been kept firmly off television not many years earlier.
Simon Fanshawe was being labelled at that time as a 'radical gay
comedian', later he came to find that label somewhat limiting, but
at the time he was pioneering the expression of alternative sexuality.

He was born in Devizes on 26 September 1956, the youngest son
of an army family. This meant that his family moved around a lot,
and he thinks that his present-day capacity for fantasy grew out of
the fact that he spent most of his holidays alone (being at boarding
school he never had time to make friends locally).

After he left school, as he remembers: 'Then I did what my mother
refers to as running away to Sussex University and becoming a
communist ... which wasn't strictly true, but when you grow up in
a middle-class family like mine the teenage desire to rebel is not
satisfied by not wearing a tie to church. . . . My parents have always
been very good about it. I took a law degree – I had a romantic
vision of being Perry Mason.'

In his last year or so at school, he spent the holidays working for
the Salisbury Festival as venue manager; this experience in arts
administration led him into the Arts Federation at university – again
he was involved with the administration. He gained his law degree –
and did nothing with it, to his parents' irritation. He then got a job at
the resource centre in Brighton; he worked for them as a community
worker and fund-raiser, and helped to put on shows for children. It
was through this that he met writer Kim Fuller, who wrote *The
Brighton Show*, which was performed by a company of four, including
Fanshawe, in the basements of various arts centres.

Then in around 1980 the resource centre burnt down. At the
benefit to raise money for rebuilding, Fanshawe succumbed to the
temptation to do a solo stand-up piece: 'The only bit I remember
was the joke: when I was a kid and we used to play doctors and
nurses, I was always the social worker. It worked at the time. Then
the panic was, I got booked! You can do it once and get by on a
combination of chutzpah and the fact that you know everybody in

the audience ... and then somebody books you! Panic!'

He got sucked into playing in the very small circuit of cabaret pubs in the Brighton area, working on one occasion on the same bill as Tony Allen: 'I died a complete death; and after the gig Tony said to me, "You'd better do it – get out there and get it right" ... which was right, though I felt sort of threatened by it.... What he was saying was, you've got something interesting to say – I was trying to make jokes about gayness, and failing miserably. And the other thing was, Tony did an amazing routine about rape, and I'd never seen anyone do anything as dangerous and as exciting.'

He began to work in the expanding London cabaret circuit – he says he learned a lot from Andy de la Tour in particular and built up a routine about being gay that had considerable impact: 'It was partly naïvety – I didn't realize quite what an impact it has if you walk on a stage and say, "Here I am, I'm gay" – people are completely thrown by it. I didn't realize that even *I* was quite thrown by it ... and I wasn't admitting to myself how much I was thrown by it! I used to say, "If you don't laugh at me, you're anti-gay." I was frightened of being heckled for being gay, and I wasn't – I was heckled because I wasn't funny.'

By March 1983, when Fanshawe took part in the recording of *Stomping on the Cat*, he had developed a good act which, though still a bit aggressively gay, was well constructed and definitely funny. In this sequence he was also the first comedian to tackle AIDS – which at that time was believed to be afflicting only homosexuals and drug addicts, and thus being classed as self-inflicted injury.

> I've just been to New York; and when I went through Immigration they asked me if I was gay. I said, 'No, but I've slept with a lot of guys who are....' ('Simon, are you gay?' – 'No, not personally, I just do it for a living....') One thing everybody is terrified of in New York at the moment is AIDS, the big killer disease ... it only kills homosexuals, Haitians, heroin addicts and haemophiliacs ... I don't know why, the big 'H' ... and I don't know why it is, neither the British nor the American governments will recognize AIDS as a disease. Now that's strange, because they both recognize homosexuality as a disease. If they think it's a disease, then if you're gay, don't go to work tomorrow – just ring in sick. 'What's wrong?' – 'Still queer' – 'Hope you get better' – 'Hope I don't' ...

He commented on the difficulty of talking to his parents' upper-class friends:

> They ask me what I'm doing ... what do I say to them? – 'Well, actually I'm really big on the radical gay comic scene.' ... Gay's so

acceptable – even to them it just means a queer with A-levels. I don't think they understand it so I had to use all the other words – nancy, poof, ponce, queer, bender ... but they think I'm just talking about one of their friends ... 'Hello, my name's Nancy Poof-Ponce-Queer-Bender, do come in' ...

He did cover other subjects at this time – 'When we were teenagers we had *avenue* credibility' – but as time went on he developed his approach so that the gay side of it was less aggressive; his later style will be examined in Chapter 16.

During 1983 Fanshawe met Jenny Lecoat, and teamed up with her and Christine Ellerbeck to perform *An Evening Of Insulting Behaviour*, given in November by New Variety at a London pub called The Old White Horse. This, and his subsequent teaming with her in a later show, made an interesting combination – his 'radical gayness' with her strong anti-men feminist approach. Though she softened it later, this strong feminist stance – which worked as well as it did because of the quality of the comedy – made a considerable impact on the circuit.

Jenny Lecoat was born on 17 May 1960; she was brought up in Jersey, which she describes as 'a lovely place to grow up when you're a kid, but a horrible place to have an adolescence, because it has all the disadvantages of a provincial town – being very small and conservative – and cut off from everywhere else by the sea'.

After grammar school – where she was 'terribly well behaved and good – which is really embarrassing if you're a comedian, you're supposed to be a rebel' – she read drama and theatre arts at Birmingham University. She had always wanted to be a performer – she had been sent to ballet lessons at the age of five, and danced at festivals and the like for ten years until she 'grew into the wrong shape' – and found that the course, which was half academic and half practical, did give her some useful experience.

More importantly for her career as a comedian, she took to singing and playing the guitar at folk clubs: 'I was playing places like rugby clubs, and I got quite a lot of work because it was a novelty to have a woman twenty years old who got up and sang filthy songs – I realized that if you said a naughty word you could get a fairly cheap laugh, and I capitalized on that. I'd hate to look back on that stuff now!'

After getting her degree she came to London, and got a job with a political theatre company called Moving Parts, which went round schools and youth clubs ('trying to change the world by coming on with plastic buckets shouting "I am inflation"') – though, more effectively, they also ran discussion groups for young people. She

found experiences like asking fifteen skinheads 'Why do you hate Pakistanis?' and reasoning with them gave her excellent experience for her later stand-up work, particularly in defusing a difficult situation.

She left Moving Parts in 1982, and went back into the folk-club circuit – moving from there into the alternative cabaret circuit because it paid more. She remembers: 'Having just come out of Moving Parts I was an absolutely rampaging flag-flying Feminist-with-a-capital-F – as only a university-educated twenty-two-year-old can be ... wearing badges saying "Exploited" and developing a strong London accent – it was just cringe-making! There was a lot of stuff about men – I did pick one thing which worked as a theme, which was an ex-boyfriend – who does exist, and who I do still genuinely dislike a good deal – I picked on him as a kind of starting point.' The material she developed from this was hard for many men to take, for she was pointing up inadequacies that few of them realized they had. This description of a one-night stand might just have given a few men pause for thought:

> You get into bed – and after about five minutes, you're lying there, and you think – 'What *is* he doing? ... He's fumbling about like he's in a bloody pottery class or something.' – Have you ever had that feeling, you know, knead it here, knead it there, slap it about and off we go ... you can't *communicate* with people like that! The problem is, right, they're all completely obsessed with their willies. Willy, willy, willy, willy, willy – that's all sex is to them. Well, it's all the *world* is to them. I mean, when those missiles go launching off Greenham Common, it won't be 200-foot clitorises flying up there. How many times have the straight women here had one of those men that parades round the bedroom for about five minutes before he gets into bed? ... 'Boinggg ... that's my willy!' ... What *are* you supposed to say? The next thing you know he's on top of you – the great white whale – going at it. And what's the next thing you hear? 'Oh ... sorry.' We all know what that means, don't we? That means, 'Thank you very much, love, it's the end of the show, we can all fuck off and have a cup of tea.' That's what 'sorry' means – there's no conception of fingers or tongues, or anything that might give us a good time. Oh no, 'Sorry, love, it's all over with my willy.' Then he fucks off into the kitchen and puts the kettle on! Of course, what they don't realize is that while they're in the kitchen making the tea ... we're in bed, having a quiet wank. It's true – I've got it down to fourteen seconds now, no problem. So by the time he comes back, he's got a nice hot cuppa, you've got an orgasm, everyone's happy. The problems really start when he pokes his head round the door half-way through to find out if you take sugar. You're there, thrashing about, having a real party all on your own – they can't handle it all. Ego drops right out the testicles.

Jenny Lecoat and Simon Fanshawe teamed the following year, 1984, with poet and comedian Oscar Mclennan (who did most of his act in the nude) in their show *Three Of A Different Kind*, which they toured and then took to the Edinburgh Festival fringe in August. The following year Jenny Lecoat appeared on Channel Four in a women's documentary series *Watch The Woman*, acting as presenter; this took up most of 1985, and when she returned to comedy (with periodic outings into straight acting) she had broadened her approach and moved away from her strong anti-men stance.

There were few enough women on the circuit in the early days, and contempt for male chauvinism provided good subject matter; interestingly, a subject avoided by Helen Lederer – who also appeared in *Stomping On The Cat* – who tended rather to deal with her own inadequacies. Being in reality slightly neurotic, she was clever enough to capitalize on this and exaggerate it, using techniques such as highlighting her own natural tendency when speaking to abandon sentences halfway through (almost in an apologetic sort of way).

Lederer was born on 24 September 1954; her father was Czech and her mother from the Isle of Wight (though there is nothing obviously Czech about her apart from the name and perhaps her face – Eastern European cheekbones and striking eyes – her attitudes in comedy are purely English). She remembers her schooldays with less than affection: 'People like me weren't really understood or tolerated; you either got married or went to teacher training college or Oxford. I was always funny, more or less, in the fact that I wasn't really a sorted-out person. All the clichés with me were there – I was fat then, I had asthma, using being funny to get friends.... I got into trouble – there were three of us who were quite subversive – unconsciously – and we were away one day, which was an innocent thing; and the headmistress gave everyone else a lecture about us – she called us Fascists, short people, said that the others weren't to be following such leadership ... this is the sort of school I went to! The next day I wondered why no one was talking to me!'

She then went to a polytechnic in London, studying social sciences – economics, basic psychology, deviancy, criminology – and went on to become a social worker. She went on studying: 'I started to do an MA, because of the chip on the shoulder about going to a polytechnic – thinking that I could be an academic person; but of course it's not my bag because I never read the books. It was in Social Policy and Deviancy ... a Marxist-type course. All these things now sound completely hollow.'

After this strange beginning her innate interest in drama finally

got the upper hand and she took a drama course at the Central School of Speech and Drama: 'I was incredibly happy because I wasn't a social worker – I had access to lectures, to theatres, we learned all sorts of technical things – it was like a dream come true for me because that was what I'd always wanted to do.'

After the course she did some auditions – not getting very far, partly because of not having an Equity card – and then got involved in a community theatre where she met Arnold Brown. He encouraged her to try some comedy, and she appeared at the Hampstead venue he was then running – Pentameters – doing a double-act with Maggie Fox. After a while she moved into working on her own, building up a very individual stand-up style.

She comments: 'I haven't chosen to use political or feminist lines in an overt sense because it wouldn't suit the way I am funny – which is by undercutting, and letting the audience deduce where I'm coming from – I can't do the "let's have a look at this" approach because it would kill my humour.'

From the beginning she exaggerated her own shyness to create a neurotic stage personality; in this later monologue she combines the stage character's neuroticism with deft observation:

I don't know if anyone's actually been in between relationships here? . . . I don't mean actually in between lots of people who are having lots of relationships, standing in the middle of group . . . no, I mean when somebody's dumped you. That's lovely, if that's ever happened, it's a good tip to experience, it's lovely . . . um . . . and the next person's too frightened of your sheer looks, beauty and talent to ask you . . . in between relationships, you know, you're with me. . . . And what you do when you're in between relationships is, you go to one of these top beauty places, um, because you've got a lot of time and nothing matters if you're in between relationships . . . so what you do, no, what you do is, you go on one of these sun-beds. I don't know if you've been – just passes the time, it's great and, um, before you get on it, you have to sign this indemnity form, obviously, saying you completely don't mind about all the accompanying perks – you know, cancer, moles, skin discoloration, that kind of thing . . . no, you tick it because you're in between relationships and nothing matters, as I say . . . anyway . . . no, you get on the sun-bed, it's a bit like a sandwich, just get in the middle, right – I don't know if you've been on this, just explain to those people who haven't, right – and you pull the top bit down, so you can just about breathe without burning your lips on the radiation tubes, which is lovely – and then you baste yourself, baste yourself in all your sweat . . . sometimes your own, sometimes some sweat that somebody's been kind enough to leave before you . . . and then when you're really red and basted, you go and have a massage – to tone down the redness, so nobody actually knows that you've ever been on the sun-bed in the first place, which is the whole point of it . . .

I don't know if you go to parties, but I got asked to this party . . . it was an invitation party actually, no, it was, because it was posted to me, it had my name on it, OK? It was *mine* . . . OK? . . . sometimes people query that . . . no, I *was* asked . . . anyway, um, I put it under my magnetic ladybird on my fridge door, so in the morning when I get my goat's milk I could actually be reminded that I had been asked to this . . . party, anyway . . . um, it was, um, it was a theme party . . . it said, 'Henrietta invites Helen', right, 'to a leave-your-partner-at-home party' . . . that's the theme, and, er, I wasn't frightfully sure if I was eligible to go to a leave-your-partner-at-home party, not having a . . . partner at home to leave at the time . . . so anyway, I phoned her up and explained the problem. I said, 'Look, I can arrange for my cousin Robert to stay in the flat for the duration of the party, to leave the phone number so he can phone in and accuse me of having a good time . . .' and, she said, no, no, she could probably squeeze me in, she said it was just a joke, she just put that on my invitation, which I thought was quite . . . witty of her . . . nobody else had that . . . and, um, I went along, very relaxed, very informal, you know, just things on sticks . . . you had to guess what they were . . . which was quite funny . . . and I was very good at it, actually. Well, I say good – I managed to eat a pound of butter – I thought they were cubes of cheese . . . guessed wrong . . . um . . . it was great, though, because I got sent home first, which was lovely, because I'd been sick on the carpet, a lot of dairy products on an empty stomach . . .

Stomping On The Cat gave Helen Lederer an excellent showcase – she projected her personality very well – and although, once again, it opened no immediate doors, she did go on to do some television and to build up her solo work.

The remaining new performer highlighted by *Stomping On The Cat*, John Hegley, had started his cabaret career by braving the Comedy Store just over two years earlier, in December 1980. He was born on 1 October 1953 and was brought up initially in Luton, subsequently going to a sixth form college in Bristol and Bradford University, where he read literature, sociology and ideas (these being about history and philosophy).

He had written poetry since he was ten, and took up the guitar when he was eighteen, combining the two in amateur performing while at university. He remembers: 'There was certainly no idea of comedy – until just after I'd left university, when someone laughed at one of my songs, and that sort of went to the back of my mind, "That's nice".'

Then he went on to work in children's theatre, working for four years at Soapbox East, an Arts Council-funded company which did 'knockabout summer shows'. He co-wrote a couple of plays – one being *There's No Smoke Without Walter* (as in Raleigh), the message of which was, 'Don't smoke'.

The company aimed at the age range nine to thirteen, and he learned a lot about handling audiences: 'They want to join in, and this can present problems unless you learn the rules for dealing with it – you direct their desire for participation into positive channels – "Come and help me row this boat to America" . . . you can't control it when they've got catapults. We had catapults once, eggs once, potatoes once . . . three times in four years isn't bad.'

He started performing at the Comedy Store at the end of 1980, his first few tries being instant gong fodder until he developed a style which suited them. He had been busking in the newly opened Covent Garden piazza; but, finding that it was too cold to play the guitar, tried speaking his lyrics as poetry and found that it worked; so he used the same idea at the Comedy Store and hit on a style which the audience would accept.

In later years he developed a style relying on a good deal of interaction with the audience; the beginnings of this came at the Earth Exchange when he was doing one of his brief poems, 'Sport':

> S – stimulating; P – popular; O – oxygenating; R – really interesting; and T – a nice cup of tea goes down a treat after a bit of Sport.

He tried asking the audience for suggestions for the letters, more by accident than design, and found that it worked well; although it was some time before he developed audience reactions into a major feature of the act. At the time one of the obsessions of his poetry was with his spectacles: 'I used to walk on and people would shout out "four-eyes" or whatever – and I thought, right, take it up, get in before they do – "Hello everybody/My name's John/What have I got/I've got my glasses on" – that was my entrance.'

His glasses featured in a good deal of his poetry:

> I look after my spectacles because they look after me
> without my spectacles, where would I be?
> I'd probably be standing here –
> but I'd have a job to see
> properly.

In December 1981 he left the children's theatre group, because in addition to his solo work he had teamed up with Sue Norton, Keith Moore and Russell Greenwood to form the comedy musical group, The Popticians; then, in a show where The Popticians appeared with

comedian and magician John Otis (who works as Otis Canneloni), he developed with Otis a routine which grew into the Brown Paper Bag Brothers. This involved a lot of jokes about paper bags – giving the audience one each and getting them to pop them all together, and bags with drawings on them (a T: tea-bag; a knight on a bag held over his head: overnight bag . . . and so on).

One of his routines with John Otis involved an attempt to 'escape from his glasses' – he would get as far as letting one arm of the frame (originally broken in an accident) hang down: 'Then I say, "I couldn't quite manage it", and then I get depressed – then I get very depressed – it's quite serious that bit, I really act it . . . "I'm sorry . . . I've got a lot of problems . . ." and the quieter audience gives you that space, and that's an interesting area to explore . . . they know I'm putting it on, but it's the suspension of disbelief; and that's something you would never get in the Comedy Store – except Rik Mayall could do it because he was so good.'

The later developments in Hegley's individual style will be dealt with in Chapter 15. Even more than most performers on the cabaret circuit, he needed an audience to play off, and thus television would be difficult for him. The problem of needing a live audience, but also needing not to exclude the viewers, is one which constantly has to be solved by producers of television comedy; some solutions work better than others.

Brian Izzard, the co-producer of *Book 'em and Risk It*, made an attempt to place alternative comedians in an alternative television setting in the six-part series *Interference*, which was independently made by his production company and transmitted on Channel Four beginning on 12 November 1983. The basic thesis of the programme is ingenious enough – although it becomes a bit strained after six episodes: each show begins with a fictitious programme, *A Friend On Four*, hosted by Fiona Richmond. On each occasion, she gets only a few seconds into her opening when there is interference to picture and sound, and 'Station S' takes over, supposedly broadcasting illicitly from various venues – much play is made of the idea that the police are hot on their trail and that they have only twenty-three minutes before they must pack up and disappear.

The shows were recorded, using lightweight cameras and video equipment, at locations including a boxing hall, a sports and social club, a comprehensive school and a river cruiser equipped for parties. Seen on the TV screen, some of the locations work well enough, with the studio audience well placed and the viewer made to feel a part of the event; but in some of the others the audience is too thin and far away from the performers – or too close; one or two sets are done from right in the middle of the audience, who are made rather tense by the cameras pointing at them.

The shows had a regular team of performers: Jim Barclay, Arnold Brown, Martin and Nikki Beaumont, and the Dialtones – Ronnie Golden, Mac MacDonald and Richie Robertson. A couple of the shows work quite well; in particular Arnold Brown looks as relaxed as he has ever done on television and projects his personality well. Jim Barclay generally comes over well, mostly using material from his stage act, with a few specially written additions; and Martin Beaumont and Nikki's routines, being rooted in music-hall and usually performed in working men's clubs, are robust enough to overcome the difficulties.

The Dialtones' musical numbers are reasonably effective; but they also perform sketches – mostly spoof advertisements – which were written at short notice and look it. Ronnie Golden was unhappy with the result: 'It was a nightmare; we were pulled in at the last minute because they needed a music act. We were getting a pittance for it – and we had to write five minutes of material every week on the Monday – we hadn't been told about that. If I'd known how bad it was going to end up I'd never have done it. But you do these things . . . I do actually put it on my c.v. because it looks quite impressive – six-part series – and nobody knows what it is.'

The show ran up against Jasper Carrott on BBC1 – and one episode was against *The Day After*, the spectacular nuclear war epic – so its audience was minuscule. If the last four episodes had worked as well as the first two – and if Golden's material had been written under more reasonable circumstances – the series might have worked better; as it is, it remains another curiosity – though good things in it include Brown's 'Campaign For Real People', including his exhortation, 'Cyclists of the world unite – you have nothing to lose but your chains'.

The show's relative failure spurred Jim Barclay on to a new approach: 'After *Interference* I suffered a reaction from doing this twenty-five-minute instant appeal, dealing with hecklers . . . I wanted to branch out into a situation where people paid to come and sit and specifically listen to me. So I devised a one-man show, because I wanted to say more involved, deeper sorts of things in my act, and I found that the lowest common denominator of the drunk Saturday night Comedy Store audience was restricting my ability to do this. But at the same time, that lowest common denominator is a valuable challenge – how do you make difficult things to say palatable?'

Barclay's one-man show, *Four Minutes To Midnight*, was first performed at the Soho Poly in June 1984, and he took it to the

Edinburgh Fringe that year. He used most of the material he had written up to that time, linking it in the form of a narrative by a visitor from outer space – Wonderwally from the planet Zanussi:

> For know thou, Earthlings – we on Zanussi are as far up shit creek as you are. The funny thing is, though, Earthlings, whereas everybody on Zanussi is running around, selling their gerbils, taking their library books back and sticking their heads in brown paper bags – you lot seem remarkably blasé under the same imminent destruction and disintegration that you are facing. And disintegration is the *mot juste*, I think you will agree. I don't know whether anybody here has ever been involved in a nuclear explosion? It's rather like having a jacuzzi bath filled with pirhana fish.

He describes his journeys trying to find someone to take his message seriously – including meetings with Marx and Christ (who had once done a gig on Earth with twelve roadies) – taking in some unlikely locations:

> I materialized myself in the Truncheon Arms, Plaistow, talent contest. A friendly pub – the sort of pub that comes alive on festive occasions like Hitler's birthday. Leaning up against the bar, there were two gentlemen discussing the repatriation of the Normans ... 'They come over here, reeking of garlic – half of them, all they've got is a suit of chain-mail and a horse ...' On the other side of the pub there's a taxi-driver translating *Mein Kampf* into Cockney rhyming slang.

He enters the Truncheon Arms talent contest as a ventriloquist, whose dummy's jokes are perhaps too political for the venue:

> I say, I say, I say – what's the difference between a pelican, the Inland Revenue, and the South-East Gas Board? – They can all stick their bills up their arses. Why has Conservative Central Office got no toilets? – Because everyone shits on everyone else. Hey, here's a cracker – what is the difference between a flock of Newfoundland geese and five hundred SS-20 missiles homing in on London and the Home Counties? – Answer, as far as the Fylingdales Early Warning System is concerned, there isn't any difference!

Finally, having failed to get his message home anywhere, he is advised by Marx to seek out the bourgeois intelligentsia:

> 'You will find them in wholefood vegetarian restaurants ... in polytechnic common rooms ... and if you are lucky you may even find them amongst late-night audiences in small repertory theatres throughout the country.' ... So, here I am. It's not just for me, you understand. It's the wife and kids as well – we've just got a home

improvement grant up there ... so, do what you can ... help ...
please.

In the period since then Barclay has done a lot of straight acting,
including a run with the National Theatre Company in the 1988
production of '*Tis a Pity She's a Whore*; he has filled in between jobs
by continuing to appear from time to time on the circuit with his
own brand of comedy-with-a-message. His contribution to the early
days in particular of alternative comedy was considerable, showing
how it was possible to take a strong political standpoint and still be
funny. He has always made his audiences laugh; perhaps he also
made some of them think.

10

The Comic Strip Presents . . .
– second series

The second series of Comic Strip films followed a year behind the first, consisting this time of seven nominally half-hour films (though in fact lengths varied up to almost forty minutes). The first to be transmitted, *Five Go Mad On Mescalin*, was, like its predecessor, transmitted ahead of the rest of the series as a 'taster' on Channel Four on 2 November 1983 – exactly a year later than the first one. The same characters appear, plus a few new ones, and the children have another exciting adventure; but the world they are in is beginning to change – they can no longer get ginger beer or ice-cream, and have to be content with 7-Up and lollies. The children themselves are more overtly fascist than before, as emerges even in the pre-title sequence of their picnic:

> **Anne:** Gosh, isn't it sad to think there are people in this world who are starving?
> **Dick:** Yes – I suppose it is.
> **George:** Still – if they didn't breed like rabbits there'd be more to go round.
> **Anne:** Yes, that's true.
> **Julian:** Mind you, half of them die in childbirth, so it must all even up in the end, I suppose.
> **Anne:** Oh, dear . . . I do wish there was *something* we could do to help.
> **Dick:** Poor old Anne – just like a girl to get het up about world problems on a lovely day like this.
> **George:** Well, it doesn't worry *me*.
> **Julian:** I agree with Dick. Africa's miles away from here – come on, let's enjoy the hols.*

Indeed, later on Dick gets rather carried away when arguing with a pushy American who reminds him that the Americans helped to win the war: 'We think it's a pity the Nazis *didn't* win, actually – because at least they cared about racial purity – and they didn't litter

* *Five Go Mad On Mescalin*, Comic Strip, Channel Four.

the country with bubble-gum wrappers'.

The series proper began on 7 January 1984 with *Dirty Movie* – an exercise by Mayall and Edmondson in their twin obsessions of weirdness and pointlessness – followed by *Susie*, a trip into something akin to D.H. Lawrence country with Dawn French as a randy schoolteacher and Peter Richardson as a drug-sodden pop star for whom she falls.

The films were again directed either by Bob Spiers or Sandy Johnson, and most of them were written by Richardson and Richens. There were ideas and scripts which never got made; Nigel Planer had several rejected: 'If you're on your own, you don't have so much power. Rik and Ade will always stick up for each other, and Peter has got Channel Four and Michael White to stand up for him; and so within the group situation I always felt a bit powerless, which was a reason for carrying on with acting work. We used to have meetings – we've given them up, thank God – we used to have meetings to give ideas to each other, and we'd even try to vote on which ones would be made – but it just doesn't work; it's much better to let people do what they're good at. Peter and [co-producer] Mike Bolland chair the selection of which films get made. It's a matter of taste whether the right ones were made – I think some of Peter's better scripts are the ones that haven't been made.'

The two second series films not written by the usual pair are *Slags* and *Eddie Monsoon – A Life*. The latter was written by Adrian Edmondson, building on the character in the first series programme which Channel Four cancelled. Edmondson: 'It's a documentary about a South African TV host who's a lush – and very violent – he's a slightly quieter version of Vivian from *The Young Ones*, but set in the real world. "Eddie Monsoon" is obviously Ed-mondson … a nickname which developed when I was drunk … all my characters are based on me when I was drunk!… there's the drunk end of my character and the sober end!'

Like *Bad News Tour*, the film is in documentary style (this time in a final edit), with the real Tony Bilbow as the interviewer. It starts with Bilbow interviewing Monsoon in a home for alcoholics:

> **Bilbow:** Eddie … in the interview granted to me by your mother, Eunice, she said – and I quote: 'At the age of twelve Eddie was a sweet boy whose only ambition was to work in an old folks' home.' And yet you see at twenty-eight you're a self-confessed drug addict, an incurable alcoholic divorcee, a bankrupt exile-stroke-fugitive of five African and South American states; and you have court cases pending in various countries on charges of tax evasion, sedition, and bestial rape. (*Kindly.*) Now, what went

wrong? . . . Are you disappointed that you failed to achieve your original ambition? . . . Eddie, does it hurt to talk about it?
Eddie: How much money am I getting for this?*

The film includes excerpts from Monsoon's understandably few TV appearances, and interviews with his ex-wife (Jennifer Saunders) and ex-manager (played by Peter Richardson with mannerisms which, if they have any similarity to those of his one-time landlord Paul Raymond, are purely accidental in their choice and no connection is implied or should be inferred). There are also some vox-pops, conducted by Monsoon with bemused members of the public.

As with *Bad News Tour*, Sandy Johnson directed the film in a naturalistic documentary style; but in *Slags*, written by Jennifer Saunders, he was given the opportunity to create an atmospheric

Adrian Edmondson as
Eddie Monsoon

* *Eddie Monsoon – A Life*, Comic Strip, Channel Four.

future dystopia where a gang of violent teenagers wars with a gang of youths in Hawaiian outfits who want everything to be 'nice'. The world they inhabit seems to be a small corner of the city in *Blade Runner*, and the film has the look of many pessimistic science-fiction films. There are also references to *The Godfather, Psycho* and *West Side Story* thrown in for good measure. Dawn French plays the leader of the gang with a splendid bad temper and lots of eye-shadow, Jennifer Saunders plays the simple-minded Little Sister with mad eyes and protuberant false teeth and Peter Richardson plays another of his crazed anarchic characters.

In *Gino – Full Story and Pics* Richardson goes to the other extreme to play an authoritarian role. *Gino*, written by Richardson and Richens, tells the story of a young man (a splendid and believable performance from Keith Allen) on the run from the police. Hijacking a taxi, he finds himself trapped into accepting fares, finally falling in with Jennifer Saunders as Angie, a spoilt girl. They get stranded in the wilds of Essex, calling at a lonely farmhouse where the wife (Dawn French) of an unpleasant cripple (Rik Mayall) recognizes Gino and murders her husband, hoping to throw the blame on him.

Gino and Angie, trying to escape, hide in a Mini-Minor when they see a milkman approach. He is in fact a policeman in disguise –

149

Peter Richardson. Richardson seems to have something of an obsession with playing policemen: 'I wish I'd been a policeman! I like the fact that somebody can be underplayed and yet have the underlying tension of being in a police situation, that you can play against. For example, in *Gino*, the line about the duvet, where he gets into a discussion about how good duvets are – I like the way he goes into a casual area, but there's always that underlying authority, that rather restricting sort of role a policeman has.'

This comes in the scene where the 'milkman' is preparing to deal with Gino. He is talking to the housewife, Frances (Dawn French):

> **Policeman:** Right, Fran – what I want you to do now is go into your living room – you got that? Now, have you got any thick cushions or a rug in there?
> **Frances:** Um, no . . . I have got a duvet.
> **Policeman:** Oh, that'll do the trick – they're nice, aren't they? Better than making the old bed every day.
> **Frances:** Yes, I'd never go back to sheets and blankets.

He then becomes business-like again, instructing her to lie on the floor under the duvet – the reason being that he and his colleagues are about to blast hell out of the Mini. Fortunately Gino and Angie aren't in it any more. Getting away, they embark on a life of crime, holding up a terrified sub-postmaster (Arnold Brown) and eventually holing up in a hotel. A waiter brings them some food – it is the same policeman. Gino threatens him with a shotgun.

> **Policeman:** I was just thinking on my way up here, Gino – thought, what's the boy done? – he's robbed a post office, stolen a few cars, and I thought, what's that worth? About five years – maybe three years with good behaviour. Out there, Gino, there are fifty armed bully-boys offering certain death in the event of an injury to a fellow officer. So I thought, what would I do in your position? Come down the station for a chat, or die in a hail of bullets?
> **Gino:** Yeah – I saw what you did to that Mini, you arsehole.
> **Policeman:** Then I thought, you lucky bastard – what a celebrity. Papers queuing to buy your story – you know, chequebook journalism – film producers paying thousands for the film rights – I thought, that's crime for you – three years in the nick, you wind up a millionaire.*

The last shot is of Gino being led into a police van – smiling happily.

There are few obvious gag lines in *Gino*, and this is true of most of the other films; even more than in the first series they depend on atmosphere rather than obvious quick jokes. Once again, this disappointed some of the audience. Adrian Edmondson: 'We became labelled as alternative comedians, which was a horrible tag to have in the first place, because it means absolutely nothing – all it does is label you as being a raving communist swearing person who shouldn't be on television and is hated by everyone who's honest and good and decent and true.... That's hampered us; and the Comic Strip series is wry, filmic, atmospheric, humoured comedy pieces; and it's a pity there was so much pressure on it to be like *The Young Ones* – the fact that they came from the same stable shouldn't have affected it. *The Young Ones* became immensely popular because it was on the bigger channel, and the Comic Strip got lost in a sort of alley; it got a few nice little crits, and a few film people interested – but it's never been appreciated enough for there to have been any genuine feedback to change the whole thing.'

Edmondson perhaps underestimates the appeal of the films. The series as a whole was never a smash hit, but a lot of people became aware of it, and subsequent repeats have offered a useful chance to reassess the individual films, many of which look better on a second viewing.

The process of making the films was of necessity highly organized.

* *Gino – Full Story and Pics*, Comic Strip, Channel Four.

Each nominally half-hour film took about two weeks to shoot, the writing having taken about two weeks on average – though *Five Go Mad In Dorset* took six days and *The Beat Generation* took two to three months. Before shooting there would be six or eight weeks pre-production – finding locations, casting, and so on; and the editing took about eight weeks to arrive at the final cut. Peter Richardson: 'I'm getting more removed from the editing in terms of the actual cutting – to start with you want to get your hand on every frame of film there is to make sure you've really got the best takes; now I find it better to leave the editors alone if something's working – if I'm not happy I'll look at every take. And editors don't like you in the cutting-room ... you learn that it *is* better to leave an editor to it; they can get a flow and a pace to it.'

Although the scripts are carefully worked out, there were cases where the ideas became elaborated in the process of filming – which would lead to an overlong film which had to be trimmed back. A case in point was the remaining second series film, *A Fistful Of Travellers' Cheques*, which ran for fifty-eight minutes on its first cut. Peter Richardson: 'What elaborated *Fistful* was all the moody walking around Spain, which takes a line of script saying "They walk into town" – and in the film they're walking along the street, the camera's tracking them, there's people looking at them – there's a whole atmosphere going on which has got comedy in it. It developed because we had a whole crowd of people watching us at the time; it was shot in Almería where they did a lot of the westerns, but because it was a parody we used the modern Almería high street rather than the western town [a standing set used for many films].'

A Fistful Of Travellers' Cheques parodies the Clint Eastwood *A Fistful Of Dollars* series. It was written by Peter Richardson, Pete Richens and Rik Mayall; one of its points of interest is the re-emergence of Nigel Planer's character, Paul, from Planer and Richardson's play, *Rank* – the 'pioneer of drug abuse'. Here he has thumbed a lift with two Australian girls, Jackie (Dawn French) and Shona (Jennifer Saunders):

> **Paul** (*getting into the van*): I dunno where it is you're going, but I'm coming with you. And staying with you. Have you got any mandys?
> (*The van drives off and he falls over.*)
> **Jackie:** I'm Jackie and this is Shona. What's your name?
> **Paul:** What's this? ... Sorry, man, I just put cigarette and ash and that all over your duvet. Shall I clean it up with this? (*Using the nearest piece of cloth.*)
> **Jackie:** No!

> **Paul:** I know, I'll turn it over so you won't see it ... Well then, I'm Paul – what's your name?
> **Jackie:** I'm Jackie and this is Shona.
> **Shona** (*unenthusiastically*): Hi.
> **Paul:** Hello, Shona ... what, you speak English, do you?
> **Shona:** Oh, yeah, we're Aussies.
> **Paul:** Oh, well hard ... look, can you cash a giro? ... I got this giro, see, and it's valid and everything, but, like, I couldn't cash it before the ferry went, all right, because Julie, that's my daughter, Julie, right, set fire to my bag, bag. Ha-ha-ha! Have you got any cash, have you?

The two main characters are Carlos (Rik Mayall) and Miguel (Peter Richardson); dressed in Mexican gunfighters' clothes, they stalk around menacingly with their guns, insisting on what bastards they are. However, we have already met them in the first series, in *War*, where it is established that they are simply local West Country boys who fancy themselves at the Clint Eastwood bit; they set up gunfights between themselves, but they are essentially harmless and the guns are loaded with blanks.

> **Carlos:** You start the row.
> **Miguel** (*threateningly*): I went first last time.
> **Carlos:** No you didn't.
> **Miguel:** Did.
> **Carlos:** Didn't.
> **Miguel:** Did.
> **Carlos:** Didn't.
> **Miguel:** Did.
> **Carlos:** Did ... not ...
> **Miguel** (*advancing, hand on gun*): Are you calling me a liar?
> **Carlos:** Er ... have we started yet?
> **Miguel** (*Lapsing into West Country accent*): Of course I have, you great tosser.
> **Carlos:** All right ... start again ...*

Ironically, at the end of the film they find themselves surrounded by armed police, called to a brawl they had no part in; as they go for their guns, the picture freezes to the sound of gunfire.

With their first two series, the Comic Strip had established their ability to make use of film to produce atmospheric comedy. They would continue to make television films, but the next step would be a move into feature films for the cinema; the next group of TV films and their first feature will be covered in Chapter 13.

* *A Fistful of Travellers' Cheques*, Comic Strip, Channel Four.

As time went on more people in the cabaret circuit were working towards their own stage shows, or shows put together with several others, such as *Three Of A Different Kind*. One such was *Brave New Comedy*, which toured for most of 1984; it comprised Arnold Brown, Paul Martin (who had been in *Stomping On The Cat*) and two performers not yet mentioned in this book – Nick Revell and Norman Lovett. Both had been around since the early days of the Comedy Store, and were gradually establishing themselves as respected stand-up performers with their own individual styles.

Nick Revell was born in Enfield on 26 December 1957; his family moved to Yorkshire when he was about seven. He went to a local grammar school, and then read English, changing to French and German, at Oxford; his interest in comedy had already emerged by this time and even before he left Oxford in June 1980 he was writing odd one-liners and sketches for Radio 4's topical comedy show *Week Ending*.

He had been in the Oxford Revue at the Edinburgh Festival in 1980, and had also formed a fringe theatre company while at Oxford – which never really came to anything – but as with so many people, it was a visit to the Comedy Store that pushed him in the direction of stand-up comedy.

He remembers: 'I was awful at first, but it was exciting to see people like Tony Allen and Rik Mayall, and see just what could be done. I didn't get gonged off the first time I went down there because I cut my losses very quickly; after that I did quite black material – my main motivation was survival rather than getting the laughs.'

In these early days he did what so many performers did – hid behind a created character, in this case a neurotic northerner – but as he gained confidence he made the step into appearing as himself: 'It took me a long time to shake the style down properly; I used to do a combination of chat as myself, and characters – and there was no integration, it was very stop-start. In about 1984 I took out all the character stuff, even though some of it was very strong – structurally it made sense to be myself, and sliding into little bits of character monologue.'

Over the following years he developed his style, still doing script-writing to bolster his income – and also writing and performing in *The Million Pound Radio Show* with Andy Hamilton on Radio 4 (he did a pilot in 1984 and the first series in 1985, with subsequent series in the following years). He also compèred the Comedy Store fairly regularly from 1985.

Nick Revell

His stand-up material is based on observation of the real world around him, including memories of his teenage years in Yorkshire (when the main entertainment was 'fighting anyone who lived further away from town than you did') and the following familiar experience on the London Underground:

> You can try and spot the miracle on the tube platform – I actually saw this once – saw somebody put thirty pence into one of those chocolate machines, and actually get a bar out. People were taking photos, you know, 'Don't move . . .' . . . It's wonderful, they never work, and it's wonderful watching different people's reactions. Every tube platform on the network, there is always, any time of the day or night, two seventeen-year-old kids . . . (*mimes thumping the machine*) 'Fucking thing!' (*thump, thump*) . . . I thought they were practice pads for Kung Fu artists, my first two years . . . 'Gary, the fucking thing ate me money' (*thump, thump*) . . . It's wonderful, you see different people reacting in different ways, you get some demure middle-aged lady who takes the thirty pence out of her handbag

very neatly ... 'Oh dear' (*rattles the machine politely*) ... 'Oh dear, oh dear' (*rattle, rattle*) ... 'Fucking thing!!!' (*thump, thump*). Or you get the yuppie ... who while waiting for a train can only strike a pose that is in that month's Jaeger catalogue ... and he gets the thirty pence out of the thirty pence page in his Filofax ... which of course is the page next to the one with the designer condoms ... where you buy them with one punched out so it looks like you've had a shag recently ... and he puts the thirty pence into the chocolate machine ... (*rattle, rattle*) ... 'Hey, what are you staring at, man – I can afford to lose thirty pence. I normally travel by taxi, actually. Here, sixty pence, and I'm still ahead, I don't care. I'm only down here investigating the possibility of converting this chocolate machine into forty flats for first-time buyers. But it's too big ... Fucking thing!!!' (*thump, thump* ...)

The other member of the *Brave New Comedy* team, Norman Lovett, specializes in a very slow, dead-pan delivery of material which is often quite surreal. He was born on 31 October 1946, and was brought up in the bracing air of Clacton-on-Sea. He went through the familiar process of being funny at school to combat his shyness, but it was not until he was thirty-two that he started actually performing. He had been through a string of boring and unsatisfactory jobs, but the comedy had been struggling to get out. He remembers: 'I started writing comedy sketches when I was twenty-one, and got nowhere – they were crap. I just didn't have a clue ... for the first four years I was performing, I had a guitar – I wanted to be like John Cooper-Clarke and Ian Dury – funny songs and stuff ... I didn't realize that all I had to be was myself.'

His early appearances were as a fill-in for rock bands on tour; but, once again, the Comedy Store provided a better springboard. He did his songs: 'I used to get pissed before I went on because I was so terrified ... and one night I went on and did well, and I did some talking about maturity tests at school – which was the first time I ever did a spoken routine; and it went down so well that Tony Allen and Andy de la Tour were saying, "You should just go out and talk." But it took me a long time to get rid of that guitar, because I had some stuff that did work.'

The piece he did first was based on a real incident when he was at school, when the boys were examined for pubertal development: 'This other boy got ten out of five ... and I got a half ... which is true ... and I say, "That's as rude as I get in my act."'

Lovett's style developed into a very distinctive technique – and one requiring a good deal of nerve, since it involves a very slow delivery and long pauses. At the beginning of his act he will some-times wait for an extraordinary length of time before starting – Paul

Jackson remembers seeing him stretch this to three or four minutes once – and even in an appearance on TV in Jackson's series *Pyja-marama* (which gave performers half of a nominally half-hour show) Lovett kept the audience waiting for thirty-nine seconds – a very long time on television. As a series *Pyjamarama* was not altogether successful, but Lovett's performance stands up well.

He has made a good reputation for himself on the circuit, and can handle difficult venues like the Tunnel with ease; the dead-pan approach – voice almost a monotone, dull expression and the skilful use of pauses – enables him to put over some very off-beat material:

> My name's Norman Lovett. That's my real name. I'd like a pound for every time someone's said, 'Lovett, I bet you do.' I'd have about six or seven pounds by now ... I was eating a hamburger. I ate it ... just finishing off this last bit ... and the hook struck. I didn't know it was bait. I went through the ceiling, through the roof, up to the clouds – where God reeled me in. He had a keep-net there with Agatha Christie in one of them ... George Orwell was in another one ... George said, 'Hello, Norman.' I just nodded, because I was coming in pretty quick. God brought me in, he took me off the hook, and threw me back. And that's why I'm here now. I landed here.... It's a good job this microphone isn't a snake, isn't it? Ssss. Ssss. It really is a good job.
>
> Cor, I'm bored now. When you do gigs – this is called a gig, and I do lots of gigs in London –I looked up gig in the dictionary, and it said 'light rowing boat' ... so I do lots of light rowing boats. Sometimes you stay at people's houses or flats, you have a drink with them afterwards. This happened with a young couple of art students who put me up. I slept on the couch. She woke me up in the morning with a cup of coffee. And proceeded to show me round the flat at eight o'clock in the morning. You just don't appreciate things like that at that time, do you, really? No, you don't. No. Then she said, let's go into the bedroom and wake him up. So we went into the bedroom, and the whole room is red, they've got these red curtains and the sun is streaming in, and the whole room is red. So I went, 'Goodness me, this is a bit much.' It hit me. So she said, 'When you wake up in the morning, and you part the curtains, it's like coming out of the womb like a freshly born baby each day.' I thought, it's a good job she only gave me coffee, and not eggs and bacon or something. Then I thought to myself, I've got brown curtains in my bedroom.

Tours such as *Brave New Comedy* mostly played in fringe theatres and other small venues in 1984; but when in the previous year *The Young Ones* toured, their exposure on television meant that they could play much larger theatres. They took with them the band from the Comic Strip stage show, Ken Bishop's Nice Twelve – there were

Norman Lovett

actually three of them; two of them, Roland Rivron and Simon Brint, went on later to become the two-piece combo, Raw Sex, appearing in a number of shows including with French and Saunders. *The Young Ones* show was compèred by Mayall as Kevin Turvey, and each of them had their own spots as well as appearing as *The Young Ones*.

The tour took in twenty-three venues, and ran from 22 February to 8 May 1983. It was organized by rock promoter Phil McIntyre, who booked them into large university and rock venues, holding one and a half to two thousand people. Rik Mayall remembers: 'The very first night we went to Sheffield University, and we went in two hours before the show went on – they said, "You're a bit early, aren't you? –the show's not until next month." Phil went on the radio, leafletted the town, and we sold it out in two hours – fifteen hundred people.'

Nigel Planer: 'That tour was when we first realized the power of television – before that we'd just been doing clubs, and here we were playing two-thousand seaters, and there were people asking for our autographs.' As well as working with the others he did a twenty-minute solo spot as Neil, which he later built up to an hour and toured by himself. (He also exploited the character in a book, *Neil's Book of the Dead*, a detailed spoof of hippydom.)

It was the last time that Adrian Edmondson did a live tour (until his 1987 tour as 'Bad News', based on the Comic Strip film). He and Mayall had already finished with 20th-Century Coyote; Adrian Edmondson: 'The last gig was in Brighton, which was dreadful – we hadn't rehearsed anything and we decided to experiment – the last thing we ever said together on stage as 20th-Century Coyote was, "Thank you for the money and good night." I used to love doing the Comedy Store, but I think the excitement just wore off – it did renew itself on *The Young Ones* tour, basically because I came on with a guitar at one point, and I'd always wanted to be a rock star – and to come on playing a guitar very loudly, and being cheered, because it was Vivian's first entrance, was a buzz. The first show lasted about four and a half hours because we'd written so much stuff – it just went on and on, interminably – but by the end of the tour it was a really tight show, we'd honed it all down. Because those characters had never been out on stage they hadn't been honed down – and a tour isn't long enough! We were just about ready by the end!'

The second series of *The Young Ones* was transmitted on BBC2 from 8 May 1984; it was again produced by Paul Jackson, working this time as a freelance. Inevitably the shock value of the first series could not be repeated, and there is a slightly different feel to the shows. Paul Jackson: 'The first series was written with a total naïvety about what television was about, which I think gave that first series a lot of its impact – they didn't know the rules, they certainly didn't know what's easy and what's difficult ... interestingly enough, nothing was rejected because the visual effects department couldn't do it ... but the writers themselves observed how long certain things took for so little reward. When the second series of scripts came in there was a marked absence of those very complicated conceits – they'd learned very quickly what takes time, and were making their own editorial decisions about where they wanted the time used.'

The programmes look a trifle more polished, although the basic style is the same; inevitably this led the fashionable critics to complain that the rawness had gone and to accuse the programme of having gone mainstream. Paul Jackson: 'I think that's stupid; certainly there is less experimentation in a way, and that seems to me to be only sensible – you try things out, and if some of them don't work it seems strange to me to stick to the things that don't.'

The general style of anarchy, with cutaway sequences and a good deal of stunt work, was maintained: one new running joke was presumably for the benefit of the owners of expensive video recorders, since it consisted of cutting in four-frame flashes which cannot possibly be grasped in real time – they include a leaping frog, a dripping tap, a skier, a potter's wheel and, finally, a notice signed by the video tape editor saying, 'I never wanted to put all these flash frames in in the first place.'

Once again the guest appearances were largely drawn from the cabaret circuit. They include Andy de la Tour, Hale and Pace, Helen Lederer, Lee Cornes, Norman Lovett and Pauline Melville (as Vivian's aggressive mum); The Oblivion Boys make several appearances, including one as ghosts with their 'eads tucked underneath their arms. Alexei Sayle makes slightly more extended appearances than before – this time not always as members of the Balowski family; in one show he is a video dealer with a Dracula fixation and in another a police officer who is a Mussolini look-alike.

The groups include Amazulu, Motorhead, and Madness – who play in the street outside in the first show, a performance which leads to an alarmingly realistically staged street riot. The plots are fairly complex, and include an appearance on *University Challenge*, Neil joining the police force in order to earn some cash, and the sudden arrival of Neil's posh parents (the lads suddenly lose their student defiance and start tidying the house up – even Sayle, who is holding them at gunpoint at the time, starts polishing his shotgun).

In the fifth programme, subtitled 'Time', Rik wakes up the morning after a party to find a girl (Jennifer Saunders) asleep in his bed. He jumps to the obvious (but incorrect) conclusion about his own part in her presence there and goes down to breakfast very full of himself. Meanwhile Vivian has his own problems:

> **Vivian** (*entering with a stick of dynamite strapped to his head*): Good morning everybody. (*He detonates it.*) I just don't seem to be able to get rid of this hangover.
> **Rik:** Well that'll teach you to mix your drinks.
> (*Cut to a cake shop; the bell rings and Alexei Sayle walks in in an eccentric manner.*)
> **Sayle:** Excuse me, is this a cheese shop?
> **Assistant:** No, sir.
> **Sayle:** That's that sketch knackered then, isn't it?
> (*Cut back to the house.*)
> **Rik:** That'll teach you to mix your drinks.
> **Vivian:** I already know how to mix my drinks, Rik.
> **Mike:** Yes, paint-stripper and bleach. Lethal.
> **Vivian:** Oh, by the way, there's a couple of strange girls in the bathroom. (*Sits down but misses the chair.*)
> **Neil:** Yeah, I saw one of them, that's what I was going to tell you

The Young Ones – Nigel Planer (in bag), Adrian Edmonson, Chris Ryan, Rik Mayall; Alexei Sayle

about earlier, that was the really freaky thing.

Mike: Don't worry about it, Neil, she probably got lost on the way to my room.

Rik: I very much doubt it, actually, Mike – because, as a matter of interest everybody, the girl in question is with me!
(*Dawn French, dressed as an oversized bunny-rabbit, enters through kitchen door.*)

Dawn (*brightly*): Hello! Hello! Easter eggs all round! (*Starts handing them out.*) Hello everybody – I'm the Easter bunny!

Rik: But it's June the twelfth.

Dawn: What?

Vivian: It's the middle of summer, big-ears.

Dawn: Oh, God. Sorry. (*She takes the eggs back, really upset.*) I'm really sorry. (*Exits.*)
(*There is a flash of a man blowing a raspberry, the lads resume their discussion where they left off.*)

Mike, Vivian & Neil: Eh!??!

Neil: What, you mean, you like, like – scored – with a chick?

Rik: Well of course I wouldn't put it in such sexist terms, Neil – but, er, (*Modestly.*) yes.

Mike: Now wait a minute, Rik, I'm the one who gets the girls round here, there could be a copyright problem.

Vivian: But I don't understand. *How?* Was she unconscious?

Rik: What, Vivian – do I detect a little spark of jealousy?

Vivian: I'm not jealous. I find the idea of spending the night with you completely revolting.

Rik: You know perfectly well what I mean. Just because I was the most raunchy and attractive guy at the party last night.

Neil: What do you mean, Rik – you passed out after half a glass of cider.

162

Rik: Did I? Blimey, that was a bit anarchic! Well, it just goes to show you, Neil – even when I'm unconscious I can pick up the birds . . . I mean, forge meaningful relationships with birds . . . er, chicks . . . tarts . . . *women*, women.

The girl turns out to be a dangerous murderess, Rik and Vivian get into a very spectacular fight over whether Rik is a virgin, the house jumps back into the middle ages, the TV shows 'Medieval Torture Hour' with Sayle as the host, and finally the house is attacked by a mob of peasants.

In the final episode, 'Summer Holiday', they get thrown out of the house, receive their examination results (Rik comes bottom in the whole world), try to rob a bank, and finally set off on holiday in a stolen London Transport bus. As they drive away, the bus crashes over a cliff; they are just congratulating themselves on a close escape when it explodes – a reflection of the team's feeling that they were satisfied with the series, and thus wanted to go on to something else. The characters re-emerged a couple of times in later years in charity appearances, but – as so often with this generation of comedians – the team had no interest in getting trapped into a long run.

The impact of *The Young Ones* was considerable. It rather surprised everyone by becoming a cult with younger schoolchildren (not really so surprising in view of the childish level of some of the jokes), and established the team firmly in the field of TV comedy. Though lacking the Pythons' patina of apparent erudition, it took the medium-bending anarchy of the Python sketches and expanded it into longer stories with characterizations that could survive two complete series; its command of television and raucous humour looks better (so far) with the passage of time. It was to prove a hard act to follow.

The Young Ones' – Planer, Mayall, 'Bamber Gascoigne' (Gryff Rhys Jones) and Ryan

The Young Ones had been Ben Elton's breakthrough as a script-writer – and he also made a few cameo appearances – but he had continued playing the cabaret circuit and trying to establish himself as a stand-up comic. His breakthrough into television came in 1982, a little before *The Young Ones* was transmitted, in youth programmes such as *White Light* and *The Oxford Road Show* – the sort of thing that was parodied in the very first *Young Ones* episode.

Though it was television, it was hardly of any importance, as he remembers: 'They were real minority kids viewing – I think the kids were watching *Starsky and Hutch*. It's always the same – middle-class producers trying to work out what people want. . . . Why should liberal and left-wing television look tatty just to prove it's got heart? There were good things about them, but they'd do things like put you in the middle of the audience, in a bunch of skinheads – what are they going to do but make V-signs at the camera and muck up your set? *I* would, if I was them. But I was inexperienced – they tried hard to make it work, but I wasn't very good at it.'

Then Rik Mayall was approached by Granada Television for a project called *Al Fresco*; he agreed tentatively but insisted that Elton should write for it. When Mayall dropped out, Elton was retained in the team, which gave him a major opportunity to try writing TV sketches.

Al Fresco was supposed to be an answer to *Not The Nine O'Clock News*; the team consisted of Elton, Robbie Coltrane, Emma Thompson, Siobhan Redmond and the urbane ex-university double-act Stephen Fry and Hugh Laurie, whose connection with the alternative comedy scene was to continue in later TV series. In the end lack of proper script editing led to Elton writing most of the series, which passed without much notice being taken of it. Elton: 'I learned an enormous amount – I was paid very well by Granada to learn not to be cocksure and young and think I was always right – and how much I needed help and criticism and guidance, which wasn't available at Granada.'

In the summer of 1983 Elton decided to get back into live comedy, and teamed up with Andy de la Tour to perform at Edinburgh that

August. They were trying to decide who to take as a third performer when they happened to meet Rik Mayall for lunch. Mayall remembers: 'I hadn't been on stage for a long time, and I'd said to Adrian Edmondson, "Let's go", and he said, "No, I don't want to work live any more, I hate it." So when Ben and Andy said they couldn't make up their minds who to take to Edinburgh, I said, "Take me." I did about forty minutes in that show – the first time I'd ever done longer than half an hour. That's when I tried to do stand-up emoting – being funny and frightening and sad and everything all at the same time. It worked really well – because it was in front of an Edinburgh-type interested arty audience. When we went on tour to civic venues with proper people who had saved up their money to come along, and who didn't want to be abused, they just wanted a good time, I had to rapidly adjust my act.'

The three of them did a couple of short tours under the name *Stand-Up*. Andy de la Tour: 'We started to get a good proportion of the audience that was very young – thirteen or fourteen – and had come to see Rik – and I was a bit worried about how I'd go down: suddenly there's this thirty-five-year-old bald comic on stage. Luckily they loved it. For example, I did a bit about anxieties about oral sex – there would be kind of shrieks from the audience, "My God, he's talking about oral sex on stage!" – a lot of youngsters were quite shocked.'

In late 1984 Phil McIntyre booked a tour for Elton and Mayall, running from 23 November to 8 December. Ben Elton: 'Rik and I both wanted to tour, and Rik was a big star so we were able to play two-thousand-seaters; he wanted me to go because we wrote together, and because I was a good support act – and because we were mates. Rik said we must have equal billing and equal money – which is probably the only time a star has ever done that! We had great times; I worked very hard on my set – I worked hard on his set as well – it's very difficult to write for Rik's live act because it's really an excuse for him to be brilliant, to be a hilarious person. It was astonishing to watch him do so much with so little. He's one of the most amazing theoreticians I've ever met – I would trust his instincts ... he *knows* how the material will go. It's difficult to put your finger on why he's funny – he's just a genius.'

In January 1985 Rik Mayall appeared with the National Theatre Company in *The Government Inspector* at the Olivier Theatre; then he and Elton toured again between 21 April and 8 May 1985, taking in fifteen venues – again, large rock gigs such as the Sunderland Empire, the Glasgow Pavilion and the Birmingham Odeon; and in August they did four days in Ibiza. Ben Elton: 'Bloody tough gig –

on at two in the morning to Club 18–30 – Rik was doing Kevin Turvey in a rabbit costume; it was 100 degrees in that club, and he had his Rik suit, the Kevin Turvey suit on top – which was a furry bomber jacket – and on top of that his rabbit suit for the first half of the set. The man was mad.'

That November they did another tour, finishing with a sell-out at the London Dominion, and in 1985 their final tour together was of Australia – twenty-seven shows between 19 April and 17 May.

Going back a little, in between these exhausting tours Elton's writing had included his first TV solo writing credit – and also his favourite script – *Happy Families*. It is a complicated six-episode serial, involving the search for the four strayed girls of the Fuddle family – all played by Jennifer Saunders, as is their grandmother. Granny Fuddle hates her grandchildren – and most of all Guy (Adrian Edmondson) – but when she is told she is dying of a rare disease she sends Guy off with the impression she has relented and firm instructions to bring them back. Each of the next four episodes deals with one girl; Cassie is a Joan Collins-type TV superstar in Hollywood, Madeleine is living in an artistic community in France, Joyce is in a convent and Roxanne is in prison.

Happy Families –
Edmondson and Saunders

The five characters gave Jennifer Saunders a chance for a considerable *tour de force* in her performances. She remembers: 'The script was excellent – I think it suffered a bit in production, it didn't seem as funny when it came out as I remember the script being.' Dawn French adds: 'It was packed full of gags – Ben writes such dense comedy, and the scripts were a joy to read.'

The series was produced and directed by Paul Jackson for BBC Manchester: 'Each of the four middle episodes was shot in a recognizable style, so the Hollywood one is shot to look like a soap opera, the second one in France is shot through gauze and in soft-focus; the convent one is shot like an Ealing comedy and the last one in prison is shot like a documentary. In the last episode they all meet up and there was a lot of technical trickery to get them all on the screen at once. It was all shot on film – a very substantial budget for a comedy, and a thirty-five-minute slot; we had a lot of support from the BBC. It remains the piece of work of which I'm proudest.'

The series was transmitted starting on 17 October 1985, on BBC1. A good deal of care has been taken with the look of each episode, but none of the participants is entirely happy with it, feeling that it has somehow misfired. Adrian Edmondson, who has the longest rôle as Guy, comments: 'Something went dreadfully wrong. I think I was appalling – I think Jennifer was great, and the scripts were great. ... Paul Jackson may be the Godfather of comedy at the BBC, but he's not a film director.'

The principal problem is the inconsistency in the pitch of the acting. Jennifer Saunders acts fairly realistically throughout, with just enough comic exaggeration. Edmondson is well over the top, and some of the supporting players – in particular Rik Mayall and Nigel Planer in the French episode – are allowed to indulge in wild over-acting. This would not matter so much if the whole series was played at that sort of pitch; but the impression left is that the performers are not all living in the same world. (This consistency of pitch is very important in comedy; for example the sort of performance which is highly suitable in, to take an extreme case, a Morecambe and Wise sketch, would stick out like a sore thumb in *Yes, Minister*.)

Many of the supporting players manage to fit in very well; Dawn French is convincing as Granny Fuddle's cook and Helen Lederer manages to be quite eccentric as the maid without seeming out of place. Stephen Fry's urbane but incompetent doctor – who has to break the bad news to Granny – is a good performance but, again, seems to belong in some other show. However, the strength of the basic idea and of the writing, and Jackson's skill in creating the

different looks of the various episodes, produce a series which is
enjoyable and effective.

In the fourth episode Guy has to get himself into Joyce's convent;
Joyce herself seems to think she is the heroine of a girls' school novel
and has been driving the other inmates out of their cowls for years.
Una Stubbs is the Mother Superior, who finds herself confronted
with Guy – dressed as a bishop:

> **Guy:** All right – nobody move, because I'm ... (*Strikes pose.*) a
> bloody bishop! And I insist ... (*Gets tangled in his sleeves.*) ... I
> insist that you return Joyce to the bosoms of her family
> immediately.
>
> **Mother Superior:** Won't you sit down, um ... Bishop? Now, do
> tell me – what is it you want with Joyce?
>
> **Guy:** Well, um, she's my sister, you see, and I want to get her back,
> so that I can be loved and wanted and be part of a family and
> discover the secret of Granny hating me ... (*Remembers he is
> supposed to be a bishop.*) ... Because the bloody Pope says so – and
> you'd better do it, missus, or else you'll be walking barefoot to
> Canterbury to say you're sorry.
>
> **Mother Superior** (*gently*): Young man – the robes you wear are
> Church of England – they command nothing but our respect
> here, I'm afraid. Look, why don't I send for novice Joyce and we
> can discuss the matter of your family. Sister Ophelia, would you
> be so kind as to fetch novice Joyce, please?
>
> **Ophelia:** I'll fetch her, but don't expect me to talk to her. (*Exits.*)
>
> **Guy:** Oh, all right, I admit it – I'm not really a bishop.
>
> **Mother Superior:** Really?
>
> (*There is a knock on the door and Joyce bounces in.*)
>
> **Joyce:** You wanted to see me, Mother Superior?
>
> **Mother Superior:** Yes, my dear.
>
> (*Guy goes into reverie, seeing himself as a child imagining he is playing
> with Joyce – who is nowhere in sight. He comes out of it.*)
>
> **Guy:** Hello, Joyce.
>
> **Joyce:** Hello, Bishop.
>
> **Mother Superior:** Joyce, dear, this is not a bishop – this is your
> brother, and he's come to take you back to live with your family –
> and with enormous reluctance I've decided to let you go, there's
> a bus that leaves the gate in about ten minutes, if you hurry you'll
> catch it, goodbye.
>
> **Joyce:** But I'm not going anywhere, Mother Superior – I'm
> deliriously happy here – I've given my life to Jesus.
>
> **Mother Superior:** But are you absolutely sure he *wants* it, dear?

In the final episode the girls arrive home to discover that Granny
wants an organ transplant from each of them to save her life; they
agree, but only if she signs her entire estate over to them. Then it is
discovered that the doctor has muddled the urine samples – Granny
is in fact merely pregnant. At the end she is left with a baby and

no money – a dramatically satisfying if physiologically unlikely conclusion.

The series got a moderately good audience. Paul Jackson: 'We made it quite intentionally for peak time on BBC1, and I think possibly that was wrong and we should have stuck with nine o'clock on BBC2 – it got six and a half to seven million, which would have put it at the top of the BBC2 chart but was nowhere on BBC1. Inevitably it was trailed as the successor to *The Young Ones*, which it clearly wasn't, but you can't stop the press quoting it as that. The major criticism seemed to be that it didn't have enough jokes – in fact it was packed with jokes but there was no laughter track to signal them in.'

The press response to the series was less than enthusiastic; for Jennifer Saunders it was the first experience of the odd behaviour of TV critics. Dawn French remembers the press-showing: 'They were provided with drinks and little interesting things on the ends of sticks – and they all came along, and ninety-nine per cent of them were plastered . . . and they were all round Jennifer like flies, saying "When's your baby due?" and "How's your marriage?" [She is married to Adrian Edmondson]. . . . They'd just watched her playing five different characters, and this was what they were interested in.'

Jennifer Saunders adds: 'They all love you to death and then go away and write shit about you. I suppose in the better papers you do get an actual criticism, but otherwise it's just opinion and gossip.'

At about the same time that *Happy Families* was showing, Dawn French and Jennifer Saunders were in their own series on ITV, together with Ruby Wax and Tracey Ullman – *Girls On Top*. It had started from the germ of an idea, simply because there were no major parts for girls in *The Young Ones*. Jennifer Saunders comments, 'Boys can't write for girls and girls can't write for boys' – Dawn French qualifies this: 'Not in our group, anyway.'

They met the boisterous American actress Ruby Wax at a party, and the idea arose from discussions with her; Tracey Ullman, an excellent comedy-character actress, was suggested by Dawn French's husband Lenny Henry, who had worked with Ullman in the TV series *Three Of A Kind*.

The idea they started from was to have the four girls in a flat – a female *Young Ones* in the basic concept, but not in the way it was presented. There were no complicated televisual tricks; instead they concentrated on characters who, though somewhat exaggerated, were recognizably real and existed in the real world. Paul Jackson produced for Central Television; the original shooting dates for the first series had to be abandoned because of an electricians' strike, and there was about a two-year delay before it finally went out, starting in October 1985.

Ruby Wax plays Shelley Dupont, a loud and rich American who wants to be an actress but has no talent; Tracey Ullman plays Candice, a common little hussy, thief, liar and calculating hypochondriac; Dawn French plays Amanda Ripley, a left-wing feminist and bossy-boots; Jennifer Saunders plays Jennifer Marsh, an old schoolfriend of Amanda's and a complete dimwit; and veteran actress Joan Greenwood plays Lady Carlton, their loopy landlady.

The scripts were written by French and Saunders with Ruby Wax, with contributions from Tracey Ullman; Ben Elton acted as script editor. The sharp distinction between the characters allowed for some good interplay within the often silly plots. Jennifer Saunders has less lines than the others, but creates a wonderfully dull-eyed and thick-witted character. Dawn French: 'The reason it was so minimalist was that Jennifer fell asleep during most of the writing ... "We've got to scene three and you haven't said anything yet!" – then she'd say "I'll say this here" and go back to sleep for another two hours.'

Jennifer Saunders adds: 'It was very difficult because you've got four prima donnas working; each of us wanted lines in a scene, so it just complicated things. Ruby is the queen of one-liners – whereas Dawn and I can let a scene go with us not doing any jokes.'

By the time the second series was made in 1986, Tracey Ullman had gone to America to star in her own show; although her character had fitted in very well, four strong characters plus Joan Greenwood's hilarious cameos had been a bit much to cram into twenty-five-minute shows; the inter-relation of Amanda and Jennifer, with Shelley siding with one or the other, worked better. The plots were becoming more unlikely; Jennifer Saunders: 'We became a lot madder in the second series, it got a lot weirder – it became more like the relationship in the room while we were writing; in the first series we were quite professional, in the second we'd just gone mad with being locked in a room with Ruby for three months.'

Dawn French: 'Ruby has extraordinary stamina, and will write for as many hours as you like – and then change it twenty times. She cannot believe that what she's written is funny so she has to re-write it a lot of times ... to us, re-write is a swear-word, because it means you haven't got time to watch *Neighbours*.'

Shelley is even louder in the second series, and Amanda just as bossy; Jennifer has become slightly more aggressive, but is no less stupid. Here she is having to sleep in Amanda's room because the lounge – where she normally sleeps – is being outlandishly redecorated by Shelley:

Jennifer: It's quite nice, this room, isn't it? – it's quite comfy, I was thinking – it's a bit like the Tardis, actually, because it's sort of bigger than you think from the outside.

Amanda: Oh, shut up, will you, Jennifer – and don't get used to this – this is just a treat while Shelley's on safari in the living-room.

Jennifer: Are you getting ready for bed now, is it time to go to sleep now?

Amanda: I haven't got a rigid schedule, actually.

Jennifer: Oh, I'm tired.

Amanda: Yes, well I'm not.

Jennifer: No, I'm not either, I just made that one up.

Amanda: Yes, well I'm tired *now*. (*Puts light out and settles down to reading* 'Playgirl' *with a pen-torch. Jennifer puts her light on.*) What's the matter, what?

Jennifer: Sorry, I just didn't know what some of the shapes were in the dark because I hadn't memorized the room properly. . . . It's all right now, I've got it. (*Puts her light out. Pause. She screams suddenly*).

Amanda: (*Putting her light on*) What? What?

Jennifer (*pointing to two socks on the floor*): Oh, it's just your socks, I didn't know what they were, I thought they were horrible black snakes crawling towards me then.

Amanda: Look, they are just my socks, all right?

Jennifer: Yes, just horrible smelly Amanda's socks – what have you got to leave them in the middle of the floor for where they can crawl into my hair in the middle of the night and make a nest and lay their eggs in it?

Amanda: Eggs? In your hair? You mean like the nits you had at school, Jennifer? Yes, only Matron and me knew about them, didn't we? But if you don't shut your gob and go to sleep I'm going to tell everybody. All right?

Jennifer: Right, I'm off to sleep now, Amanda.

Amanda: Yes. (*Switches her light off and goes back to* 'Playgirl'. *Pause.*)

Jennifer: Amanda . . . do you think you could get me a glass of water?

The second series went out starting on 30 October 1986. Strangely, *Girls On Top* was the only time French and Saunders ever had any real problems over censorship, although they did not have to deal with it themselves. Dawn French: 'The great thing about Paul Jackson is he will put his neck on the line to fight for you to keep things in you think are funny. He did for that for us at Central – we didn't have to deal with any of that – he did a lot of shouting and screaming and throwing wobblies.' Central had even got to the stage where they were nervous of fictitious characters. Jennifer Saunders:

'The lawyers were very picky because they actually thought Irma La Douce might sue us for calling her a prostitute.'

At the end of the series the entire house and all the characters are destroyed by an explosion, caused by Lady Carlton igniting a large hoard of petrol she had accumulated for no very intelligent reason. Like *The Young Ones*, the writers were evidently determined not to get sucked into a long-running series. Paul Jackson: 'All the TV companies found this very difficult to cope with – the days when you walked in with a contract for three years with six a year, and people were falling at your feet ... they suddenly found the complete opposite – people didn't want to know how much and how long, they wanted to know who was writing, how it was going to be done. People have consistently wanted to do something different ... the BBC were desperate for a third series of *The Young Ones*; no way; and we could have done a second series of *Happy Families*.'

It is a characteristic of the people covered in this book that no TV show has run to more than two series, with the exception of *The Comic Strip Presents* ... and that only because every film is different. French and Saunders would move on from *Girls On Top* to a different approach to TV; and indeed the Comic Strip provided them with further opportunities to experiment and expand their style.

After the second Comic Strip series in 1984 there was a long hiatus before the next proper series – which did not go out until 1988 (and will be covered in Chapter 18) – partly because that series was shot over a much longer period. In the intervening time there were three TV specials (in the sense of being isolated from a main series) and a couple of feature films (the second of which, *Eat The Rich*, will also be covered in Chapter 18).

The first special, *The Bullshitters* (transmitted on Channel Four on 3 November 1984) is not strictly speaking a Comic Strip film; written by Keith Allen and Peter Richardson, it was made under a different production name, largely because Keith Allen did not want to be associated with the Comic Strip. Directed by Stephen Frears, it is a parody of *The Professionals*, the British TV series glorifying a group of Secret Service men dealing with spies. Keith Allen plays Bonehead and Peter Richardson Foyle, two one-time members of 'D15' who are called back into service by Commander Jackson (Robbie Coltrane) when his daughter is kidnapped. Foyle is acting in a left-wing play; Bonehead is running a school for TV toughguys. Here he lectures them on the proper way to get into a car:

> **Bonehead:** The camera's running – the sound's rolling – I've got to get inside that car. What's the first thing I do – Troy?
> **Troy:** Start the engine, sir?
> **Bonehead:** No! Anybody – Quickly, come along.
> **Chuck:** Door acting, sir?
> **Bonehead:** Very good, well done Chuck – all right, what's the first thing I do with this door handle, Stig?
> **Stig:** Press it down, sir?
> **Bonehead:** No! I do not press it down. The first thing you do with a door handle is you do not look at it. Now this is a good opportunity for a nice profile shot. Use it – you might not get another opportunity. Plenty of looking up and down that street – international terrorists in town – the TV tough guy never does what – Wayne?
> **Wayne:** Locks his car, sir.
> **Bonehead:** And why?
> **Chuck:** Wasting film, sir.

The Bullshitters – Peter Richardson and Keith Allen

Bonehead: Well done – very good indeed, Chuck, very good. OK, we're getting inside this car – come along, gather round. (*Gets in.*) Right then, I'm in the car – what's the first thing I do, Dean?
Dean: Seat belt, sir.
Bonehead: Dean . . . I've got thirty seconds of film time to get across London, where fourteen armed terrorists are waiting to pump me full of lead. Now, I'm going to take this and push it in there? . . . perhaps I ought to get out and check the tread on the tyres? . . . All right, gentlemen, joke over . . . remember, there's no clunk click on these trips.*

Bonehead and Foyle are used to fast cars and walkie-talkies – but this is an undercover operation and they are issued with bus passes and coins for phone-boxes; they launch into action with a good deal of shouting 'Let's go!' and running around clad only in leather jackets and briefs. The film ends with them shooting everyone in sight and leaving in a helicopter.

The two specials under the Comic Strip umbrella proper went out on Channel Four on 1 and 2 January 1986. The first, *Consuela*,

* *The Bullshitters*, Channel Four.

was written by French and Saunders and directed by Stephen Frears; it is a sustained parody of the Hitchcock film *Rebecca*, with references to *The Birds*, *Georgy Girl*, *Suspicion* and *Don't Look Now* thrown in for good measure. Jennifer Saunders is Jessica, the new wife of John (Adrian Edmondson) who is hated from the first by the housekeeper, Consuela (Dawn French). Consuela's unfailing but menacing politeness stifles Jessica:

> **Jessica:** I don't want to keep you from your duties, Consuela – I shall just pop into the village and pick up John's shoes from the cobblers.
> **Consuela:** I've taken care of that, madam. They're in his wardrobe.
> **Jessica:** Oh good . . . well, I shall get some flowers to arrange, then – the house looks so drab.
> **Consuela:** I did that this morning, madam.
> **Jessica:** Thank you, Consuela. Then I shall be able to go out this afternoon and sketch some ducks.
> **Consuela:** Took the liberty, madam. (*Holds up a drawing of a duck.*)*

Peter Richardson appears as Consuela's son – a randy Spaniard whose attentions frighten Jessica – and Rik Mayall in the relatively straight part of the estate manager. In the end Jessica is driven sufficiently distraught to shoot nearly everyone with John's shotgun.

The other film, *Private Enterprise*, was written and directed by Adrian Edmondson. Neatly constructed, it tells the story of Keith (Richardson), a van driver on parole who is fiddling his company by selling some of their stock of toilet rolls on the cheap. Delivering to a recording studio, he hears a fairly awful band, fronted by Alistair (Mayall), steals a demo cassette and takes it to an A&R manager, Derek (Planer). At first uninterested, Derek subsequently asks Keith to produce the band – but the band has split up and gone abroad. Keith does manage to steal the unmixed master tape from the studio, and Derek issues it – intending to make a tax loss. The record's success embarrasses Keith, who can't produce the band. He and his friend Brian (Edmondson) – whom he is breaking his parole by seeing – get the band's tour cancelled by setting fire to several of the venues just before the concert; but in the end Derek's demands that the band gives a press conference means they have to dress up as two of the band members. The re-emergence of Alistair causes problems – as does the appearance of Keith's parole officer (Dawn French) with two policemen to arrest Keith for stealing the toilet rolls. Keith solves this by being 'shot' by Brian and, together with Keith's girlfriend (Jennifer Saunders), they drive off to look for a

* *Consuela*, Comic Strip, Channel Four.

new life – taking the profits of the record with them.

The plot is one of the most logical and tightly constructed of all the Comic Strip TV films, with the acting and the level of the humour well under control; a sardonic look at the pop world, always a fascination of Edmondson's.

Peter Richardson and Pete Richens, meanwhile, had been concentrating on writing the team's first foray into full-length cinema features – *The Supergrass*. Produced in association with Channel Four, and directed by Peter Richardson, it was released in November 1985; it is a well-crafted, coherently told story – although Richardson feels that it is perhaps a little too gentle for the Comic Strip. Certainly the anarchy is well under control – although according to Nigel Planer the actual filming was chaos; he was amazed by how well it turned out.

Dennis (Adrian Edmondson) is a nerd. Returning from a holiday with his mother in the West Country, he tries to impress his girlfriend Andrea (Dawn French) by inventing a story that he is involved in a drug-smuggling ring. Overheard by a policeman (Michael Elphick), he is arrested and interrogated by Commander Robertson (Ronald Allen) – who makes his first appearance in a Dracula outfit, having just come from a party. (Dennis shrinks back in his cell and makes a cross with his fingers.)

Determined to nail the smugglers, Robertson persuades Dennis to turn supergrass – which Dennis does because he fancies the idea of a holiday in the West Country paid for by the police. Robertson brings in a detective, Harvey Duncan (Peter Richardson), who doesn't believe a word of this nonsense but has to go along with it. A girlfriend has to be provided to maintain Dennis's cover – WPC Lesley Reynolds (Jennifer Saunders) – unfortunately for Harvey she is his ex-lover. Equipped with a Jaguar at Dennis's suggestion, they make for the West Country; but Dennis's exuberant driving lands them in trouble with a traffic cop, Perryman, played by Alexei Sayle.

Although it is only a small part, Richardson cast Sayle for a good reason. Peter Richardson: 'What people in the Comic Strip are good at doing is finding some sort of angle to the characters, to make them slightly unusual as opposed to like a straight comedy performance. I really like Michael Elphick – he was in *The Supergrass*, and he was originally going to play Perryman; then I started thinking it would be better to be more unpredictable – Alexei gave it a very quirky side. That's what I like about the people in the Comic Strip, they're able to do something which is quite strong and individual.'

Sayle plays Perryman with a combination of delicate sarcasm and frustration at being only a traffic cop. He overtakes the car on his

The Supergrass – Adrian
Edmondson

The Supergrass – Jennifer
Saunders and Peter
Richardson

179

motorcycle and halts it. As he strides over, Dennis admits to the others that he hasn't got a driving licence:

Harvey (*prompting from the back seat*): Tell him we're on holiday.
Dennis: We're going on holiday.
Perryman: Oh yeah – where's that, then – France?
Dennis: No, no, West Country – you know, cream teas, surf-boarding, all that.
Perryman: No, you see the reason I said France was, I thought you might be getting in some practice, you know, for driving on the wrong side of the road. (*Dennis laughs.*) Name?
Dennis: Dennis Carter.
Perryman: Dennis Carter. I'm going to show you something, Dennis. (*Halts the oncoming traffic and stands in the middle of the road.*) What's that, Dennis?
Harvey (*prompting quietly*): White line.
Dennis: White line.
Perryman: A white line. Yes. Now, in France, going *that* way, they would drive on *this* side of the road – the *right* side. But, in Angleterre, Monsieur Dennis, we still drive on the . . .?
Harvey: Left.
Dennis: Left.
Perryman: The *left!* (*Jumps balletically across the white line.*) Correct! But *you* were driving on *this* (*jumps across the white line*) side of the road when you should have been driving on (*jumps again*) *this* side of the road. Comprenez-vous, Monsieur Dennis?
Dennis: You must be the funniest copper in the world!
Perryman: What did you say?
Harvey (*to Perryman*): He says he's very sorry, officer, and he'll never do it again.
Perryman: Documents?
Harvey (*prompting*): In the post.
Dennis: In the post.
Perryman: Can't you speak for yourself?
Harvey: Yes.
Dennis: Yes.
Perryman: I don't like you. Now I could have been *difficult* with you, Dennis. But instead (*taking the car keys*) I'm going to be *unreasonably* difficult. Get out of the car.
Harvey (*showing his ID*): Hello.
Perryman: Er, could I have a look at that, please, sir?
Harvey: You're looking at it.
Perryman: Well, do you think I could have a quick word with you?

Harvey gets out of the car, but Perryman's attempts to find out what is going on come to nothing, as do his offers of help:

Perryman (*pathetically*): Oh, how do you get into plain clothes? You see, I'd love to work undercover – I've applied three times but they don't seem to want me, you know, but the thing is that

I feel somehow that I'd make a really good detective.

Harvey: I'm sorry, it's not my problem.

Perryman: Maybe I could just come with you, you know, sort of hang around, because then at least I'd be mixing with people who could really help me. . . .*

They have some trouble in shaking Perryman off . . . in fact a chase develops which ends in Harvey writing off the car.

Once at the resort, Dennis has to stall Harvey, getting deeper and deeper into ridiculous stories about submarine deliveries of the drugs. Harvey is still sceptical – but now events conspire to back up Dennis's fantasy as he loses control of the situation. Two real drug-runners (Keith Allen and Nigel Planer) are staking out the beach, disguised as a family (with children hired from a model agency); and the menacing Sergeant Troy (Robbie Coltrane) arrives. Then Dennis stumbles on a real subterranean cache, and – as the film takes a sudden twist into a darker tone – his local friend Jim is murdered. Dennis tries to confess his deception, but Troy is having none of that and beats him up until he is forced to make up yet more details. Meanwhile Lesley – who has been pretending at a developing

The Supergrass – Jennifer Saunders and Adrian Edmondson

* *The Supergrass*, Comic Strip, Channel Four, Michael White Ltd.

The Supergrass – Robbie Coltrane

relationship with Dennis in order to taunt Harvey – is reconciled with Harvey after the three get drunk and indulge in a 'truth' game. Dennis narrowly escapes being murdered by the real drug-runners; and then Troy takes a chain-saw to a perfectly innocent yacht that seems to fulfil Dennis's fantasy. As Harvey and Troy abandon the case, the real smugglers drive off with the heroin – but incautiously they leave a clue and drive into the distance with Perryman on their trail. . . .

The Supergrass is a remarkable first full-length film for Peter Richardson as co-writer and director; he also gives an excellent performance as Harvey, mixing quiet authority with the strain of the affair with Lesley. Adrian Edmondson's character has similarities with Guy in *Happy Families*, but this time the performance is tightly controlled and fits perfectly into the atmosphere of the film. All the characters blend together well, producing a film whose complicated plot is confidently handled and which balances the humour and the darker aspects of the story well. Its success enabled Richardson to make a further step into the medium of cinema; but the next film would be a much more anarchic affair.

The term 'alternative comedy' embraces a wide field, from the politically committed pioneers of the Comedy Store to the more mainstream comedy of some of the later performers. A group who touch the fringe of alternative comedy are Fascinating Aïda – three glamorous women who perform witty and pointed songs. The founder of the group was Dillie Keane, and in her book *Fascinating Who?* she details the formation of the group in 1981 as a result of getting bookings to write songs for Radio 4's *Stop The Week*; she had met the other original members, Marilyn Cutts and Lizzie Richardson when they were working in repertory theatre at Crewe in 1979. After a couple of changes the personnel settled down to Dillie Keane as organizer and composer, Adèle Anderson and Denise Wharmby – the latter an Australian recruited to replace Marilyn Cutts. Nica Burns – who runs the Donmar Warehouse theatre in Covent Garden – acted as director, and together they developed a very individual style.

Early on they had played one or two cabaret gigs, but their style demanded a theatrical setting, if only for economic reasons. Dillie Keane remembers playing at Jongleurs in their early days: 'It's a great atmosphere, but it's not our atmosphere any more – great fun, but an awful lot of smoke ... and we'd find we weren't on until two o'clock sometimes, and that's just exhausting. And they can't pay us enough – we have two roadies, book-keeper, accountant, lawyer, director, agency, plus ourselves to pay.' Because of this they have of necessity to play to larger audiences than cabaret gigs can provide; and in any case they have developed a style more suitable to theatres.

A lot of work goes into the look of the show; whereas the cabaret circuit has necessarily abandoned any attempt to look glamorous, the costumes, lighting and make-up are an important part of Fascinating Aïda. Dillie Keane: 'You win over the men immediately if you try and look your best – and you win over almost all the women as well, because there's nothing women appreciate more than other women looking as well as possible – they've paid good money and you plough it back into the show. But feminist groups are terribly unpredictable – one group walked out, but we've always had great reviews in *Spare*

Fascinating Aïda – Adèle
Anderson, Dillie Keane,
Denise Wharmby.

Rib [the feminist magazine] and feminist friends have said how great it is. . . . We did have a woman in Kendal who said, "I really enjoyed the show, but why do you shave your armpits?" . . .'

She does not feel related to the alternative comedy field: 'We've existed like a little island on our own, we're not at all part of it. I like some of the stuff they do – we often set out to say something that we feel is deeply political, and people say we're much less satirical . . . it's difficult to see how we can be when we've got pointed songs like "Radiating Love" – the message is so clear in that – it's varnished, but it's still very clear. I think it's very political.'

> Would you love me at all if I lost all my hair?
> Would you still hold my hand if my skin wasn't there?
> For I can't help but feel you won't find me attractive
> When the isotopes render me radioactive;
> Will you whisper the sweet words I so long to hear
> In the hole that denotes where I once had an ear?
> When I'm gaunt and exhausted, unable to crawl,
> Will you love me then at all?

Dillie Keane: 'It's my favourite – this week – because it's got such a pretty tune and such horrid words. In fact Marilyn refused to sing it when she was in the group because she said it turned her stomach. Denise has a stronger stomach. We had to do a lot of research – I went to a CND-style bookstall and got various pamphlets, and read the medical reports after Hiroshima, to get it right.'

As with Jim Barclay's *Four Minutes To Midnight*, the distance that comedy provides enables the audience to think about the unthinkable; the message goes home better for being sweetened. The group's songs cover a wide range of subjects – taking in Yuppies, Brechtian songs, and tights; Dillie Keane: 'With songs you can be more personal – it's not gags; I personally think the greatest songwriter of the second half of the twentieth century is Randy Newman – he can be very witty and acerbic, and writes the most crushingly personal songs which are very funny. We did a TV special in Dublin, and Arnold Brown was with us; he said he hadn't realized how much every song is a drama – he said, "You inhabit the songs, you don't perform them – you *are* that person singing the song." So for instance, before the song "Whites Blues" Adèle comes on with the coffee-cups and we do a conversation: "How's Tamsin?" – "I'm a bit worried about her, she's coming out with some really bizarre ideas, for instance she asked me the other day at breakfast, could she have a frilly pink party frock" – "God, how embarrassing" . . . so that people can identify whose point of view we're singing the songs from.'

I live in Nelson Mandela Close, and my rubbish bags are grey;
If someone mentions 'blackmail' I put him right;
But when I gave a party, just the other day
I noticed all my friends but one were white ...
We always go National Health; our GP's really super;
But you never know when you'll need a new hip so we're insured
     with BUPA;
Oh I ain't got the blues;
I've got those God-I-hate-the-Tories but-Militant-Tendency-give-
     me-the-willies
I-wished-it-was-Dennis-Healey, and-did-I-really-vote-Alliance?
Smoked salmon socialist – that's smoked salmon for everyone....
Angst-ridden middle-class whites.

Dillie Keane does not see the group as either alternative or Estab-lishment: 'I think we're an anachronism. The people we get compared to consistently are Tom Lehrer, Flanders and Swann, Noël Coward ... occasionally Beatrice Lillie, Joyce Grenfell ... we don't get compared with Victoria Wood, ever, which surprises me in a way, women doing songs.... I'm glad, because I think she's such a genius that we wouldn't come off very well compared with her....'

But Wood's approach is, of course, very different; for one thing she eschews traditional feminine glamour – although she always looks smart unless playing a scruffy character – preferring to present herself as a more ordinary person. After her 1982 TV series *Wood and Walters* she was approached by various TV companies to make a new series. She remembers: 'I eventually decided BBC2 would be best, and I just got a contract to write six shows – "Starring Victoria Wood", that's all it said. There's not many formats you can come up with, apart from coming on, saying "Hullo, good evening" and then lots of sketches.... I knew I wanted a continuity announcer, I knew I wanted to have documentaries, I knew I wanted to have a soap opera – and that was about it. I just worked it out as I went along – I wrote as much as I could, and threw half of it away, and thank God I had enough for six half-hours at the end of it.'

The first series of six, under the title *Victoria Wood As Seen On TV*, went out in January and February 1985, with a second series of six starting on 10 November 1986. By this time she was also estab-lished with her one-woman show in the larger theatres. The other regular performers in the TV series were Julie Walters, Celia Imrie, Duncan Preston and Susie Blake, and the show was unusual in being entirely written by Victoria Wood – most sketch shows are written by a team of anything from three to fifteen people. Victoria Wood: 'The same people are writing all the shows – that's why it's very hard for a show to have an individual feel about it. If you write it all yourself, good or bad, it is at least your style – you can either take the credit or take the blame!'

Each show begins with a short stand-up set (as do a number of other personality-sketch shows; perhaps the influence of the cabaret circuit permeating mainstream television). Mostly the material was new rather than drawn from the then current stage act, because once a sequence had been done on television it would be old hat to a stage audience. The monologues show a sharp observation and skilful use of language.

> I've got this terrible posh friend – she lives in this old place they're doing up – it's a converted mill chimney. It's nice – the rooms are quite small but they have nice high ceilings. She was sitting in the kitchen which she'd just decorated – which was pale yellow with touches of green – she'd based it round a Marks and Spencer's broccoli quiche – and she was all depressed about the veins on her legs. She'd had shorts on the other day, and her husband had used her left thigh to direct someone to the motorway. She was low, really, because she had post-natal depression. She showed me the baby ... and then *I* had it as well. They can't *do* anything, little babies, can they? – I mean, they can't crack jokes, they can't shift pianos ... what I hate about going to visit someone with a little baby is they always get it out, plonk it on the living-room carpet, rip all its clothes off, grab it by the ankles, and start scraping away at its bottom with a cotton-wool ball. You're trying to be chatty, and there's this terrible smell, like the elephant-house. They lift it up and there's a little patch where the carpet's stopped growing. My friend – she didn't know what sort of birth to have, because she's quite frightened of pain ... in fact she had an epidural before she had sex ...

Among the regular performers was Susie Blake as a splendidly individual continuity announcer, colouring her linking announcements with personal comments:

> **Susie:** ... and later on this evening on the alternative channel we have a new series dealing with all aspects of women's health, called 'Well Woman' ... that's original ... programme one looks into that very distressing and all too common ailment ... that's not a word I care to read out, I don't think. Fortunately it's not something I'm ever likely to get ... and if I did get it I certainly wouldn't put yoghourt on it.

Another regular item is a justifiably spiteful spoof of *Crossroads*, called *Acorn Antiques*. Most of the jokes centre on the incompetence of the actors – and the technicians – as things go wrong and the actors struggle to carry on. Victoria Wood: 'All the cameramen

started to put their oar in once they realized it was supposed to be funny ... I put in things like wobbly scenery and people banging into microphone booms, and then the cameramen put in things like going out of focus and banging into the furniture – which they were doing anyway, but they did it more. When I first wrote it I actually put jokes in the script, but I found they were getting completely buried by all the other things that were happening.'

Two books have been published containing scripts from the series – *Up To You, Porky* (Methuen, 1985) and *Barmy* (Methuen, 1987) – the latter containing all twelve episodes of *Acorn Antiques*. The series also contains a number of spoof documentaries and sharp jabs at various styles of television programmes – including this look at holiday programmes, with Victoria Wood as Joan and Julie Walters as Marjorie:

> **Joan:** And as Philippa climbs out of that piranha tank I'm sure she won't mind if I let you into a little secret – she's actually into the fourth week of a very serious nervous breakdown. Now I turn to Marjorie who's been finding out what's available holiday-wise for those of us who aren't going abroad this summer. Hello, Marjorie. What's available holiday-wise for those of us who aren't going abroad this summer?
>
> **Marjorie** (*to camera*): Hello Joan – well, believe it or not, not every holidaymaker will be flying off to Marbella or Alicante with a suitcase full of velour leisure shorts singing 'Y Viva España'.
>
> **Joan:** And why is that, Marjorie?
>
> **Marjorie:** Possibly because they don't know the words to the second verse, Joan.
>
> **Joan:** So a lot of people will be looking for a reasonably priced package in this country.
>
> **Marjorie:** That's right, Joan.
>
> **Joan:** OK, so, I don't have very much money, I'm single, I can't afford to go abroad, I don't make friends easily – what can I do?
>
> **Marjorie** (*to Joan*): We had all this out in the wine bar. (*To camera*) Well, there's lots of alternatives available, Joan – the cheapest being a two-week conservation holiday in the West Midlands, dragging old bedsteads out of the Grand Union Canal and living on pulses.
>
> **Joan:** And what would I need to take with me?
>
> **Marjorie:** Well, if they haven't been soaked, a can of air-freshener.
>
> **Joan:** And if I'm a book-lover, and would like nothing better than to meet my favourite authors?
>
> **Marjorie:** Then hie yourself along to the Swan Hotel, Warwick, where you can mingle with popular novelists, or have the chance to examine such literary treasures as the original manuscript of *Wuthering Heights*, James Herriot's collection of rubber gloves, and, most exciting of all, Jeffrey Archer's very first bank statement.

Victoria Wood as Seen on TV – Acorn Antiques – Duncan Preston, Victoria Wood, Julie Walters, Celia Imrie

Victoria Wood as Seen on TV – Victoria Wood and Julie Walters

Joan: But you've also been looking at singles holidays, haven't you, Marjorie?

Marjorie: That's right, Joan, because for every outgoing popular, physically attractive swinger like me, there's an emotionally repressed lumpy old pongo like Joan.

Unlike some others, Victoria Wood had few problems with censorship at the BBC: 'I don't think they even know what I'm doing – nobody's ever come and said "hello" or anything – they don't seem to know I'm there. I just sneak in and make a series and go home again. The only thing was in the first series, they said I couldn't say "Lil-lets".'

Despite her modesty, it is interesting to note that, unlike most of those covered in this book, the programmes were popular with the television establishment, receiving several BAFTA [British Association of Film and Television Arts] awards.

Victoria Wood As Seen On TV falls into the same mathematical rule as most of the other programmes mentioned – no more than two series; after a forty-minute special transmitted on 18 December 1987 she decided to do no more shows: 'I love television, and if it was possible for me to work in it more, then I would; but because of the position I've put myself in of being the only writer on the show, I can't physically work in it that often. I've just had it with sketch shows for a bit – people have liked it, and I want to stop while they still like it.'

The problems of writing a lot of material never seem to have worried Ben Elton, who has continued to turn out material at a quite extraordinary rate. Apart from *Happy Families* and his own stand-up material, he also became involved in co-writing a successor to Rowan Atkinson's 1984 series *Blackadder*. This had placed Atkinson in the middle ages, at the centre of intrigue and skulduggery, and had been written by Atkinson and Richard Curtis.

Ben Elton: 'Richard Curtis had an idea to write a sitcom for the pop group Madness – a sort of modern *Monkees* – and we did a lot of work on that and it never quite made it. Then Rowan dropped out of writing *Blackadder*, and I co-wrote *Blackadder 2* – we write a script each, and then swop and work on each other's script; and we have good rules, like try not to look back – "Oh, you cut my favourite joke" – you accept what happens and move on.'

Blackadder 2 places Atkinson at the court of Queen Elizabeth I – a splendid performance by Miranda Richardson in the style of a spoilt pre-Sloane teenager (a complete contrast from her best-known, and stunning, performance in the film *Dance With A Stranger*).

Edmund Blackadder himself is a man with a modern outlook, trapped in a historical setting and surrounded by idiot servants and associates; the series is well-written and performed, and was considered more successful than the original.

Here Edmund is summoned by the Queen because the elderly Lord Melchett (Stephen Fry) is ill; he is being attended by the Queen's thick-witted nurse (Patsy Byrne):

> **Queen:** It all started last night at about two o'clock – I was tucked into bed having this absolutely scrummy dream about ponies, when I was wakened by a terrific banging from Lord Melchett.
> **Edmund:** Well . . . I never knew he had it in him.
> **Queen:** It's true, I promise – he was banging on the castle gates, and falling over – and singing a strange song about a girl who possessed a thing called a . . . dicky dido?
> **Edmund:** Oh, yes – it's a lovely old hymn, isn't it? Well, ma'am, I *think* I know what's wrong with Lord Melchett – and unfortunately, it isn't fatal.
> **Queen:** Well, hurry up and cure the horrible man, I'm fed up with him lying there moaning and groaning.
> **Nurse:** And letting off such great and fruitsome flabby woof-woofs one can't believe one's tiny nosey.

Blackadder 2 was transmitted on BBC1 from 9 January 1986; and a further series, *Blackadder the Third* – placing his descendant (and his servant's descendant) in the service of the Prince Regent – began on 17 September 1987. This last series was something of a strain, even for the indefatigable Elton, because at the time of writing it he was closely involved with the later developments of a new television series growing out of alternative comedy, which had begun with a pilot programme early in 1985: *Saturday Live.*

Saturday Live was another Paul Jackson project, this time attempting to mix cabaret performers with rock groups, sketches and pre-filmed items in a show which would have the extra adrenalin factor of going out live. The pilot, mounted for Channel Four by London Weekend Television, was produced and directed by Jackson, and went out on 12 January 1985 from 8.30 to 10 pm. It was linked by Lenny Henry with confident aplomb, and included Andy de la Tour, Chris Barrie, French and Saunders (with Dawn still on the YOP scheme from the job centre), the Dangerous Brothers (Mayall and Edmondson in pre-recorded mayhem) and groups Style Council and Slade. A complicated and jazzy staging was built, with the audience partly standing in a floor area close to the performers and partly on the more normal tiered seats – and a few bemused audience members going round and round on a genuine fairground roundabout. All the performers came over well, and there was a general air of excitement in the live sections; a filmed parody of *On The Waterfront* with Henry in the Marlon Brando part was effective, though perhaps a bit out of place in such a programme.

Plans were laid for a series of ten; but difficulties began to arise. Paul Jackson: 'We were misled by the runaway success of the pilot, which had gone marvellously. When we came to do a run of ten, the mood of broadcasting in general had changed radically in the year since the pilot, which ran us into unexpected content problems [for one thing, Winston Churchill (Jnr.) had been making complaints about decency in broadcasting]; LWT was taking more notice of this programme which was taking over a studio for ten consecutive weekends – there were more technical problems, safety problems – there was a promulgation about the number of audience on the floor, and on the first show it was reduced to almost nothing; the comics don't play to the seated audience, it's too far away, and there was no atmosphere at all. That first show was dreadful; Lenny Henry did the second show – he was *par excellence* the man to do it, and he just about got away with it – he worked his bollocks off.'

The middle programmes of the series were a very difficult time for Jackson; there were objections raised over some of the material,

Saturday Live *overleaf*

and with a new compère each week it was difficult to give the show an identity; only towards the end of the series did the show start to work as they got the atmosphere right.

The series was produced by Paul Jackson and Geoff Posner, and ran from January to March 1986. Many of the individual items came off well; Peter Cook and John Wells appeared in one show in several pointed sketches (Cook reviving his Harold Macmillan [Lord Stockton] impersonation); Stephen Fry and Hugh Laurie contributed a series of witty sketches; and there were appearances by American comics including Rita Rudner, Emo Philips and Louis Anderson. Simon Fanshawe, Helen Lederer, Pamela Stephenson and Rowan Atkinson also appeared; and Harry Enfield contributed regular comments as 'Stavros', a Greek kebab-shop owner (whose Cockney-Greek accent and malapropisms led to complaints of racism which dogged his continued use of the character). The various rock groups who appeared were well staged in the flamboyant set.

There were appearances each week by Mayall and Edmondson as the Dangerous Brothers, Richard and Adrian (now promoted to Sir Adrian), which were pre-recorded and allowed them to exploit the full range of stunts, breakaway sets, explosions and the like. Adrian Edmondson: 'We love doing stunts – we're both quite agile, and not particularly afraid of hurting ourselves. I don't know how we developed it – we do it well now because we've been doing it together for so long. It's very hard if [as in a couple of the Comic Strip films] Nigel has to head-butt me because we haven't worked together in a relationship that much; but with Rik, we know how our bodies relate to each other. There was only one serious thing, when I caught fire in the *Saturday Live* pilot – we had to stop the tape and start again – I burnt my eyebrows off.'

There were regular appearances by Ben Elton, who also compèred one of the shows. By this time he had done the three major tours with Rik Mayall as well as many individual gigs, but *Saturday Live* was his big breakthrough on to television – which would of course reflect back into the stage work and increase his popularity enormously. He was initially asked to write for the show, but suggested that he might perform; he was hired for five shows with an option on the remainder, which was taken up when it became apparent that he could work well on TV. Ben Elton: 'It was another of those watersheds; I didn't know whether I could make it work in six-minute slots, I didn't know whether I could make it work without swearing, I didn't know whether my fast live patter would work ... now it seems obvious, but it didn't then – I just did what I did on stage, except that I didn't swear. I did six minutes near the end of each programme – and I used up the material I'd spent five years putting together. I was really scared, I thought it would take me another five years to put together that much material again, but what I've since discovered is that I can write more, it's coming out of my ears.'

The risk of using up material – which he would then not have been able to tour with, since many of his audience would already have heard it – was worth taking, since the programme established him firmly as a leading stand-up comic.

Whatever the faults of the first series of *Saturday Live* (the second series will be covered later), it did introduce something of the alternative cabaret scene to a wider audience for the first time – those who lived outside London, or who for whatever reason did not go to live gigs – and may have been a contributing factor to the continuing expansion of the cabaret circuit.

By the end of 1986 the London circuit, now expanded to around fifty venues, had stabilized. Although some venues came and went, all the principal ones continued through the next couple of years (with the exception of the Crown and Castle, which closed in early 1987). The range of performers had expanded considerably; again, over the next couple of years the main ones continued to work in much the same way, although more minor ones appeared and disappeared. More pubs had woken up to the possibilities; the Chuckle Club, in the Black Horse just off Oxford Street, was a particularly good venue which, though small, had a good atmosphere – as time went on it has become more and more crowded. The Meccano Club at the Cambden Head, Banana Cabaret at the Bedford in Balham, and the Punchline Comedy Club at The Railway, West Hampstead, were other pub venues; and meanwhile the Albany Empire did occasional cabaret shows, and Jongleurs, the Comedy Store, the Earth Exchange and the Tunnel Palladium continued to do good business.

Of the many performers developing their styles, one of the most interesting is John Hegley. From his earlier appearances simply reading his poetry he had built up a relationship with the audience which depended upon them heckling him. He developed a characterization which allowed him to be wittily sarcastic to hecklers, apparently contemptuous of the audience and irritated with the inevitable procession of people fetching drinks or going out for a pee – anyone crossing in front of him with a handful of drinks invited sarcastic comments or simply sharp looks which were the more hilarious for Hegley's excellent timing.

The act itself, which has continued to develop, consists of songs to guitar or mandolin, or poems – often about his dog or his brother-in-law – all presented as being far above the comprehension of his audience. He will break off a poem to glare at an interrupter, or even refuse to read one altogether as a punishment for inattention. He reacts to the audience laughter as if it is an insult – this of course makes them laugh the more. He comments: 'Some people believe it – "You were really annoyed with the audience tonight" . . . sometimes I really am! – that's a good thing, that there is an element of it . . . sometimes I am pissed off with audiences.'

The poems themselves are quietly witty, often non-rhyming and sometimes non-scanning. Some of them are very terse, as in the one called 'Liverpool':

> on the ferry across the Mersey
> it was cold
> and I wore my jersey

Some are sharper than they appear at first sight:

> sister you can turn boredom into joy
> and make toys from the rubbish
> sister you are an alchemist
> but you have not done a very good job with your husband

Indeed his brother-in-law comes in for a good deal of poetic flak:

> After his favourite vegetarian meal
> consisting of seventeen pints of lager
> my brother in law offers me a lift home.
> On the way we stop off for a drink.
> At the bar I ask for two halves of lager
> my brother in law says there is no such thing as a half of lager
> I suggest we get a bus the rest of the way.
> My brother in law says that buses are only for scum
> and that if he comes in his car
> he leaves in his car
> before we leave and discover his car has been stolen
> my brother in law tells me
> how he likes to stop and ask hitchhikers where they are going
> and then tell them that he will get there first.

He is more interested in continuous development of his act than in honing it to a fixed set-piece: 'It's a process not a product. While it's a process it's much more alive. Which could be said about the cabaret circuit – to what extent is cabaret now a product? – whereas it was a *process* once.'

John Dowie, who had been touring the university circuit for much of the time the alternative cabaret circuit was building up, also finds that a good deal of his material grows out of improvisation – although in his case he is rather more interested in developing it into a fixed routine. The version of his act recorded live and issued on a gramophone record in 1985 contains some material which started as improvisations. He comments: 'A lot of the stuff in that was improvised on stage – and also in therapy sessions, which were very useful for creating new material . . . it might start off having two laughs in five minutes; then the next night you might do three minutes and get four laughs; then if you're lucky you'll do six minutes and it'll all be funny.'

He is not afraid to go into difficult areas – for example, he does a sequence about haemorrhoids: 'When you've got them, what else do you talk about? If you have an appalling haemorrhoid problem you can't walk on stage and make mother-in-law jokes because that's of no value or interest to you.'

The feeling that comedy should be a form of therapy is one that seems to be shared by a number of performers on the circuit; but Dowie has a low opinion of most of them: 'I would dispute that there are people on the alternative cabaret circuit going into areas where other people haven't gone before. Tony Allen is one who does attempt that, and does it, often; most people go on and pretend to be somebody who's not very bright, thus encouraging the audience to feel more intelligent than that. I don't think there's many areas I go into that haven't been covered in some form before – plays, films; artists can go anywhere they like – and I think comedy has as much value as literature and stuff, it's a shame that people don't make more use of that.'

Dowie's hour-long act covers a wide range of subjects; like Keith Allen, he speaks as himself rather than as some character, but instead of weaving extended webs of fantasy narrative he relays his thoughts and opinions, backed by occasional forays into speculation. He breaks the speech up with music, usually self-accompanied on the piano in minimalist style; he learned to play from a correspondence course (he was robbed). He has had from the first what Ronnie Golden calls a certain kamikaze element in his comedy, but it is by now well under control, so that he can go into touchy areas and still be extremely funny.

> The Vatican said two things not long ago, guaranteed to make everyone's life so much better and happier . . . the Vatican said, *'It's still a sin to be a homosexual, and it's still a sin to wank'*. Well, the Vatican didn't say 'wank', obviously, did they – they said pull your plonker, I think, I can't remember . . . but *what? What? A sin* to

wank? A sin? Eternal hell-fire and damnation because you've had a wank? That's a bit heavy, isn't it? I mean, can you think of a better way to stitch up the entire planet? And what's wrong with homosexuals? What do homosexuals do? – 'I'll tell you what homosexuals do – I'll tell you what they do – homosexuals get into bed – *with each other* – and then – *they play with each other's bits!!* If you're going to get into bed with somebody, and play with their bits, they have to have *different bits from the bits that you've got ... and you can't play with your own bits either! I ought to know – I'm the fucking Pope! And I don't play with any bits at all!*' ... The reason why the Pope doesn't like homosexuals and masturbators is because they don't breed – hardly at all. The Pope likes people to be Catholics, and breed. And make more Catholics – and they breed – and make more Catholics and more Catholics and more Catholics ... all those Catholics go round to the church and give all their money to the Pope! And he spends their money on a long white dress with an artificial hand, and underneath – he's wanking all the time. 'I'm doing it and nobody else is! And I'm doing it in Latin. Veni, veni, veni ...' I'd like to go back 2000 years, stand at the foot of the crucifix and say to Jesus Christ, 'Do you know what you're doing *means*!' – 'Yes, I know what it means, actually, thank you very much, I know what it means ... I don't get nailed to a piece of wood for no fucking reason. Of course I know what it means. I'm taking the sins of the world on my shoulders – through me you shall be redeemed.' – 'It's got fuck all to do with that, pal – 2000 years from now, no wanking.' – 'What? No wanking? Are you mad? No wanking? You think I got nailed to a piece of wood to stop people wanking? It stops *me* wanking, I agree ... no wanking?' – 'And no homosexuals.' – '*What*? No homosexuals? Do me a favour! Haven't you noticed I hang around with twelve men all the time? It was snogging with Judas that got me into this mess in the first place. Who's been filling your head full of all this crap?' – 'The Pope.' – 'Who's he?' – 'He's in charge.' – '*I'm* in fucking charge, pal – I'm in charge – I'm the Bruce Forsyth of this particular gig.' – 'Yes, but you're just like a tiny little corner shop, aren't you? – he's like Tesco's – he's got the entire market sewn up – you're fucked! Sorry!' ... Interesting, also, isn't it? – the Pope drives around in a car with bullet-proof glass in the windows ... and Jesus Christ never wore nail-proof gloves, did he?

He goes on to visualize the original act of creation as being performed by a God who is pissed out of his mind; here God is explaining Himself:

> ... and I see hanging up in the sky, this little blue ball. I thought, I know what I'll do for a laugh – I'll get that little blue ball, and I'll cover it with little intelligent bipeds ... then, to fuck them up, I'll give them a sense of logic. And I'll make 'em all different colours, that'll give them something to talk about, I expect ... I'll make eight or nine different sexes and say there's only two ... and I'll get these

ones, I'll call them Hebrews, and I'll give them a really fucking hard time. For ever. And I'll say that they're the Chosen People. Ha-ha-ha. Of course, I won't tell them what they've been chosen *for*. . . .

Despite Dowie's criticisms of the cabaret circuit, he has a family interest in it in a way, for his sister Claire has been establishing herself on it. She was born on 23 September 1956, and after a period as a dancer (in staged numbers in night-clubs on the Continent) she turned to poetry. She came to London when she was about twenty-one and made some appearances reading her poems, and appearing in a double-act with Elaine Costa, in the cabaret circuit and the smaller poetry circuit that has existed, almost underground, for some years. By 1982 she had added some stand-up routines to the poetry, and was beginning to appear in venues like the Finborough Arms or the Croydon Warehouse.

She has become identified with lesbian material; she comments: 'I started with a non-sexual act, then it was a heterosexual act, then it was a sort of lesbian act – now it's getting back to being just sexual, not any one thing. I did do a full-blooded lesbian act before, but not so much now. It just changes as I change, I think.'

Her lesbian material could cause some of the men in the audience to sit stony-faced as she embroidered real-life experiences.

> You've got to be fit to be gay – 'cos all you've got is discos and marches – it's true – all this just to get laid! And the Gay Pride march – march – I mean, it's *walking* . . . I had to walk everywhere – with a banner. . . . Aren't I persecuted enough? Why can't I sit in a pub and be proud? – occasionally march to the bar, perhaps. . . . And then, I slept with a man. I didn't know – I thought it was OK, I thought it was right-on radical . . . 'cos he was gay as well . . . it's true, he's one of my best friends, and he's lovely, he's so camp . . . but anyway, I ended up in bed with him – don't try it. If you're a butch dyke, and you go to bed with a very camp man, don't try it. Don't. I thought it would be a giggle . . . I thought, oh this'll be a laugh – I was a bit drunk . . . I'd been being proud . . . I ended up on Valium for three weeks . . . it was awful . . . we're in bed together and it's like . . . I can't explain it . . . it was like there was a penis running round the bed and we weren't too sure who it belonged to. . . . It was like, 'Is that yours?' – 'No, that's not mine, mine's bigger than that'. . . .
>
> I'll tell you another true story – so embarrassing. . . . I have a lot of trouble going into ladies' toilets. It's not that I can't, physically – you know, can't get in – it's 'cos I've got short hair and I wear trousers. Well, I obviously look like a boy. How stupid – I get mistaken for a boy lots of times in ladies' toilets. I keep getting told to get out, things like that – 'Who are you, you pervert? – get out of here' . . . and it happened to me one time, I went in – it was

Victoria Coach Station toilets, actually – and there was this woman about my age, looking at me really hard, and I thought, Oh God, she's going to come over, she's going to tell me I'm in the wrong toilet and all that crap, and I can't be bothered with it, it really gets on my nerves . . . so I thought, right, I'm going to show this woman, I've had enough of this – I'm going to show her I can be aggressive and assertive . . . that's how you're supposed to be – right, I'll show her. And I grabbed my shirt and my jumper, and I went . . . (*mimes raising jumper*) . . . I wasn't wearing a bra . . . 'cos I'm a lesbian. . . . I stood there like this, and this woman came over to me – and she said, 'Excuse me – aren't you Claire Dowie?'. . . . I was so embarrassed . . . I stood there for about ten minutes while she was telling me about this gig she saw me at in Brixton . . . and I was going, 'Gosh, isn't it hot? . . . just taking the air, you know how it is . . .' – about ten minutes, I stood there rigid . . . meantime all the other women were walking by saying, 'Look at that boy with tits, isn't he odd'. . . .

More than most performers, she puts her own personal life on stage: 'I can't do it any other way. I can't make stuff up – I can't write jokes, I can only do it from my own perspective.'

On the tendency of her material to upset audiences, she comments: 'That's half why I do it – because it is absurd – because they shouldn't be uneasy about it – everybody has sex in one form or another, and making it into some sort of some big deal – that's the absurdity of it. I wouldn't like the audience to agree with me all the time! I once did it to a quite theatrical audience of elderly farmers and their wives – and Sensible Footwear had been on before me, they were a mild feminist trio, and they went down really awfully . . . and I went out and did this lesbian stuff, and they loved it. I was really amazed . . . middle-aged farm people, clapping and cheering . . . there must be a lot of it about. I had one gig once, I wasn't going down with the young audience at all, and there was this one older woman – she was the mother of somebody who ran the place – she was about sixty – she was killing herself laughing . . . she said, "I've seen it all before, you can't tell me anything!" Funnily enough, the most problems I get, if anybody's going to complain, is usually from other lesbians. Lesbians take it incredibly seriously – not all of them, but there are a few. What I like about doing comedy is, maybe you have a problem, you can stand on stage and make it a joke, and it makes you feel better. It's very therapeutic.'

Subsequently she has moved away from doing particularly lesbian material; and indeed has expanded her range away from comedy with her drama-monologue *Adult Child, Dead Child*, first performed in 1987, which mixes poetry and narrative to explore a neurotic character in a sensitive and moving way.

There were few enough women on the circuit in the earlier days, and even more recently they have continued to be in a minority. One who, like Claire Dowie, came in from the poetry circuit is Jenny Eclair, whose off-beat approach mixes deliberately silly poems with monologue material all delivered in a very individual husky voice. She was born on 16 March 1961 to an army family – which meant that, moving about a lot, she had to keep making new friends quickly. She says: 'You do tend to show off, because you don't have friends for very long . . . and I was fat, let's be brutally honest about it, and not particularly clever at anything – so nobody wants to copy your homework . . . so I had to be vaguely amusing. I went on to Manchester Polytechnic School of Theatre . . . it was one of the few that would let me in, my headmistress wrote the worst school report any drama school has ever seen apparently. They were very wary of letting me in because it said I was disruptive – I'd had problems at school with disruptiveness, for a long time they thought I had glandular fever, but it was boredom.'

She proceeded to get anorexia; and then when she left she fell in with a man who had seen the early cabaret circuit in London and was proposing to clean up by starting one in Manchester: 'I was vaguely his girlfriend, because he had a warped interest in girls with the bodies of twelve-year-olds. . . .' She took up performing with a band – buffooning around between numbers – but all this did encourage her to write some funny poems. When the inevitable split-up came, around 1982, she moved to London and began appearing on the poetry circuit . . . she was also 'the world's worst waitress' for a time. Finding the poetry circuit too dreary for her tastes she began to move into the cabaret circuit.

She has developed an outgoing and eccentric style (having recovered completely from the anorexia) with a sense of sheer mischief, taking in subjects such as what to do with your pets while you're on holiday:

> . . . you can't trust anyone else to look after them properly, and however clever you think your goldfish is, they're not much cop with a can-opener. Anyway, if you do leave them to their own devices they only have all-night pyjama parties, smoke dope and wreck the joint, so it's best if you kill them first.

The poems also feature in the act. Having killed her pets successfully she goes to Greece:

> We are on holiday in Greece.
> It is night-time in Nico's bar. (Because there's always

some complete bastard called Nico who always comes
from Macclesfield or somewhere.)
Nico says, 'You should have been here last night.
This giant turtle just strolled in from the beach,
Tame as anything.
Ate a bit of souvlaki, sat under that table.'
We are excited!
Every night we go to Nico's bar
And every night Nico says:
'You should have been here last night.
This giant turtle just strolled in from the beach,
Tame as anything.
Ate a bit of souvlaki, sat under that table.'
We never see the turtle.
I'm not really surprised.
The beach is six miles away.

She feels that the cabaret circuit is a bit precarious and might just disappear one day, taking her livelihood with it; so she has done some writing, beginning with an article for *Company* magazine: 'That's such a thrill – I was always labelled an illiterate Goth at school – lots of imagination but no spelling or grammar, so nought out of ten. People are actually saying, "I'll pay you to write" – that's nice . . . an enormous boost to my confidence.'

There are still not many women on the circuit compared to men, although the proportion is higher than in the early days when there were literally only three or four. One who started as late as 1985 but has made a firm impression is Kit Hollerbach, an American; a number of performers from the well-established American comedy circuit have performed during visits, but her visit turned into a welcome permanency.

She grew up in Nevada, and studied urban economics at Berkeley University, doing drama as a side course: 'Their drama department is notoriously bad – it got me interested enough that I enrolled in some private classes, and as I went along economics became less and less important to me.' After leaving university she worked with a theatre group that did improvisational drama: 'I never got to be in enough sketches, so I decided to be a stand-up comic – because on my own I had all the lines, provided I wrote them!'

America has a more established tradition of stand-up comics in clubs, but the women were still in a minority. Kit Hollerbach: 'They didn't like the idea of a girl telling jokes – it wasn't the audience so much, it was my fellow performers; sadly I do have some rather bad memories of some of the people I used to work with.'

Some of her material at the time was rather weirder than her later

act: 'I used to tell the audience that there had been an accident in the club – that some comedian tripped and fell into the audience – and went on to describe this virtual blood-bath! I think it was amusing to the other comics – I don't think the audience had a clue as to what I was on about.' She also did a range of American characters – something she dropped later because English audiences cannot appreciate the subtleties of different American accents – in the same way that she herself could not tell Welsh from Cockney when she first arrived.

She worked in the original Comedy Stores in both Los Angeles and San Francisco; then in 1985 she came to work in a girlfriend's art gallery in Ireland because she felt she needed a break. She flew to London at weekends and did a few gigs, mostly by asking to appear on open spots (a regular way for new performers to break into the circuit; many venues would allow newcomers to try doing a five-minute set). When she did an open spot at Jongleurs she overran her five minutes – to thirty-five – and in the end had to be taken off by the compère; but the audience loved it, and she was increasingly establishing herself in the circuit.

Her earlier style was slightly gentler, but she had to develop a more aggressive approach: 'I'm not particularly happy about it – I've been playing the Comedy Store and Jongleurs, and the problem with that is, there's a lot of pissed-up people, so I spend a lot of time dealing with them, which gives me the impression of being a lot more hard-assed than I really am. If I play a gentler club, it's apparent; but I play the Comedy Store and Jongleurs a lot, and get those habits – like, the audience is so drunk you can't have a joke that's too long, because they can't think that long. And fast and furious – you can't leave a pause because they'll nail your butt. So there's a style that's come from a need. . . . I don't think that's such a good change, but the alternative is to make less money, which I've never been that keen on. . . .'

Her stage character is a slightly noisier development of her own outgoing personality, which combines American brashness with a good deal of genuine warmth; she looks at Britain with the bemused eye of the foreigner.

> I'm married to an English guy, he's a typical English guy, he's very reserved – in fact, it wasn't until after we were married that I actually knew he wanted to go out with me. I used to get these love letters from him that would begin with, 'To whom it may concern' . . . but I'm glad I'm married because I never had very good luck meeting men – I don't know what it was, I'd be in a pub or something, there'd be a million really cute guys around. . . . OK,

maybe only one ... but invariably Mr Nerd-wad-wally-dick-brain of the Universe would fly in from another planet just to be with me. When I first came here I met this guy who was wearing a badge, it said 'Sainsbury's – assistant manager – Jim'. That kind of takes the guesswork out of it, doesn't it? But Jim was so cool – he had one of those shirts with the hair attached – he came up to my table, he goes, 'Hey, darling, I like you' ... I'm thinking, lucky, lucky me, uh?! 'You know, darling, you're OK in my book' ... yeah, apparently not a best-seller! He wouldn't let up, either – he took my glasses off and he said, 'Without your glasses, why, you're beautiful.' I said, 'Without my glasses, you're not half bad either.' Finally I had to get rid of him, get him away from my table – give him subtle little hints, you know, things like ... (*mimes sticking two fingers down throat and vomiting.*)

I've been a little depressed lately, what with the impending nuclear war and my most recent haircut – I can't get my hair to do anything I want it to, like the housework ... so I figured to cheer myself up I'd go down to Harrods, I thought I'd buy myself a lipstick ... Harrods – what a snotty store! I mean, even the window dummies have attitudes ... I go in there, I go to the Clinique counter in the hall of beauty – what an amazing place, the Clinique counter – the women are wearing white laboratory jackets. I'm thinking, there's some serious stuff going on here! What have they got – girls in the back on stretchers, OD'd on mascara? I went in there for a lipstick – I thought they'd ask me for a urine sample. The woman who was helping me was incredible – she had one of those hair-does that veer up in the front and make little shelf units. She told me what I had was 'combination skin' – combination skin, that loosely translates, 'I'll have to buy the entire store.'

Her husband, referred to at the beginning of that excerpt, is another comedian on the circuit, and one who has been very influential: Jeremy Hardy. He began working on the circuit in 1984, about a year before Kit Hollerbach, and his dry laconic style and sharp observation has made him a rôle model for many newer performers.

He was born in Farnborough, Hampshire, on 17 July 1961, and grew up in a small village in Surrey, the youngest of five children. He studied modern history and politics at Southampton University, but when he left there in 1982 he was unable to get a job. He had done some writing when at school, and thought perhaps he might get into journalism or perhaps comedy scriptwriting; however, it took some time before he finally had some items accepted by Radio 4's *Week Ending* – not a programme he particularly enjoyed, but which did give him an entry into writing.

He then decided to try writing an act and performing on the expanding comedy circuit. He remembers: 'At that time there weren't a lot of new people; there was a bit of a vacuum – the Comic Strip by that time were no longer performing, Jim Barclay was moving more into acting, Tony Allen was taking a bit of a back seat for a while, Andy de la Tour and Pauline Melville had gone off into acting. There was quite a lot of work to be had, because you could get an open spot within a week, and a booking within about a month – whereas now it takes about three months to get an open spot. The Comedy Store was closed at the time – which I was quite thankful for, because if I'd gone on there and had a rough night it might have severely dented my confidence.'

He was lucky in being able to go to the Edinburgh fringe in 1984 with a lunchtime revue, where he did some sketches and some stand-up. His first set round the circuit was a *Blue Peter* spoof about making fall-out shelters for teddy-bears; but although it was a good – and rather black – sketch, he became tired of it after a few months and moved into simply talking as himself.

He talks in a very dry manner, drawing much of his material from observation of reality, slightly exaggerated; despite the apparent laid-back approach, the material is very carefully crafted: 'I'm very guilty of that, in a sense, because I think it would be good to be a bit more loose with it. I'm quite obsessive about language, about finding the exact wording – I like quaint expressions and English words – like "flummoxed" – and once I've got the precise phraseology, because I've got a parrot memory for words it tends to come out verbatim.'

The feeling that material ought to be partly improvised is a common one on the circuit – Tony Allen seems to have been partially responsible for starting it – and has led to a lot of rubbish being performed as well as some genuine flashes of brilliance. Hardy's careful choice of language suits his material well, and though he has experimented with improvisation it is the finely crafted approach which has earned him his considerable reputation. Here he remembers his schooldays in the Surrey village:

> I went to Mychett County Primary School, and our bully was called Guido, because his mother was Italian – that's not racist, it's true. Guido was fat, weak, stupid and cowardly, but we accepted him as our bully. By virtue of his being extremely violent, I suppose. If you've ever wondered why slugs have no legs, it's because they were pulled off by Guido's ancestors. Another feature of my school was its proximity to the Broadmoor Hospital for the Criminally Insane – this is true, in Camberley, there – and the thing about the Broadmoor Hospital was the siren, which was tested on Monday mornings at ten o'clock – and local people familiarized themselves with the sound of the siren, because we knew, if we heard it at any other time than ten o'clock Monday morning when it was tested, it meant there'd

211

been an escape – somebody, possibly a dangerous psychotic, was on the loose, and the local people and the police would be on their guard. So, at ten o'clock every Monday morning, five hundred dangerous psychotics would escape, and not be rounded up until Thursday afternoon – by which time they'd have successfully infiltrated the local Rotary Club, and the local battalion of the Territorial Army. I should explain, if anyone's unfamiliar with the Territorials, they're a group of paramilitary insurance salesmen. They're called Territorial because, like dogs, they mark out their territory by urinating everywhere they go. Luckily the escapees kept away from my school, because they were frightened of Guido as well. I think the reason we allowed ourselves to be dominated by a bully of Guido's calibre is that all the young people of my generation, in the early sixties, had so much less confidence than today's young people.

I find myself today as an adult wanting to be stern and disciplinarian with young children – I want to say things like, 'I'll have none of your lip' ... 'You watch your step, young feller-me-lad, or I'll fetch you a clip round the ear' ... '*I can hear you in the staff room*'.... And the kids say, 'Do you want a lolly-stick up your bum?' I think it's video. I think video has spoiled our young people. In my day, we *read*. We had books – we had creative, imaginative children's books – like *War and Killing for Boys* ... *A Hundred Favourite Wars* ... *Paddington Invades Vietnam* ... and we learned things. Like the fact that you must never ask a Gurkha to show you his sword – because according to custom, once a Gurkha has withdrawn his sword from its sheath, he must then draw blood, before he can return it to its sheath. Well, bear it in mind.... We also learned that you must never say anything to a paratrooper –

because once you've done that, according to custom, he must then hit you over the head with a nailed piece of wood. I learned that on Aldershot High Street, actually. I suppose I probably asked for it – cocky young four-year-old, I was. . . .

Though they do not perform together on the cabaret circuit, Kit Hollerbach and Jeremy Hardy have appeared on Radio 4 in two series of their situation comedy, co-written with Paul B. Davies – *Unnatural Acts*. The first series of six started on 28 March 1987, and took as its starting point the home-life of Mr and Mrs Hardy – Kit Hollerbach running the kitchen is a bit like a sitcom in real life (unless it's put on for visiting interviewers) – and goes on from there into plots which, although deliberately structured like a 1950s radio sitcom, manage to get in a few sharp digs. Kit Hollerbach: 'We nailed the concept of royalty, without naming names – Jeremy found out he was the rightful king, but because he was married to an American he had to abdicate – his speech was pretty much verbatim Edward VIII – on *Video Box* . . . and we targeted the National Health – I was in hospital, and they were selling it off to the Americans.'

They were lucky with their BBC producer, David Tyler; Kit Hollerbach: 'You work on projects, and it's a collective effort – if you've got a few wankers in there you're at their mercy, you've got to do whatever they ask, and they could be demented – a lot of producers are, they haven't got a clue about comedy . . . it's true in Los Angeles, and it's true here. . . . With *Unnatural Acts* David Tyler was very good – he took a back seat – a lot of producers would want to get involved, but if you have a good team of writers the best thing is to stay away from them and just produce the show.'

The show, which stars Paul B. Davies and Caroline Leddy as well as the Hardys, is entertaining and comes over well despite being a first effort in the field. It was followed by a second series of six beginning on 19 March 1988 (and a stage version, *At Home With The Hardys*, at the Hackney Empire in April 1988). The series is an interesting example of performers from the cabaret circuit taking over the conventions of mainstream comedy and gently subverting it to their own ends.

The Hackney Empire; the circuit and the
audiences; Brown Blues; Jenny Lecoat;
Simon Fanshawe; Gerry Sadowitz;
Victoria Wood; Ben Elton

16

Through the period while the cabaret circuit was developing, there
was a parallel strain building up – a development from Roland
Muldoon's political theatre company, CAST, which had been in the
forefront of political theatre in the 1970s. By the time the Comedy
Store had opened, CAST was finding it increasingly difficult to
recruit suitable people.

Roland Muldoon comments: 'The actors coming in were either
professional – who didn't like the notion of improvisation – or the
enthusiast or activist who joins but after two years can't take the
strain, because they're not professionals. We thought the answer
would be in finding a strain of people who played out to the audience,
and to set up "New Variety", touring London in the same way that
CAST had toured Britain. What the Comedy Store had done was to
win the battle about whether there was going to be sexist or racist
comedy, whether just anybody was going to come in – and they won
that battle, to their great credit, that humour was to be open and
you weren't to expect the old clichés ... except that they were the
next generation into television, and we as a theatre company had
always said we can't be absorbed if theatre's going to be the last
place of freedom of expression. So we argued that what was not
needed was five male stand-up comics being naughty in Soho *à la*
America, but that the tradition in Britain would be back to variety.
This coincided with our need to recruit people who could play out
to the audience and the idea of setting up in London a circuit with
specific interest in promoting entertaining performers as opposed to
entertaining comedians – so we would take on jugglers, acting groups,
comedy – anything. So there was a deliberate attempt by us *not* to
be the Comedy Store.'

New Variety ran only a handful of gigs compared with the main
cabaret circuit, although there were strong links between the two,
and many performers from the circuit appeared for New Variety. At
the end of 1986 they were lucky enough to be able to obtain the
Hackney Empire – the last of the old variety theatres left in Greater
London. It had been run since the 1960s – at a loss – by Mecca
Bingo, who fortunately had been too financially restrained to make

any serious alterations; so that the theatre was substantially in its original state apart from the rear of the stalls having been raised to form a level area with tables and a bar.

New Variety opened at the Hackney Empire on 9 December 1986, slowly building up the theatre as a recognized venue. They put on a wide range of shows, including Ken Dodd, Lenny Henry, feminist evenings, shows by alternative comedians. In June 1987 Tony Allen, who had gone into management with the excellent mime and comedian Roy Hutchins to form Crystal Productions, put on an evening to showcase his artists – including comedy band The Howlers, singer Sharon Landau, musical duo The Frugivores, and others including Hutchins and Allen themselves.

The Hackney Empire makes a splendid venue for variety – which is exactly what it was designed for – and just to stand on the stage when the theatre is empty and the house lights up demonstrates the genius of its architect; the entire audience seems within easy reach, despite the sheer size of the place. Roland Muldoon: 'Not all the performers know how to play off the big stage; but then others really shine on that stage – John Hegley, Otis Canneloni – they do better here than in pubs; and Jenny Lecoat did extremely well here.'

Muldoon has high hopes for the future of the theatre: 'It could quite easily become the comics' venue – Ben Elton or Lenny Henry can make enough money here because it's a one-thousand-seater – there isn't another theatre as good or as available.... You do have to come to Hackney, but you can park, and the seats can be cheaper than in the West End. There's nowhere in the West End the comics can play, except the Dominion and the Hammersmith Odeon, and they're rather big venues.'

The theatre is under the control of the Hackney Empire Preservation Trust, effectively run by New Variety, and was in the process of being bought from Mecca; however, the insistence of English Heritage, the government department in charge of listed buildings, that the original roof domes – removed by Mecca in the 1970s – must be replaced by Mecca forced the price of the sale up to £150,000. The Preservation Trust became a charity, borrowing some of the extra £50,000 caused by the revision, and working to raise the rest by May 1989. The Trust also hopes eventually to raise a further three million pounds for a complete refurbishment.

One major financial success for the Empire was a special show on 30 April 1988, transmitted live by satellite to a huge audience by the American cable TV company, Home Box Office, and starring many of the established names in the comedy circuit.

Over 1987 and 1988 the cabaret circuit had settled to something much more predictable; although some venues still came and went there was a much more stable list of gigs – now occupying nearly two pages of small print in *Time Out* (and in February 1988 even achieving a partial listing in the newly revamped *Guardian* newspaper – a sign of respectability?).

The performers also stabilized – there were by now a rather larger number than in earlier days, but fewer new people were coming up (partly because of the difficulties of breaking in: open spots were besieged by hopefuls, but each could only accommodate one a week). While there were many good performers, inevitably there were also many mediocre ones; and while there were always some willing to experiment, the whole scene seemed to be settling down into a predictable form of entertainment – as John Hegley says, the product at the end of the process.

One experiment which was started at the Comedy Store in late 1986 by Kit Hollerbach, an improvisational workshop, led on to regular Sunday night improvised performances. The original concept arose out of the difficulty of trying more outlandish ideas in a stand-up set. Kit Hollerbach: 'If people are paying you can't just go, "Like, I'm going to try this really different thing – I'm going to be a carrot for an hour . . ." You can't do that. . . . It was the same in the States, when things were first starting in what you guys call alternative comedy, it was much more adventurous. There was a lot less at stake – there was no TV dangling like a carrot, people did it just because they liked it, and it was entertaining to the audience – so a lot of what was done was much more risky. Sadly, TV and money and stuff – at the end of the day I'd love to have all that, but it's when they get their claws into it . . . you go to Los Angeles, where every single stand-up comic sounds exactly like the last one.'

She started the improvisation workshop to teach the people who later made up the Comedy Store Players – doing the improvised Sunday night show – and also to teach new people the techniques of comedy: 'A lot of recent comics have come out of the workshop – and a handful of women . . . which is wonderful, because it wouldn't kill anybody to have a few more women stand-ups.'

The workshops were on Saturday afternoons, and in the end proved not to be an economic proposition for the Comedy Store. Don Ward: 'There wasn't sufficient turnout, and I had problems getting staff in – you'd get twenty kids come in, at £2 entry, and there was nothing much coming out of it. . . . I suggested putting it in a largish room above a pub – we had to have every light in the place on, that's ten kilowatts. The best thing is if people get up and perform in front of an audience – we do "open mike" for people trying out new material on Fridays, and on Saturdays there's an open spot – throw it open to the audience at the end of the evening. We do get the odd one up . . . and we've had people buy a ticket and kid us – Emo Philips and Charles Fleischer [both established on the American comedy circuit] asked to do a bit, and went a storm.'

The Sunday night shows have gained a fairly regular following. Kit Hollerbach herself dropped out for lack of time after a year or so, but others have carried on, including Josie Lawrence, Paul Merton and Neil Mullarkey. The routines are based on the sort of 'actors' games' taught in drama schools, but are genuinely improvised within the given framework – which can include asking the audience for a locale and a closing line, or for an object to base songs in various styles on. Much of the humour is funny largely because of the 'buzz' of being improvised on the spot, but there is a good deal of real wit brought into play.

The audience for these shows is genial and responsive; but this is not always true of other events. The late shows at the Comedy Store are notorious for audiences which can be very rowdy and occasionally hostile; and there has been a general change in the type of person coming to events. In the early days many gigs would attract almost entirely young, radical left, often unemployed people who would be sympathetic to – and indeed expect – a left-wing viewpoint in the acts. This is on the whole no longer true; particularly at the more expensive venues, the audiences can certainly afford £5 admission plus an evening's serious drinking, and are just as likely to be right-wing – if they actually have any political views at all.

Most performers still tend to the left side of the fence, although few would claim to be making specifically left-wing political points – which Roland Muldoon views with a certain irony: 'One of them said to me, "We're the most Thatcherite of all people, because we're self-employed – if we work we get paid, if we don't work we don't get paid." And yet they're identifying with trade unions, who are not like that at all. They're in love with the notion of the mass, and the people in opposition. They all did everything they possibly could to support the miners' strike – it was noticeable if artists didn't. That miners' strike was the most political thing that has happened in Britain for years, and for a whole generation of acts to identify with a clear class struggle must mean something – whatever they say in their dressing-rooms about "If people want to construe this or that from what I'm saying. . . ." In the end they don't want to get so involved with politics that they lose their comedy, but they all are associated with a critique of society as it stands.'

But increasingly the audiences are not interested in politics. Jongleurs, as the most trendy place on the circuit, naturally attracts the most comments from the performers, many of whom find it difficult going. Nick Revell: 'The main thing I like is that it's so much bigger than anywhere else on the circuit that it's a good place to play to get the technique of playing big places; but it's interesting how that place has changed since Battersea's changed – in terms of yupp-ification – it's a long night there, and the order of acts is very important in terms of their concentration level. You always feel that even if you're doing well there's a fickle strain – you could lose them the next second – which is not true at the Comedy Store. If you're really going well there, then you've got them, unless you blow it . . . whereas at Jongleurs, it doesn't happen that much, but you always feel there is a chance they will just switch off.'

Some performers object to the politics of the Jongleurs audience, an attitude Maria Kempinska has little time for: 'The circuit did have the attitude of "let's convert the working class". I object to that premise – my parents were working-class, and what does that mean? Convert them to what? And at the end of the day, the people who go to fringe theatres are not working-class; if you've been working in a factory the last place you want to go is the top of a grotty pub – you want to go somewhere that's a bit more glitzy where you can forget about the politics of working in a factory. Some performers say, "My material is too left for a yuppie audience" – I find that irresponsible, that somebody who is out to change people's attitudes won't perform at our venue – if they feel like that they should find a way to convert these people. There's only two or three people who won't play here . . . but it does happen.'

Not all the problems are political. Jeremy Hardy has reservations about the Jongleurification of some parts of the circuit: 'I think in a sense there is an imbalance on the circuit because there are so many street entertainers, people who don't require a great deal of listening or thought – that makes it harder for the stand-ups. If you're on a bill with music, acrobats, jugglers, impressionists – if the audience has suddenly got to sit and listen to one person for twenty minutes, it can be like an eternity for them.'

Of course, pre-war variety consisted of a mixture of acts, quite successfully; but the audience is very different in the present-day circuit. Drunkenness has already been mentioned; there is also the problem of destructive heckling. The late-night shows at the Comedy Store provide the most spectacular examples of this; Jeremy Hardy: 'Sometimes there's only a small destructive element in the audience, but there are people who go determined to wreck what is happening – which doesn't happen anywhere else. The Tunnel isn't like that –

there's an element sometimes at the Tunnel that wants to get people off, but most people actually want to enjoy themselves. Though you have to appreciate that the open spots are Christians and lions, that's the whole point of that. But I have never had a large contingent at the Tunnel being hostile to me; whereas at the Comedy Store there can be a large group of people that just want you off the stage, and the rest of the audience doesn't really care either way. At the Tunnel people want the hecklers to be beaten, at the Comedy Store they're quite happy for the hecklers to win.'

There are various techniques for dealing with hecklers – well-worn put-downs include, 'I remember when I had *my* first drink' or 'Sit back in your chair, I'll get someone to plug it in later'; sometimes a heckle can inspire a sharp return line – Kit Hollerbach, faced with heckling from both sides, commented: 'What is this, stereo arseholes?' The worst heckling tends to be of women by men, largely consisting of witticisms such as 'Show us your tits'; one man who asked Kit Hollerbach 'Are you a lesbian?' got the response 'Are you the alternative?'

Heckling beyond a certain level makes it difficult for any comic to give of his best; but when it has the extra unpleasantness of sexual aggressiveness often directed at women it adds an unwelcome element of nervous strain to the already tense business of performing. Helen Lederer comments about the Comedy Store: 'A lot of the audiences who come in at midnight have rather mixed motives – and it's late licensing ... if I'm not going down well, plus I'm doing it badly, plus I'm a woman – it's my being a woman is the major thing they don't like ... that audience wants to attack you and they are really disappointed if they succeed. It's a very strange dynamic, and it's very tiring.'

Kit Hollerbach has experienced a lot of destructive sexist heckling at various venues, and has lost all sympathy with it: 'Even before you get on stage you're not accepted in a neutral position. These things never used to bother me, but year after year of this kind of stuff, you say, this isn't fair – why should I go on stage and have to dig myself out of a ditch? Why is it socially acceptable in Britain for an audience to go to a woman, "Show us your tits", and not to say to a black man, "Hey, nigger" – to me, it's the same goddamn thing. I don't think it's acceptable. They have a much tighter attitude towards hecklers in the States – if somebody's calling you a fucking asshole twice they're thrown out – I don't know where British audiences get off thinking this is actually helpful. A lot of comics' styles don't lend themselves to that – and shouldn't. I'm not saying you shouldn't have heckling at all, some comics do very well with

it – but it's important to accept that there are many different styles.'

Don Ward has had to address the problem of the late-night shows by hiring a couple of bouncers to keep an eye on potential trouble-makers. He explains: 'People are out to enjoy themselves; we don't restrict the comics as to what they do – except racist and sexist stuff, we don't want to hear that. We gave the audience a little opportunity to say their piece, because you can get some very good banter; but time moves on, and football supporters have become ruthless bloody hooligans – you get some of those on a Saturday night, wandering up here and want to come in – you have to stop that at source, so one of us goes along the queue at nights, susses out who's going to be a problem, and then refuses them admission. And if someone's had too much to drink, we refuse admission. Otherwise the mob just takes the place over. So we stamp on stupidity.'

Another reason for heckling can be an audience's over-familiarity with the material – Kit Hollerbach responded to people heckling her because they'd heard the set before by saying, 'What is this, comedy police? Pull over?'; but with the same performers going round the same relatively small circuit repetition can be a problem. It is simply not possible for a comedian to write a completely new twenty-minute act of any quality every few weeks.

Lee Cornes: 'It's a great myth that the old comedians changed over their material – it's just impossible to do, unless you've got a whole bank of writers behind you. Without TV, these guys were doing ten minutes of material for thirty years. Television is the great eater of material – this is why mainstream comedians are often appalling on TV – they're not going to blow, for a few hundred quid, what will clearly make them far more money doing the clubs. The thing about TV is to be seen on it, not to do well.'

The solution most performers have found is to re-work the act a bit at a time – altering perhaps five minutes a month – so that anyone in the audience who has seen them before will at least get some new material – and perhaps will enjoy hearing some of the old again. The Comedy Store gets a large turnover of audience, but Jongleurs and the Tunnel have a regular contingent, and this can present problems – it is unwise for anyone to play two gigs at the Tunnel closer than several months apart. Most other places seem to get a mixture of old and new audience, and comedians who cannot create new material, even gradually, are bound to disappear from the circuit eventually.

The increasing number of gigs outside London does help to alleviate the problem, and many performers are able to get away from the rather enclosed London circuit. In addition to running the Tunnel, Malcolm Hardee has been attempting to get a small provincial circuit going, starting a regular gig in Bracknell and various one-offs; he lists some of the other venues: 'There's one in Nottingham called Spots, one in Blackburn called Laughing Gas – started by Phil Cool – someone's trying to start a five-day circuit round Scotland; Devon seems to be popular from the old hippy days; I've got one going in Totnes, of all places. . . . Certain towns for some reason have a high population of twenty- to thirty-year-olds, and others don't – I don't know why that is. Provincial audiences are dead easy – the only difference is they might get upset by what they see as the outrageousness.'

As time goes on venues come and go, just as in the London circuit's earlier days; but with *Saturday Live* and other publicity about the Comedy Store and the alternative circuit, there is an increasingly wide knowledge of this sort of humour in the country as a whole. The fringe of the Edinburgh Festival has of course long provided a chance for alternative comedians; and in 1987 it seemed that most of the circuit had gone there – London was almost denuded of them for most of August that year.

Recognition for cabaret has been given in the form of the Perrier Award for the best performer at Edinburgh – £1,500 plus a booking at London's Donmar Warehouse theatre for the winner, with booking at the Donmar for the runners-up as well; in 1987 the winner was *Brown Blues*, consisting of the blues-based singers Barb Jungr and Michael Parker in the first half, and Arnold Brown in the second – ending with the unusual spectacle of Brown sort-of singing some of his material to their accompaniment.

Brown's style has remained very much what it was at the beginning, although he has relaxed into it – prowling the stage with the microphone, fixing the audience with a genial and glinting Scots eye, and developing his own bland of quiet lunacy. Here are some samples of his later material:

> When I was seven at school, one of my classmates told me that all Jewish people were wealthy. Nice one. You know, I remember that day even now – running home excitedly to break the news to my mother and father. We spent that weekend taking up the floorboards.
>
> As there's only a few of us here tonight, I'll let you into a secret . . . it's a bit difficult for a masculine comedian to talk about this . . . I cannot achieve an erection under a Conservative administration. But don't feel any sympathy for me – I was particularly active under the Wilson government. And so was Wilson. Actually, sex is not a problem with me, it only starts getting complicated when other people get involved. This is true: I used to be an accountant, and if you're an accountant, it does flavour your sex-life adversely, it makes it a little bland. Actually, half of the accountants I know talk about

the strength of the pound during foreplay. And the other half think that talking about the strength of the pound *is* foreplay. I'm probably being a bit technical here, but in these matters I favour the monetarist position – that's the one with the bank manager on top.

Topical matters get his attention in a suitably off-beat way. Commenting on the discreditable affair in which Tory politician Jeffrey Archer was accused of paying a prostitute – who was allegedly blackmailing him – £2,000 to leave the country, Brown claimed that before the 1987 election he had overheard Margaret Thatcher offering Jeffrey Archer £2,000 to leave the country. And here he comments on the proposed Zircon spy satellite (an attempted TV exposé of the way that plans for financing this had been concealed from Parliament had recently got BBC Scotland done over by the Special Branch):

> The Zircon spy satellite ... it's a bit frightening isn't it? ... Zir-con ... no wonder the Russians are worried. Zir-con ... I suggest, in the interests of easing international tension, the name should be changed to something more harmless-sounding ... something like ... "Keith". I mean, the Russians wouldn't mind being watched by, er ... Keith. (*looks upward*) Ach, it's only Keith. What does *he* know?

The other performers at Edinburgh all had to solve the usual solo performer's problem of filling a show of reasonable length. Nick Revell had expanded his material effectively to around an hour; on his return to London he appeared at the Donmar theatre, teamed with another performer who had been to Edinburgh, character-comedian John Sparkes, so that each could do half the show. Sparkes' act was divided into several characterizations – Frank Hovis, the determinedly drunk northern club compère, and Siadwel, the dim Welshman, being the most effective.

Helen Lederer took a show which she had already performed at the King's Head earlier in the summer. The first half was filled by 'Raw Sex' (Simon Brint and Roland Rivron as a marvellously tatty music duo, with an act expanded from their earlier fill-ins when touring with Mayall and French and Saunders); Lederer did fifty minutes in the second half, alternating monologues – in a style which built on and refined her earlier work – with character pieces. This is a standard device for breaking up what would otherwise be a solid monologue, and the character pieces were well crafted; the problem of integrating them always remains, and there was a tendency for the personal monologue simply to lurch into the character piece; but the whole show was enjoyable and effective.

Helen Lederer used some music to break up her act, finishing

with a spectacular number in the style of an American TV personality show. The use of music is, again, a standard technique to break up a monologue. Jenny Lecoat had previously used songs to her own guitar accompaniment; at Edinburgh in 1987 she teamed with The Diamantes to make music the major part of the act.

She had broadened her approach from her earlier days when she took a strong anti-men stance. She comments: 'I used to get accused of picking a very easy target, and that was quite true. In my own defence, I'd say that that really hadn't been done at that stage, and I was probably the first person who really did it successfully and got laughs from it. It would be appalling to do it now, and it makes me cringe when I see women getting up five or six years later and still doing that kind of material – because it is too easy, and it's very hypocritical, if you're a heterosexual and you have male friends, to just go up and slag men off generally. I would say I'm far more pleasant on stage now than I was then – when I first started it was, "This is happening and I'm going to tell you about it"; whereas now it's, "Do you have this experience?" – it's a different attitude to the way I relate to the audience.'

For the women in her audience, an aspect of her act is reassurance; not the 'everything's all right really' reassurance of mainstream situation comedy, but, as she says: 'reassuring women that experiences they may have had in a certain area are common ones – jokes that make them think, "Yes, I do that." That's not cosy reassurance, that's shared experience reassurance.'

In her 1986 Edinburgh show she covered subjects such as depression, being overweight, sanitary towels and the problems they cause, and the difficulties women have when nature calls in natural surroundings ('piss in the country – nettles up the bum'). The 1987 Edinburgh show consisted largely of songs, with herself on guitar and the Diamantes supporting her on guitar and piano. This song takes a gentler but still pointed look at women's attitudes:

> I rang the DHSS this morning
> I've been waiting on eight weeks pay;
> They said, 'We're sorry but we've lost your file
> You're gonna have to start again.'
> I felt my heart a-pumping and my temper rising
> I said: (*spoken*) 'Oh, don't worry about it, it's probably my fault, I'll
>   come in next week ...'
>
> Bottle it up ... Bottle it up ...
> Cultivate a tumour ... Bottle it up ...
> For Christ's sake never say what you mean
> Bottle it up.

I walked into the kitchen
The pots were piled high
It wasn't my turn to wash them
It wasn't even my turn to dry;
My flat-mate walked in, I said, 'Now look –
(*spoken*) I'm sorry about the mess, I'll have it cleaned up in just a
    minute . . .'

> Bottle it up . . . Bottle it up . . .
> Grow that ulcer . . . Bottle it up . . .
> For Christ's sake never say what you mean
> Bottle it, bottle it, bottle it up.

Jenny Lecoat

227

Jenny Lecoat's co-star in *Three Of A Different Kind*, Simon Fanshawe, had also broadened his approach as he gained experience. The 'radical gay' label tended to stick to him, but a major turning point came when he was touring Canada in 1986. He was working one evening in a club in Hamilton, which was known for having a difficult audience, and his usual gay material was not going over well. He remembers: 'I was doing about three minutes about being gay, just coming straight out with it; and somebody shouted, "Boring". I completely flipped – I hurled a glass at the floor, threw the microphone down, and stormed off stage. It gashed some woman's hand ... not very badly, and the whole incident was smoothed over; but I went through three days of absolute panic ... and a nice man called Howard Lapidis said, "It's no good saying you don't know what to do – you've *got* to know what to do. If you're going to do this sort of material, you're just going to have to find a way of writing your way out of this situation." It was a traumatic situation, but it made me face up to it. So, I wrote fifteen minutes of material, which I used for a year, which was about America and Canada – soft, easy material. Then I'd go into the gay stuff after about fifteen minutes. Then I found an absolutely perfect line to get into it; I used to do a routine about personal freedom in the States, which involved a Supreme Court decision about anal and oral sex. The tag to that is saying, "Being gay, that really pissed me off". One night I saw this person reacting, and I said, "Did I just say I was gay, did I just mention that?" – and they nodded – and I said, "I thought so, because all I could hear was the sound of arses tightening across the floor." This got an enormous laugh – and I suddenly understood this thing of setting up a tension and releasing it – you've got to allow the audience the space to cope as well as yourself.'

By this approach he has been able to allow the audience to accept his homosexuality, and not feel threatened by it; an attitude that they might perhaps keep with them when they leave the gig.

In his 1987 Edinburgh show (which subsequently played at the Donmar), he included a lot of material about America ('Americans think things that are seventy-five years old are really valuable ... and should be elected'), some remarks on Mrs Thatcher's re-election to a third term ('Did you vote Tory? Did you see a film on lemmings and think, oh, we'll do that?'), and some inter-relation with the audience – which usually involved gentle insults delivered with enough charm to be inoffensive.

Once again he tackled the subject which had increasingly been obsessing everybody since earlier in the year – AIDS. The government's campaign about it had led to a spate of condom jokes –

in the mainstream of comedy as well; indeed, the first mainstream
routine about AIDS on television was performed by Jasper Carrott
and written by Fanshawe. Here, in his own routine, Fanshawe talks
about its impact on him as regards dating:

> I'm finding it difficult at the moment, with AIDS and everything –
> that's changed my lifestyle a lot. I used to go out every night, and
> try and get laid, and fail – and I'd call that sexual frustration. Now
> I go out every night and try and get laid, and fail, but I can call it
> a 'healthy lifestyle'. Funny Government leaflet about sex though –
> there was an amusing aspect to that in the sense that they'd spent
> about six years trying to keep sex education out of schools – and
> then we force them to put twenty-three million leaflets through
> everybody's letterbox telling them how to give a blow-job. It was
> something the pensioners liked, too ... no, it was something they
> could do without their teeth. But, you know, a Government leaflet
> about sex? I'm not really sure that when I'm in bed with the person
> I most love in the world, I actually want to follow instructions issued
> to me by an employee of the Department of Health and Social
> Security. I mean, what do you do when you have an orgasm – shout
> out your National Insurance number? Oh ... WV/12/1451/A ...' –
> or, if you're a woman, 'WV/12/1451/A ... WV/12/1451/A ...
> WV/12/1451/A ... WV ...' – there's a group of men looking very
> confused down there. Never been there when that happened? Nearest
> they got was, 'Oh, WV ... (snore)'

The broadening of approach, which a number of performers have
found enables them to relate better to their audiences, is rejected by
some. The most spectacular example of a refusal to compromise
could also be seen at Edinburgh in 1987, in the person of a relatively
new entrant to the cabaret circuit: Gerry Sadowitz. Starting about
two years earlier, he had established himself as a favourite at the
Comedy Store in particular. His ranting, raucous and extremely foul-
mouthed style carried something of the impact of Alexei Sayle in his
early days, before audiences had switched on to that sort of comedy;
but whereas Sayle, even in his more outlandish moments, always
had a responsible left-wing viewpoint somewhere in the background,
Sadowitz is fired by a largely negative viewpoint.

> I fucking hate everything, right – the only reason I haven't slagged
> off the socialist party so far is that there isn't one. But I tell you, if
> there was one, I fucking would. I think Neil Kinnock's got a certain
> amount of street credibility, you know – from a certain angle he
> looks like a fucking Belisha beacon. Silly bastard. Ken Livingstone,
> the thinking man's Gerald Kaufman ... what a total prick. He
> thinks all the things that we think, only he gets paid eighteen fucking
> thousand quid a year to say them. I'd love to get Ken Livingstone
> into a pub and say, 'OK Ken, there's the bitter, there's the lager,

half an hour for lunch, *get to fucking work*!' What I actually believe, deep down, I suppose, is that life is a piece of shit. Absolutely convinced of it – life is fucking shite. Doesn't matter what *I* say – life is fucking shite. I'll say whatever the fuck I want, sometimes even for spite – for example: Nelson Mandela – what a cunt! Terry Waite – fucking bastard – I don't know, you lend some people a fiver, you never see them again. I'm the sort of person, if you lent me a fiver and never saw me again, it would be worth it.

His one-man show at Edinburgh was a considerable achievement for someone relatively new to the scene; in with the swearing and the deliberate bad taste there were flashes of brilliance; but only time will show whether Sadowitz can develop as a comedian or whether he will burn himself out. At least he has the courage to attempt to stretch the medium – even if it is in a direction that many people would not care to follow.

There is certainly no likelihood of his being acceptable to a wider audience; but it is interesting that a number of performers have managed to appeal to a quite different audience without compromising their style. Jeremy Hardy, in particular – who also appeared in Edinburgh in 1987 and, the following year, won the Perrier Award against stiff competition – is one who has been booked to perform to audiences of, for example, advertising men at conferences, through a bookings system set up by John Davy as an offshoot of Jongleurs.

John Davy comments: 'We've got companies like Saatchi and Saatchi who want entertainment – they want something inventive; because Jongleurs Promotions exists, they feel safe enough to come to us to supply them. They won't scrabble around amongst the cabaret circuit – they might come up against people who are doing open spots, and aren't reliable – but if it's good enough for Jongleurs, it's good enough for them. When people perform at Jongleurs it opens up all sorts of other avenues – and the money is much better.'

Jeremy Hardy is just one performer who can make biting remarks against the type of people in these audiences, and get them to laugh at themselves. Whether he can really cause them to think about things is another matter. John Davy: 'If someone points something out to you in a particular pertinent and intelligent way, it's going to make an effect. The people looking at Jeremy are looking at him as their intellectual equal. If they've got someone standing up and just ranting at them, that's dismissible.'

This sort of entertainment at private functions is something Victoria Wood has already been doing for some time: 'I did one for some Unit Trust managers – four hundred men and ten women …

And one for British Airways – they'd had a one-day conference, and at the end of it, instead of going home – which they must have been dying to do – they had me, in a marquee, with the sun blazing down at half-past-five in the afternoon.'

She finds that this is the only sort of performance where she is aware of being a woman, as opposed to just a comic: 'It's only at these business conferences, which are predominantly male – and a particular sort of man ... it's middle-fifties top management. You really are hitting your head against a brick wall because they've just not heard of a lot of the things you're talking about – like sex. If you make a joke about British Airways they absolutely die laughing. If you say the word "privatization" they think you're the funniest thing on God's earth. If you say "tampon" it would be little blank faces all round.'

It is in the theatres that she can work to her best advantage, to a sympathetic and informed audience. In October 1987 she finished a tour by playing a season at the London Palladium – a very successful show, which was well appreciated by the audiences (who seemed to be an equal mixture of those who had come because it was her and those who had come because it was the Palladium). Commenting, 'This is the theatre where Sooty was heckled', she did about two hours including interval, mixing songs and patter. She ended the first half with a sad song – something she had also done in *Lucky Bag* – and handled the difficult problem of having to come on a second time by doing a strong character monologue. The theatre itself, though a sympathetic venue, long famous as a variety theatre, is very large, and her command of the material and the audience demonstrated the depth of her experience gained over more than a decade of performing.

Although he is not really part of the comedy covered in this book, it is worth mentioning an even more stunning display of sheer technique demonstrated by Billy Connolly at the Royal Albert Hall in July 1987; the venue is alarmingly huge (uncomfortably large even for orchestral concerts, never mind stand-up), but – assisted by some extremely professional sound reinforcement and a large projection TV screen which showed his face in detail for those so far away they could barely even see him – Connolly held a mainstream audience spellbound for over two hours of solid speech. He rambled in an apparently artless fashion, covering some of the subjects dear to the hearts of alternative comedians (including the perfect excuse for being caught wanking – tarantula up the trousers), hiding his vast technical experience behind his natural communication with the audience.

However, for endurance the palm must surely go to Ben Elton – a workaholic if ever there was one. Following his last tour with Rik Mayall in 1986, Elton did a six-day run in Dublin starting on September 29, followed by a national tour, taking in twenty-seven large venues, from 14 November to 11 December. The following year, 1987, he toured again – with all new material (no mean feat in itself) – from 5 November to 12 December, again taking in twenty-seven venues and ending with a five-night sell-out at the Hammersmith Odeon – a record for a stand-up comic there. His ability to write a complete new act at about yearly intervals must also be some kind of record, and although his television appearances in *Saturday Live* helped to create his large following, they are inevitably watered down compared with what he is like on a live tour.

What is most valuable in all this is that, whether it is Connolly at the Royal Albert Hall, Ben Elton at the Hammersmith Odeon or a new untried comic in the Chuckle Club, there is a firmly established tradition of live comedy which fills the gap left in the 1960s and 1970s by the death of the old-fashioned variety circuit. Even though live performers can never reach the same numbers as those on television, nor work in glamorous surroundings (for the most part), live comedy – and in particular, subversive live comedy – is a vital part of Britain's heritage, and one can only hope that its regeneration in the decade following the opening of the Comedy Store will prove to be a permanent and expanding facet of popular entertainment.

Ben Elton

17

Comic Relief; Just For Laughs;
Various TV shows; Lenny Henry;
Filthy Rich and Catflap;
Saturday Live; French and Saunders

If one of the achievements of the alternative comedians is the resurgence of live comedy, another is their infiltration of television. For the Young Ones and the Comic Strip it happened quite quickly; for the later generation it has been a slower and more difficult business, but even so they are making their mark.

An interesting aspect of their work, and one in which they worked with an older generation of comics, is the charity shows such as *Comic Relief*, an offshoot of Bob Geldof's 'Band-Aid' fund-raising work for Africa. The tradition of late-night charity theatre shows was started by the Monty Python/Goodies generation of comics in 1976, with the first of the shows in aid of Amnesty International; the first *Comic Relief* gig took place in April 1986 and was televised on 25 April on BBC1. French and Saunders – who had by then had their successful first series in *Girls On Top* – appeared in a sketch; Nigel Planer resurrected Neil to introduce Ben Elton; Lenny Henry, Rowan Atkinson, Ronnie Corbett and Billy Connolly represented the more established stream of comedy; and the Young Ones performed 'Living Doll' with the aid of the real Cliff Richard (who commented, 'I realize that tonight it's *me* that's the alternative').

French and Saunders and Victoria Wood were among those who appeared in *Comedians Do It On Stage*, a stage show – transmitted on Channel Four on 23 December 1986 – in aid of the Oncology Fund (which assists in the training of cancer specialists). Then on 5 February 1988 BBC1 mounted *A Night of Comic Relief*, running for well over six hours; it was hosted by Lenny Henry and Griff Rhys Jones, with help from Jonathan Ross, and included most of comedy show business – mainstream and alternative. Archive material (including a sketch in which a tall young man complained about a dead parrot) was mixed with live contributions from many performers, including Victoria Wood, Ben Elton, French and Saunders, and Phil Cool. The exercise raised over thirteen and a half million pounds.

Less spectacularly, there have been many gigs on the cabaret circuit in aid of various charities; Jongleurs has raised large amounts of money by mounting special shows, and there have been a number of charity shows at the Hackney Empire (including one to save the Hackney Empire).

Apart from these worthy occasions, the mainstream of television has tended to ignore the cabaret circuit; the days when TV producers would go to the Comedy Store and the Comic Strip to look for new talent are over, and it is much more difficult for newer performers to break in. Brief appearances in variety-type shows remain the usual platform – a mixed blessing, since the two or three minutes which is all that can usually be spared is a very short time in which to make an impact. In a live gig it would take many performers that long to establish their rapport with the audience.

This was one of the disadvantages faced by those who appeared on *Just For Laughs*, two series of shows consisting of excerpts from the Canadian 'Just For Laughs' Festival of Comedy held in the summers of 1986 and 1987, packaged by Paul Jackson into half-hour programmes. The first series of six started on Channel Four on 17 March 1987, and the second on 27 October 1987. The performers were mostly American and Canadian, with one British act in each show – these included Helen Lederer, Lenny Henry, Jeremy Hardy, Stephen Fry, Rowan Atkinson, Harry Enfield and Norman Lovett. Lovett in particular suffered in the television version, being a slow comedian and needing more than the two-and-a-half minutes that was all he could be allowed; but Jackson handled the shows efficiently within the necessary limitations, taking a separate feed of the Canadian TV crew's cameras so that he could edit in the gentler British style. The main problem is that the shows really needed to run for an hour and not thirty minutes in order to allow the performers room to breathe.

Getting a few minutes of your act into someone else's programme is a well-established way of managing the perils of television; John Dowie was invited by impressionist Rory Bremner to appear in his series *And Now – Something Else* on BBC2 in March 1986; Dowie contributed to and appeared in sketches, and also had several minutes of stand-up in each show, in which he performed one of his songs and a section from an old stage act which he had recently replaced – thus avoiding the problem of burning out material on television before it has outlived its usefulness in live shows.

Ruby Wax attacked television in another way – again with the connivance of Paul Jackson – by hosting a chat show in her own exuberant style. The first series of *Don't Miss Wax* began on Channel Four in April 1987, with a second starting in January 1988. Chat shows are a staple of the bland television diet, but Wax managed to get a more varied collection of guests than is usual, and her style –

not much more subdued than Shelley in *Girls On Top* – shook the programme loose from the comfortable moorings of the accepted format. The shows also gave Norman Lovett a chance to make brief contributions in his own dead-pan style; since his pieces, though short, were specially written each week for the show and he was able to make an effective impression.

Shortly after the second series began Lovett also appeared in the BBC2 comedy series *Red Dwarf*, starting on 15 February 1988. Written by Rob Grant and Bob Naylor it starred Chris Barrie and Craig Charles as the inhabitants of an almost empty spaceship marooned in the far future by an accident; Lovett played Holly, a super-intelligent computer with no time for whingeing humans ('I'm a computer with an IQ of 6,000, not your mother').

What everybody wants, of course, is their own series. Norman Lovett has laid out detailed plans for a series of his own, but getting the ideas to become reality is always a long business. Helen Lederer – who had also appeared in sketches in the more mainstream series *Naked Video* – teamed with Clive Mantle and Nick Wilton for their own show, *Hello Mum*. They had previously made three series of the radio show *In One Ear*, and in *Hello Mum* they followed that show's tradition of live transmissions. The problem with this was that most of the show – apart from a few pre-filmed inserts – took place in the same studio set. In the first show they made great play with the fact that it *was* only a set; this left them little to do for the rest of the series than bicker with each other. The comedy band, Bermuda Triangle, provided some musical relief, and Arnold Brown sat seraphically above them in a special part of the set and injected occasional one-liners. In later shows he sat in the audience or went up to the roof of Television Centre; but he looked nervous throughout and the very short time he was given allowed him little opportunity to establish his style. (He has been unlucky with television – he came over better in *Interference*, but the audience for that was minuscule.) The scripts were written by a large team including John Dowie, Jeremy Hardy, Nigel Planer's brother Roger, Simon Brint and Roland Rivron, and Jamie Rix and Nick Wilton.

Helen Lederer comments: 'I think it was a brave attempt to do something outside what had been done before, but there's a beginning and an end to the power of being different. You have to look at what's funny. I don't think we had time to develop characters – I would have liked to have known who I was in relation to them.' She found that, despite the supposed resurgence of women in comedy, the mostly male production and writing team was uneasy about any attempts to contribute to the planning: 'We are nowhere near men being comfortable in women's company in a more formalized way, like in script meetings. If you want to make a point you're seen as difficult – which will cause half-an-hour's discussion if you want to change a line. I think people are alarmed by women, particularly in comedy – comedy seems to be such a serious business, everyone has their own opinions. Women who have been known to do things on their own – whether it's good or bad – are seen as eccentric, are defined as feminist, their sexuality is sometimes questioned ... we're not absorbed. There's a subversion going on about your presence – particularly at meetings – they're punishing you slightly for thinking you can occupy their world ... it's a terribly passionate industry! On the other hand, one's own limitations have to be recognized – this situation does exist, but I feel it's important not to blame it for any shortcomings which are mine. And on *Hello Mum* we had eighteen or nineteen writers, and I asked if Morwenna Banks and Abi Grant could come to the first script meeting because they might be writing – if they hadn't come, there'd have been no women in that room! – and then they got on to the writing team ... so I'm proud of that.'

Hello Mum, although in the end it didn't really work, was at least an attempt to tackle the problems of television in a fresh way, and it is perhaps better that a show should try something a bit different and fail, than simply go on ploughing a well-established and comfortable furrow. The different methods by which various performers and writers approach the problems of television are interesting. Lenny Henry, who though not part of the alternative comedy scene, has been influenced by it – not least by his marriage in 1984 to Dawn French – came to success on television after a long hard slog. In 1975 – when at the age of seventeen – he made a hit on *New Faces* (the ITV talent show), he left his engineering apprenticeship and embarked on some years' work in summer seasons, appearances on BBC's *The Black and White Minstrel Show*, in the touring version of it with Cannon and Ball, and on *Tiswas* – an ITV children's programme consisting largely of throwing water over everybody in sight. His first real chance came in Central Television's early 1980s' late-night comedy series *OTT* (standing for 'Over the Top', which it certainly was); the programme was excessively silly but did give a good platform to both Henry and Alexei Sayle, then just establishing himself.

Up to this time Henry had been using any material he could lay his hands on, including some fairly racist material – standard enough fodder, and no less offensive for being performed by a black man. Gradually, as he began to develop as a comedian, he discarded this sort of material; his appearances with Tracey Ullman in *Three Of A*

239

Kind gave him access to some sympathetic production from Paul Jackson and skilful scriptwriting, particularly from Kim Fuller, and he developed characterizations such as Algernon Razzamatazz, the heavily sexist Theophilus T. Wildebeeste and the elderly survivor of the first wave of Jamaican immigrants into Britain, Deakus; he also developed a friendly and relaxed stand-up style. Deakus in particular enabled him to make observations about the rôle of blacks in British society in a wry and effective way.

When in September 1984 he got his own series on BBC1, *The Lenny Henry Show*, he came to it having gained a good deal of experience and was able to make excellent use of the medium. The show was written by a large team – often a recipe for blandness and lack of individuality, but this time the disparate elements gave Henry a chance to develop a wide range of personalities in sketches, as well as opening each programme with several minutes of stand-up. His acting ability enabled him to create characters so strong that sometimes one has to look quite hard to be sure it really is Lenny Henry and not a visiting black actor.

Later series allowed him to develop characters at greater length. The run of six programmes which started on 27 October 1987 was built entirely round one character – Delbert Wilkins, a street-wise Brixton hustler who runs a pirate radio station, dresses 'real sharp', but underneath it all is insecure and a bit of a loser. The character would probably be offensive if attempted by a white man; in Henry's hands it becomes a complex, sympathetic (and very funny) look at a certain type of black lifestyle. Interviewed for ITV's *The South Bank Show* by Melvyn Bragg, Henry commented: 'I like Delbert because he's political, because he has a point, because he talks about black people in Britain now and the way they're perceived – he talks about the police, and the bomb, and South Africa – and I can't do that when I do stand-up on stage, because they don't expect me to come out with stuff about politics; but as Delbert I can be very political, and get away with it. As soon as I grew into what my point of view was, to do with politics, the world, women, being black, etc. – that's when my comedy started to go right into the socket – I miss sometimes, but at least I've got a point of view.'

This is a sample (co-written by Henry and Kim Fuller) of Delbert as a stand-up character:

> I went to this club, right, and the bouncer on the door was typical, you know, big guy – he had 'hate' tattooed on one fist, and 'fist' tattooed on the other fist. . . . I walked towards him, I knew no fear, you know 'at I mean? – 'cos I'm from the Brixton posse, right? My hair was slicked back – my hair was so slick there was guys surfin'

on it, you know'at I mean? That's how slick my hair was, guy – I was feelin' mean – I was feelin' so mean I was refusing to lend money to *myself*. That's how mean I was feelin', guy. So I walked up to this geezer on the door, right, I said, 'Step aside, Quasimodo – Delbert Wilkins has *arrived!*' And when I came to, this policeman was standin' over me saying, 'You're nicked, sonny.' And that's what we have to put up with in Brixton all the time, right? Complete and utter hassle from the police, every single day.

For instance, yesterday I was stopped by the police fifteen times, right? On the same street! I kept saying, 'Look, I was nowhere near the *Belgrano*, you know'at I mean? I was steamin' in the opposite direction, guy, towards the paper shop.' All the time they keep stopping me – I say, 'Why?' – they say, 'Suspicion.' I been stopped that many times I'm beginning to suspect *myself*. You know, I look in the mirror and go, 'Well, maybe I *did* do something', you know'at I mean? I tell you something else they're trying to get off the ground round our way, right – the neighbourhood watch scheme – you know the one, where you're supposed to grass on your next-door neighbour. People are getting carried away with it round our way – they've been arresting themselves, beating themselves up, and then denying it the next day, man, you know'at I mean? It's well out of order, guy. I tell you the worst thing – check this, because this is seriously funny, right? – check this – the government are trying to give the police extra powers! What for, man? The police don't need any more bloody extra powers! That's like puttin' a spear on the end of a Cruise missile, you just don't need it, you know'at I mean?

The 'Delbert' series, written by Stan Hey and Andrew Nickolds, is also interesting because it presents not only Delbert but other black characters as fully rounded people, with all their flaws and humanities, and not simply as stereotype black Brixtoners. Similarly his stand-up material – much of it about family life as a child or his own experiences in the normal course of living – does much to bridge the gap between the perceptions of black and white. By presenting – as do many alternative comedians – shared experiences as opposed to strings of jokes, he enables the white members of his audience to accept a black person's experiences as being similar to their own.

As he came up in the entertainment business through a mainstream route, few people would class Henry as a member of the alternative comedy scene; but his links into it include appearances on *Saturday Live*, a cameo in *Happy Families*, and indeed much of his approach to comedy. His resounding success in mainstream television gives a demonstration to his more alternative colleagues that the problems of creating fresh TV comedy *can* be solved without appealing to the lowest common denominator favoured by some mainstream comics.

When Ben Elton and Rik Mayall came to attempt a follow-up to *The Young Ones* they had to solve not only the problems of any television show, but also the problems of following a highly successful and innovative series. Rik Mayall: 'I had this basic idea that I wanted to live in a flat with Ade Edmondson, so I went to Ben Elton and said, let's write it together. Ben being the kind of writer that he is, wrote ninety-five per cent of it, so I had my name taken off the front. It was rushed – we went into the studio too early – Ben had a hernia when he was writing them so he was in hospital for a lot of the time.'

Ben Elton: 'It was the most unhappy experience of my life, writing that show, because I never really knew where I was – was Rik writing it with me or not? In the end he said, "I haven't written a word, so you'd better have the credit", but by that time I'd spent four months trying to write something as part of a team, so it wasn't easy. Having said that, I'm very proud of it – all right, it's loud, it's dirty, it's noisy, but there are some good bits in it – we got more fan mail than for *The Young Ones* – we also got the most vitriolic critical panning I've ever seen in my life.'

In the series Mayall played seedy showbiz failure Richie Rich, Edmondson played his minder, Eddie Catflap, and Nigel Planer played his agent, the decrepit Ralph Filthy – hence the title, *Filthy Rich and Catflap*. Richie Rich thinks he is a famous stand-up comic and celebrity, but in reality is a talentless and self-centred failure who desperately pretends that he is friendly with half of show-business. Eddie Catflap knows perfectly well that Richie is useless, but being mainly interested in drinking himself into oblivion, his observations, though shrewd, carry little weight with Richie. Ralph Filthy, himself a total failure as a theatrical agent and porn merchant, is not at all well and can do little to help. In the shows these characters appear as themselves, so that in effect they are acting out plots which to them are not real – hence the constant remarks about poor gags or the plot itself, and periodic reactions to camera – particularly from Richie whenever Eddie is being particularly obtuse. This convention is a bit off-putting at first; but once one understands that while the characters are 'real' the plots aren't, the whole thing makes (slightly) more sense.

The series of six started on 7 January 1987 on BBC2, going out at 9.25 pm. The first show in particular was very raucous, and the whole series received a total critical panning. Adrian Edmondson: 'All these critics were saying things like, "Of course, I was a big *Young Ones* fan" – *no one* was a big *Young Ones* fan in the press, at all – there wasn't one good review of *The Young Ones* until halfway through the second re-run. That was a cult programme – not by design, it just was – and it was hated by the press.'

Nigel Planer adds: 'We said at the time, even if it was brilliant it

243

would attract flak – TV critics are the most impotent people – they write about something after everyone's seen it, whereas at least a theatre critic can make sure that a show closes. And because they're impotent, they're much more vitriolic, because they don't have any effect on the ratings – people watch what they want to watch.'

Looked at again, with the criticisms in the past and the format borne in mind, there are some good things in *Filthy Rich and Catflap*. There is a devastating spoof of the panel show *Blankety Blank* – under the title *Oo-er, sounds a bit rude* – which is vicious, barbed, unkind and thoroughly deserved, and an extended sequence in which Richie and Eddie squabble while playing *Trivial Pursuit* (a board game for know-it-alls). The plots are deliberately absurd, but sometimes the signalling of the unreality of the plot and the grimacing to camera gets a little out of control; Nigel Planer's characterization of Ralph Filthy is excellent but is not really given sufficient room to develop, and Mayall and Edmondson are sometimes allowed to become self-indulgent; but there are plenty of good laugh-lines and the series is much funnier than its reputation would suggest.

Rick Mayall: 'I'm still very proud of it – I think it's as funny and probably more useful than *The Young Ones* – particularly the last three programmes. I think it's the most neolistic piece of telly we've ever done – it's completely anti-television, it's anti-fame, it's anti the media generally, and anti-privilege; whereas *The Young Ones* was anti rock-and-roll and anti complacent youth – my feeling was that it was trying to destroy the stranglehold that rock-and-roll had on kids – because in the 1920s, there was no rock-and-roll, there was politics, and kids used to go out and talk to each other at meetings, and things like that. Now it's not only rock-and-roll that does that to kids but television itself – bland entertainment itself – and *Filthy Rich and Catflap* was trying to attack that. And we wanted to be as ugly and unpleasant as possible, which we did in *The Young Ones*, and *Filthy* ... was having a proper grown-up crack at that. It looked more like grown-ups being unpleasant on television – I think maybe the calculation backfired a little bit ... you write something ironically, assuming that everyone feels the same as you do, and they don't see the irony because they see things differently from you.'

The series was produced and directed by Paul Jackson, who comments: 'I think it attracted exactly the flak we anticipated – the protectors of our moral standards, this time forewarned – *The Young Ones* had crept up on them before they recognized it ... in fact there was far less of the "filth" in *Filthy Rich and Catflap*, but people got in with that complaint. And a lot of *Young Ones* fans, now three or four years older, were disappointed because there'd been a change.

Filthy Rich and Catflap –
Planer, Edmondson and
Mayall

But if you look at the best ones you'll see some very funny comedy, with more jokes in them than the average sitcom.'

One of the main targets of the show is the artificial friendliness of showbusiness, where who you know matters altogether too much. Here Richie and Eddie are bored stiff:

Eddie: (*Sighs*)

Richie: Oh, stop *sighing*, Eddie.

Eddie: I'm not sighing. (*Sighs.*)

Richie: Pardon me, but I think you *are* sighing.

Eddie: I'm not. I'm idly collecting phlegm at the back of my throat. And when I've got enough, I'm going to gob at you.

Richie: Wouldn't blame you if you were sighing, actually. The hours are not exactly charging by at the mome. No work, nothing to do – I wonder what Tom O'Connor's up to. Imposs to say, really. The man is such a sparkling multi-faceted genius that one simply cannot predict what amazing thing he'll get up to next. Actually, there's an interesting thing about Tom O'Connor . . .

Eddie: Well congratulations Richie. I had thought that today I had plumbed the very depths of tedium – a level of boredom beneath which I could not sink – but now Richie Rich has started to burble on about Tom O'Connor. What shall we do – stare at the wall or chat about Tom O'Connor? Oh, well I've got a bit of a weak heart condition, so staring at the wall would probably be too exciting, probably safest if we chat about Tom O'Connor!

Richie: You don't fancy watching a couple of episodes of *Name That Tune* on the vid, then?
(*Eddie nods, gets up, walks over to the TV set, smashes it with a hammer.*)

Eddie: Oh, no, the telly's broken.

Richie (*after a pause*): Tom O'Connor's probably playing golf now – him and a few of the guys – probably only just realized that I'm not there . . . 'I thought you were going to ask him, Bob Monkhouse' – 'No, you said you'd do it, Tom' – 'Oh bother, that's the whole game ruined then'. Bob Hope will chip in . . . 'Bother bother bother. . . .'

Eddie: Richie, please – I'm begging you – no, I'm not, I'm threatening you – if you don't shut up, I shall ram your head into the microwave!

Richie: All right, all right . . . the subject is closed . . . (*pause*) I see Brucey Forsyth's got a new series . . . *Spot the Catchphrase* . . . Brucey trots out a series of meaningless catchphrases, and the celeb panel have to guess which one's going to annoy the general public most. Could be very big, Eddie . . .

Eddie: Richie, do you think we could possibly avoid the subject of Brucey Forsyth as well? I mean, in terms of boredom it's much the same as talking about . . . Michael Barrymore, really, isn't it?

Later in 1987 Rik Mayall appeared in a much more conventional TV series – *The New Statesman*, written by Laurence Marks and Maurice Gran. Following the fortunes of an unpleasant Tory MP called Alan B'Stard (played by Mayall) there were six episodes on ITV, starting on 13 September 1987. Comparisons with *Yes, Minister* are inevitable, since the series revolves partly around political manoeuvring in the House of Commons, but the whole approach is rather broader. Mayall gave a good performance – since the character is unpleasant he was originally going to launch into one of his grotesqueries, but was persuaded to play it straight, with preferable results. Before making a second series in 1988 Mayall appeared with Stephen Fry, John Sessions and John Gordon Sinclair in a new production of Simon Gray's play *The Common Pursuit* at the Phoenix Theatre, London.

In the meantime the variety-show approach to television had been represented by the return in February 1987 of *Saturday Live*, which ran for ten shows from 7 February. Learning from their mistakes in the previous series, the production team restricted the length to a more manageable hour-and-a-quarter (the originals had been 90 minutes) placed later in the evening, at 10 pm (instead of 8 pm).

Paul Jackson had withdrawn from the project, leaving the production to Geoff Posner and Geoffrey Perkins. Jackson comments: 'I think it had its act much more together, it had a slicker, much cleaner presentation; the first of the second series was the best ever – and the next best was the pilot – and if you take the second series and compare it with the original programme specification it's so far removed from it that … it's not that I didn't like the second series, I thought it was excellent, but because it was so far removed from the original idea it had ceased to interest me. A kind of variety show with two bands and a few stand-ups was never what it was supposed to be. As that, it was excellent.'

Certainly the whole show had gelled this time, conveying a genuine air of live excitement. Ben Elton compèred throughout the series, and Stephen Fry and Hugh Laurie made regular appearances in sketches. Harry Enfield appeared as Stavros in most programmes, as well as creating some new characters. Comedy guests included Simon Fanshawe, Craig Charles, Rowan Atkinson, Lenny Henry, Jenny Lecoat, Kit Hollerbach and Andy de la Tour. Importantly, the series also gave an opportunity for newer performers on the cabaret circuit to have a chance at television. They included Skint Video, Punt and Dennis, 'Bing Hitler', the eccentric Randolph the Remarkable, and a most effective performance from Julian Cleary in his persona as the Joan Collins Fan Club (one very camp young man and a soppy dog).

Elton emerged as the star of the series, hosting the programmes and doing two sets in each; the first written specially and based on the week's news, and a longer one near the end drawn from his recent stage act (with the swearing removed to keep the Channel Four executives quiet). Taking into account the complete re-working of his stage act after blowing it on each series of *Saturday Live* and the short topical sequences in each of the second series programmes, Elton produced a frightening amount of material in those two years – most comics could only ever produce a fraction of that amount.

The topical sets were inevitably more politically orientated than most of his stage act. He comments: 'People say it's biased – but comedians have to be satirical, and if you've got a government in for eight years, they're up for grabs in my opinion. People say, "Why don't you have a go at the opposition?" – I mean, why? They're in a minority, what's the point? – you might as well have a go at the cat. There's one power – that's who you go for! As it happens I hate Mrs Thatcher more than most of them, but in a way that's a coincidence – she's the Prime Minister, so what's a comic supposed to do? I don't think he's supposed to do what Tarbuck and Davidson do, which is to say, "Isn't it wonderful to be British, Maggie's a wonderful woman, and don't you hate that Arthur Scargill?" Scargill's miners struck for thirteen months and nearly starved to death – I don't consider that's something to be knocked by a comedian, whether you agreed with the strike or not. (I happen to agree with it very much.)'

Choosing a sample of topical material is always difficult because so much explanation is required to set up the background. In this excerpt from 21 February 1987 he deals with the privatization sales of Leyland Trucks and British Airways – comments which, with the continuing policy of privatization, have a continuing relevance:

> Ladies and gentlemen, a week in politics when the party that has been in power for eight years chose to spend the entire week telling the opposition they're not fit to govern – well, it hasn't worried *them* for a while, has it? They've sold off British Leyland, they've sold off British Leyland Trucks to DAF Trucks. Well, isn't that nice? – that's a very dignified name for our trucks, isn't it? DAF. Some big butch bloke goes in a transport cafe – 'What you driving, mate?' – 'Well, I'm driving a DAF!' ... that's lovely! Of course, they say we haven't sold it – oh, no, we haven't sold it – we've *merged*! Big difference – we haven't sold our trucks, we've merged. So, next time you're down the butcher's, picking up a half a pound of sausages for your tea, just remember you're not buying them – you're *merging* with 'em – for the mutual good of you and the sausages! Ooh! – bit of a political image there, I've been to university, I don't mind

showing off, fair enough.

Anyway, been a lot of things going on – all this selling, selling everything – British Airways has been sold, and we are now told to rejoice, because the value of the shares has gone through the roof! The value of British Airways has almost doubled, and we're told what a good idea it was to sell it. Well, I'm not so sure, because if the value's doubled in a couple of weeks, that means the previous owner must have got a bum deal – and since the previous owner was *us*, I'm not too happy about it, are you?

These and other directly political statements invite comparisons with the classic satire programme from 1962, *That Was The Week That Was*; but whereas that was withdrawn because of the 1963 election (and may perhaps have helped in some small way to remove the Tory government), *Saturday Live*'s small audience of about one and a half million could hardly have any significant effect, whether they sympathized with Elton's stance or not. Certainly Margaret Thatcher was returned for a third term in June 1987 with a thumping majority – a clear demonstration to anyone who thought alternative comedy was going to change anything. Elton himself was under no illusions about it, and regarded his sets as comic satirical comment, not an attempt to influence people politically.

The show returned a year later, on a different night and hence under a different title – *Friday Night Live*, starting its run on Channel Four on 19 February 1988 at the later time of 10.30. The format was the same, although an attempt to introduce a spoof game show in the first episode failed to come off and was hastily abandoned. Harry Enfield's Stavros was a regular once again, plus another creation of his, the rich plasterer Loadsamoney – a deliberately unsympathetic creation, but one which Enfield found becoming irritatingly popular at its face value. Josie Lawrence (of the Comedy Store's improvisational team) appeared in monologues and sketches, and there were regular appearances by Hunter and Docherty, a Scots double-act. In fact, there were almost too many regular performers; but on the whole the series worked well, with guests including Nick Revell, Ronnie Golden with Mac MacDonald, Hattie Hayridge and several American performers. It is to the credit of this and the previous series that stand-up performers were allowed a longer time – often six or seven minutes instead of the three or four permitted by most programmes. Elton sported a villainous beard for the first three episodes – shaving it off for the fourth, claiming that he had done so to annoy the producers, who had annoyed him by truncating his set the previous week. (The presence of the beard in some sets and not in others would make the re-editing for the autumn highlight a nightmare.) His sets – again mixing new topical material with re-workings of sections from his stage material – were by now very polished, using pace and rhythm with complete assurance.

The series generated a good deal of the excitement of the earlier shows, although, inevitably, once any show – however innovatory – has become established it is bound to lose the freshness it had when it started. Despite the difficulties – there was more and more censorship of Elton's material during rehearsals as the climate of public opinion was increasingly manipulated against television by the government – and despite the small audience, it is still important for an alternative comic viewpoint to have a voice, and important that it should be allowed some political expression. Once or twice Elton has come perilously close to fulfilling the accusations of preaching – in fact he admitted it at the end of one or two of the shorter sets – but better that than to lack commitment in his approach to comedy.

The last of the ten editions of *Friday Night Live*, broadcast on 29 April 1988, was graced by the presence of 'superstar' Dame Edna Everage (who described the programme as the *Opportunity Knocks* of alternative comedy, with Elton in the Bob Monkhouse rôle). At the end, Elton announced that it would be the last of the *Saturday/Friday Live* programmes; although Channel Four would have liked another series, he and the other principal participants wanted to put an end to it while it was still successful.

Saturday Live and *Friday Night Live* remained in effect alternative TV variety shows, and a more-or-less straight variety bill was adopted by *Cabaret at the Jongleurs*, recorded at Jongleurs and transmitted on BBC2 starting on 25 February 1988; the series included many of the Jongleurs regulars such as Jeremy Hardy, Nick Revell and Mark Steel, and was notable for being the first independently made light entertainment production to go out on the BBC.

When Dawn French and Jennifer Saunders embarked on their own television *French and Saunders* series for the BBC, they managed to some extent to bridge the gap between mainstream and alternative television. Basically the shows consisted of sketches in their usual style, plus spoof documentaries and TV films; but in order to avoid the all-too-common format of one sketch backed on to another backed on to another, the first series packaged the sketches into a fake – and very tatty – TV variety show.

The series of six began on 9 March 1987, being placed at the

familiar time of 9 pm on BBC2. Once again Jennifer played the star and Dawn the YOP-scheme unpaid and unwilling assistant, and Raw Sex provided the music. The show also boasted a team of incompetent dancers, the 'Hot Hoofers', managed by Madame Betty Marsden. Much of the show took place in the studio apparently in front of a tiny audience (specially shot – the real audience was never shown) and consisted of the girls' attempts to present glamorous entertainment, the Hot Hoofers' clumsy dancing, and bits of Raw Sex's act. From time to time the girls would wander off into their dressing-room to argue, or into various back-stage areas. They also played some of the behind-the-scenes characters, such as the chain-smoking wardrobe ladies. The 'real' sketches were then simply inserted into this framework, almost as if they had fallen out of some other show (performed by professionals).

The format, though ingenious, was also self-limiting and became tiresome; indeed, the best show is number four, in which the Hot Hoofers go on strike, and the girls and Raw Sex – locked out of their own studio – break into the Blue Peter studio and mount the show themselves.

They were lucky that their producer, Geoff Posner, was willing to give them the tacky look the show required. Dawn French: 'People have been trained by the BBC to be clever dickies, and to have a snappy sharp show – there's lots of shows that are right to be like that, but our stuff is much better when it's all languid and gentler.' Jennifer Saunders: 'We write a lot of it by imagining what it's going to look like, and if you write like that it's very annoying to have people change it.'

When they did *Girls On Top* they had been unhappy about the flat look of the lighting. Dawn French: 'Everyone says, "Well, video, that's always the case" – and that's not true, because they do dramas on video with interesting lighting, and depth . . . but they will not take the risk of doing it in Light Entertainment. We'd love to use technicians from drama – our stuff is much more drama based – but the big TV companies don't ever let you do it. Which is why the Comic Strip is great, because you have the freedom to use people in the crews that you respect. People in those crews will give you suggestions . . . whereas in the BBC there are obstacles.'

Jennifer Saunders' comments are similar to Helen Lederer's on this subject: 'You're not expected to be in certain meetings, you're not expected to suggest certain things – I'm sure we were considered incredibly difficult – if you write something and perform it, you obviously have an idea how you want it to look.'

With *French and Saunders* they were successful in getting the show mounted much as they wanted it; Posner is an experienced producer of alternative comedy and gave them the sort of sets and lighting they needed. Apart from the tacky variety-show framework, the individual sketches are well conceived and presented in whatever style the material suggests, and there are neat spoofs of *The Avengers*, fashion shows, *A Chorus Line* and freestyle swimming. Various guests, including Julie T. Wallace and Joan Armatrading, were included in the variety framework and were suitably insulted; and in show four the girls try to convince Michael Grade (then still with the BBC) not to axe the show.

The second series, again of six, began on 4 March 1988. The constricting variety framework had been abandoned, leaving a much looser construction. In the first show the sketches are separated – as opposed to linked – by the girls arguing in Jennifer's flat (Dawn still the underling but becoming more assertive); in later shows they run their own breakfast TV cable station, go pot-holing, and mount a devastating spoof of ITV's trendy *Night Network*.

Like much of their stage material, many of the sketches are conceived as character studies and look flat on paper; they come to life only when performed, the tone of voice and facial expressions providing most of the laughs. Jennifer Saunders' ability to sink herself into a character remains outstanding, with Dawn French also displaying a considerable range. Some of the characters appear in several sketches through the series; the two in the sketch quoted below have had a longer life. As younger schoolchildren, discussing sex in knowledgeable but wildly inaccurate terms, they first appeared in the earlier stage show; in the first series of *French and Saunders* they were just reaching menstruation; there they are presented as teenagers at a bus stop, discussing contraception. With Dawn French as the bossy and ill-informed know-it-all and Jennifer Saunders as the dim impressionable one, the characters are almost Amanda and Jennifer from *Girls On Top*, in their younger days. Only a handful of the sketches in *French and Saunders* go into areas such as contraception; but it is noteworthy that a semi-mainstream TV show – and at 9 pm not even in a late-night placing – can mention subjects which only a few years before would have been firmly banned:

> **Dawn:** What are you going to the doctor for – have you got a fungus, or a thrush, or what?
> **Jennifer:** No.
> **Dawn:** Well that's a shame, because if you did have, I could cure it. All you get is some raw lemon-rind and Deep Heat and rub it on, that's all you do. Well what *are* you going to the doctor for, then?

Jennifer: Well I'm not supposed to say. (*Pause.*) I'm going to get a contraception.

Dawn (*superior*): Ooo-ooh!

Jennifer: You know the pill?

Dawn: Yes.

Jennifer: What is it, then?

Dawn: Do you know about contraception, or not?

Jennifer: Not.

Dawn: Right. The first most important thing about contraception is to choose the right contraceptive utensil – like, for instance, I personally would not choose the pill.

Jennifer: Why?

Dawn: Because all it does is block your philippine tubes and makes your bosoms five times as big, which in your case is unnecessary and careless, frankly.

Jennifer: Well I might not go on the pill, then, I might go on something else.

Dawn: Like what, like what? – they're all as bad. If you told the doctor you don't want to go on the pill, you know what he'll do?

Jennifer: What?

Dawn: He'll insert a UFO inside you. Do you know what one of those is, or not?

Jennifer: Not.

Dawn: Right. Other name, coil. Do you know what a slinky looks like?

Jennifer: Yes.

Dawn: Well, it's like a huge slinky, and it's got barbed wire on it, and they squish it all up and stuff it up inside your bladder, and it hooks on, and stops babies. The only drawback is, you can get out of control going up and down stairs, that's all.

Jennifer: What, it just stays in there – doesn't it go rusty?

Dawn: No, because it's got a rope on it, hasn't it, to pull it out. Well, *you're* not allowed to pull it out. A certified medical practitioner has to pull it out. Not a social worker, and not a meals-on-wheels lady, right?

At the other end of the scale is a documentary with them as ballet dancers – very few verbal gags, simply a joke about their own overweight compared with the genuine ballerinas they danced beside. Because they are able to project the *characters'* belief that they really are skinny dancers, the whole joke works sympathetically – whereas other comedians' attempts at similar sketches would simply be an unkind gibe at over-sized women. Similarly, a sketch in which they are incompetent schoolgirl athletes works well because of their ability to project conviction – and indeed Dawn French's genuine grace of movement.

In the last show they share a dressingroom with one of the most experienced comedy actresses in the business – June Whitfield; and in a spoof on Hollywood documentaries on itself, Dawn French successfully repeats the dancing joke as Cyd Charisse, and Jennifer Saunders contributes a remarkable impersonation of Doris Day (sugary song and all).

With its range of subjects and depth of observation and acting, *French and Saunders* is one of the most successful forays into television from the alternative comedy tradition; a series which is acceptable to a wide audience while remaining true to its performers' roots.

Eat The Rich; The Comic Strip Presents ... – third series; Alexei Sayle's Stuff

18

After the Comic Strip specials transmitted in January 1986 there was a two-year gap before any new Comic Strip TV films appeared; the team made three nominally hour-long films in 1986 and three in 1987, for transmission early in 1988. In the meantime, Peter Richardson also directed a second feature film, *Eat The Rich*, released in October 1987. Strictly speaking this is not a Comic Strip production, in the sense that the usual team were restricted to cameo roles; the leading parts were taken by actors who had made minor appearances in earlier Comic Strip TV films: Jimmy Fagg, Ron Tarr, 'Nosher' Powell and black trans-sexual Lanah Pellay (who, as Alan Pellay, had appeared in the earlier films).

Peter Richardson had some difficulty setting the film up: 'I went through a year of traipsing around offices to raise money – it was a very hard one to sell because we had no stars in the lead roles. We were holding out to have these infamous mavericks in the lead parts – we wanted people who were interesting personalities ... you cannot get people to *act* Jimmy Fagg, or Lanah Pellay, or Nosher Powell.'

Eat The Rich is a deliberate move away from the more gentle humour and careful structure of *The Supergrass*. Set in the near

Eat the Rich – Lanah Pellay

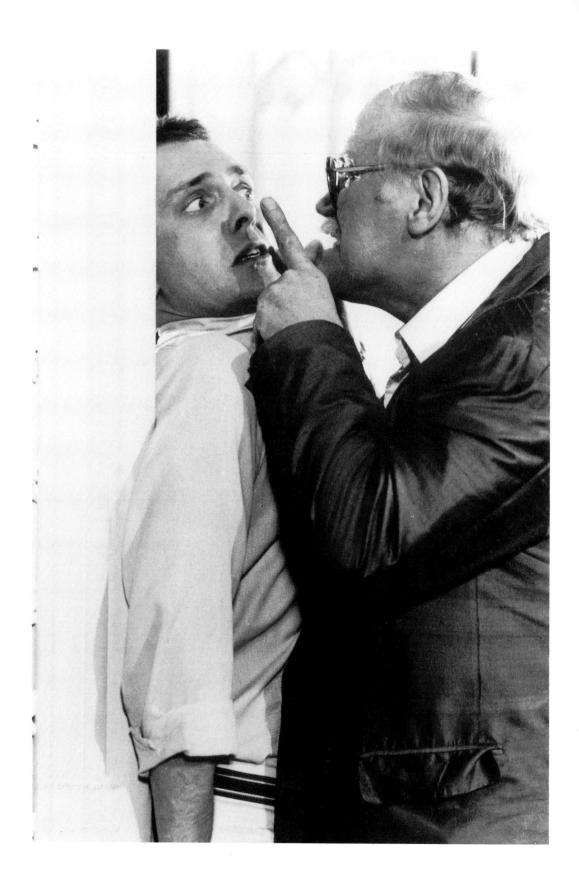

future, where the British Home Secretary is a loud-mouthed middle-aged yob (Powell), the head of MI5 is a Russian spy (Ronald Allen), and the rich patronize trendy restaurants while terrorists roam the streets and the poor starve, the film presents a complicated and unlikely plot as a vehicle for its stars; there are also numerous cameos from the rest of the Comic Strip team, plus Miranda Richardson (excellent as a bitchy DHSS employee), Koo Stark, Paul McCartney, Jools Holland and – as the Israeli Ambassador caught in a terrorist siege – a certain Peter Rosengard.

Lanah Pellay plays Alex, a black waiter sacked from the yuppie restaurant Bastards. He teams up with a tramp (Ron Tarr) and attempts to start a revolution against the government of people like Nosher Powell (who ends a strike by direct negotiation with the union leader – a swift punch in the balls). Alex and Ron team up with a farmer (Jimmy Fagg) and a call-girl (Fiona Richmond) recently found in a compromising position with Nosher; they take over Bastards, killing the staff and clientèle, and re-open it serving up minced human being to the new customers. Meanwhile Nosher has been slung out by his wife (Sandra Dorne) after flirting with the Queen at a banquet; the MI5's Commander Fortune (Ronald Allen), who has been trying to ruin Nosher, manages to get a photograph of Nosher at Bastards, eating minced Prime Minister.

In the end Fiona gives birth to Nosher's much desired son; Nosher and Ron fight over custody – Nosher's wife eventually killing Ron – but Commander Fortune steals the child and returns it to Fiona. Fiona and Jimmy drive off to hide in the country, while Alex and Nosher shoot each other and lie dying in a country lane as the film ends.

The film's writers – Richardson and Richens – were not aiming for restraint, and Richardson's direction gives the film a wildly over-the-top style. Its representation of a violent futuristic Britain is well-staged, with an impressive look to it; the satire is uncontrolled but does hit a number of targets effectively; and, even though some of the cameos are a trifle distracting as they turn into a star-spotting game, the overall effect of the film is as scurrilous, violent and anarchic as anyone could wish for.

Richardson is plainly attracted to the idea of making feature films, and has drawn up detailed plans for a full-length film following the Famous Five characters as adults – now grown into unpleasant older versions of themselves; Julian, for example, has become a corrupt diplomat. The Graham Greene-style adventures include their being captured by Sandinistas.

The next stage after the writing (and re-writing) will be the difficult task of raising the money. One advantage of feature films is that more money is available to create an impressive look; the corresponding disadvantage is that, unlike the TV films – where Channel Four on the whole allow the team to get on with it – the features have to be sold in detail to the money men, who are difficult to convince. (Indeed it is the tragedy of cinema as a whole that it is financed and largely run by businessmen who have no interest in or idea of cinema as a medium, but only as a financial investment; the pre-war Hollywood moguls were monsters but at least they loved films – today the last word goes to people who understand little and care less.)

Given all this, it comes as no surprise that the first of the new Comic Strip series should be aimed at the cavalier behaviour of film producers. The series of six began its run on Channel Four on 20 February 1988 – five of the films having had a limited theatrical release the preceding autumn. The films mostly run about fifty-two minutes for an hour-long slot, thus giving the various writers more time to explore their ideas, and are all of a high quality in their different ways (although arguably one or two of them might have benefited from being trimmed for a forty-five-minute slot).

The first film, *The Strike*, runs fifty-nine minutes (for a seventy-five-minute slot) and is Richardson and Richens' satire on film producers – an obvious target, but deserving of the sharp treatment it gets. Richardson directed what is in effect two films – the story of the attempts to make a film about the 1985 miners' strike, and excerpts from the film itself, shot in a glossy Hollywood style.

In the main story, Paul (Alexei Sayle in subdued mood) has written from first-hand experience a script about the miners' strike. He and the director, Bernard (Nigel Planer), put it up to producer Goldstein (Robbie Coltrane). At the first meeting Goldstein and his secretary Verity (Dawn French) give Paul and Bernard the good news:

> Goldstein: I'm here to tell you that Golden Pictures would like to be part of your movie. Now, my partner and I are both of the opinion that this property has a very good chance of doing very good box-office business in the United States – however, we feel, too, for this to be a possibility, we'll have to make one or two tiny changes to the screenplay.
> Paul: Well, we did feel that there would be some re-writes, you know ... um, which bits did you think might need more? ...
> Goldstein: Well, um, every five pages or so there should be an event – an event – maybe ... a mining disaster, a whole heap of miners trapped underground and a big flash flood – death, destruction ... what, am I a writer? ... boys ...
> Paul (*tentatively*): Excuse me, Mr Goldstein ... the whole point of

the story is that the miners are on strike ... it's the miners' strike, and, er, that means that the mines are closed. They're not working.

Goldstein: So you're saying that this Scarface ...

Verity: Scar*gill* ...

Goldstein: Scargill, schmargill ... you're saying that this guy, the hunky hero, the head of the miners, you're saying that he's too chicken-shit scared to go down the mine and dig out Meryl Streep!?

Bernard: I'm sorry ... what's Meryl Streep got to do with it?

Goldstein: I dunno ... she's available in July.

Things get worse. The designer (Adrian Edmondson) visits the real village ('It doesn't say mining village to me') and makes it over as a 1930s village complete with cobbled streets and a blacksmith's shop. Al Pacino (Peter Richardson) is brought in to play Scargill. Having taken over a small local cottage (and fitted it out with a tennis court and a jacuzzi) he makes his own contribution to the script:

Pacino: I've read it now a couple of times ... um ... not all of it ... um ... it's great. Um ... I dunno ... it's just something about these last ten pages, you know ... um ... I feel there's something kind of ... important missing. Um ... I dunno ... maybe it's a typing foul-up ...

Bernard: Um ... do you have all the pages?

Pacino: I think so. OK, what I'm really trying to say is, er, it seems to me this Arthur Scargill character is ... um ... seems to me to be some kind of ... um ... loser. Yeah ... that's the way it reads to me, I think.

Bernard: Um ... yes, he loses, yes.

Goldstein: Yeah, well what Al's trying to say ... forgive me, Al ...

Pacino: No, please.

Goldstein: ... is that we don't like the end of the picture.

Bernard: In what way?

Goldstein: Well, he *loses* – so he's a schmuck!

Pacino: Let me say this – I like what you guys are trying to do, you know ... um ... I'm a Democrat, so, uh ... but, uh, all my instincts are, this Scargill guy, this ... this great human being ... um ... after all the shit he's been through ... should in the end, somehow ... some way ... uh ... win this strike.

Goldstein: *And* get the girl out.

Pacino: Right.

Bernard: Yes, well with all due respect, Mr Pacino, um, this strike was probably the biggest blow to the British Labour movement in the last sixty years, and ...

Pacino (*to Verity*): Could you get me a Perrier water?

Verity: With lime?

Pacino: Yeah.

Bernard: ... and people in this country are extremely aware, actually, of how the strike did in fact end, and that Scargill did, in fact, lose.

Goldstein: Oh, really? Well watch my lips – nobody in Wyoming
gives a god-damned shit about that, 'old boy'!

Bernard: Yes, well, I'm sorry, Mr Goldstein, but Paul and I here
do give 'a god-damned shit' and we're actually not prepared to
compromise on what is essentially the whole point of this film.

Goldstein: Verity!

Verity: Yes?

Goldstein: Pay this guy off, will you?*

The end result is predictable. The finished film – with a new,
American, director – is a complete nonsense, ending with Scargill
rescuing his small daughter from a caved-in mine and then rushing
to London on a huge motor-bike to plead with Parliament to let the
miners go back to work before the deadline when the militants will
blow up the Sellafield nuclear plant. In the main story, Paul returns
to his village to be ostracized by his disgusted friends.

The whole story is pointedly told, with some excellent performances. Jennifer Saunders gives a stunning imitation of Meryl Streep,
looking quite alarmingly like her as she wanders through the film-
within-the-film endlessly peeling oranges (a mannerism picked up
from *Out of Africa*). Keith Allen makes brief appearances as a jaded
film executive and – at the BAFTA awards ceremony – as a celebrity
with a striking resemblance to Jack Nicholson. At the same ceremony
Dawn French appears as another celebrity who is suspiciously like
Joan Collins; Peter Richardson plays Pacino as a mumbling bundle
of sexual tension; and, in the film-within-the-film, Rik Mayall
appears as a grotesque one-eyed hunchback in the village, and as
the Harry Davenport-like Speaker of the House of Commons (whose
members all wear formal suits and top hats). Alexei Sayle underplays
effectively as the helpless writer, watching his original idea turned
into overblown commercial rubbish; and the whole film is neatly
constructed – with the excerpts from the completed *Strike – The
Bloodbath Begins* integrated into the story.

The film was entered in the Montreux Festival in May 1988,
winning both the Golden Rose and the Press Award against competition which included an episode of *Blackadder the Third*.

The second Comic Strip film, *More Bad News*, was written and
directed by Adrian Edmondson, and presented a further look at the
heavy metal band featured in the first series. In autumn 1987, as a
prelude to the film, Edmondson, Mayall, Planer and Richardson
went on tour as Bad News. The show ran about an hour and twenty

* *The Strike*, Comic Strip, Channel Four.

The Strike – Jennifer
Saunders

The Strike – Peter
Richardson

minutes, with the band performing six or seven numbers in a very disorganized style.

Adrian Edmondson: 'It turned into a huge heavy metal pantomime by the end of the tour . . . it wasn't the most satisfying show that I've worked on – it got too close . . . because we were actually being like a band, having to do sound checks . . . the line between being comic and being musical was getting more and more blurred.'

The film of *More Bad News* looks at the band five years on; the style is similar to the original, and provides plenty of opportunities for sharp digs at the world of rock. At the end the band plays at a (genuine) heavy metal gig at Castle Donnington, to an audience of 70,000 (and the real bands at the event make their own comments to the documentary camera).

The third film in the series was also written by Edmondson, together with Mayall, and was directed by Stephen Frears. Called *Mr Jolly Lives Next Door*, it chronicles the adventures of a couple of alcohol-crazed idiots who run an escort agency next door to what turns out to be the office of an axe murderer (a splendidly dry performance from Peter Cook). The two, played by Mayall and Edmondson, are given no names, but are in effect the Dangerous Brothers, grown older, seedier and drunker. Though largely an excuse for the two to indulge their delight in spectacular and destructive stunts, the logic of the plot holds together well, and the whole effect is genuinely funny provided no one expects subtlety.

Keith Allen and Daniel Peacock wrote the next film, *The Yob*, a direct parody of the 1987 remake of the classic silly horror film *The Fly*. In *The Yob* there is a psychic transformation between a football hooligan (Gary Olsen) and a trendy director of pop videos (a bravura performance from Allen, particularly as his character begins to exhibit the social behaviour of the yob). The film is certainly over the top – and perhaps by the end has run the idea rather out of steam – but gets in some barbed jibes at the expense of the pop promo world.

Shown last in the series, Nigel Planer's first script for the Comic Strip – written with Doug Lucie – takes a sour look at the Mediterranean world of organizations such as 'Club 18–30'. Directed by Baz Taylor and called *Fun Seekers*, the film follows the story of a group on one of these sex-orientated holidays, and in particular Tony (Planer) who is hoping to hide the fact that he is thirty-four and shouldn't be there. Peter Richardson is the holiday organizer – a seedy master of ceremonies at games designed for plebeian titillation – and Mark Elliott and Keith Allen are among the holiday-makers. The plot is fairly straightforward as Tony is exposed by

Jamie (Mark Elliott), whose supposedly single room Tony has invited himself to stay in; there is a sub-plot concerning a pregnant local girl who is being ostracized by the villagers, and one of the girls on holiday who bears a striking resemblance to the local church's portrait of the Madonna. (In a neat and understated joke Tony leads the girl home on a donkey, their clothing accidentally making them look like Joseph and Mary searching for the inn.) In the end the local girl goes into labour in the deserted church, and Tony comes to the rescue – thus winning back the respect of his juniors.

The most arresting of the six films, shown fifth, was written by Alexei Sayle, Pauline Melville and David Stafford, and directed by Bob Spiers: it took its title, *Didn't You Kill My Brother?* from a line in Sayle's early stage act. Very densely written, with numerous understated references to Sayle's stage act, it tells the story of twin criminal brothers, Carl and Sterling Moss (both played by Sayle). After five years in prison, Carl emerges with 428 academic qualifications, a gentle nature and a Liverpool accent. His probation officer, Pauline Sneak (Pauline Melville), hoping to bask in the glory

Didn't You Kill My Brother? – Pauline Melville

reflected from a famous criminal, introduces him to the youth centre where he will be an Unstructured Activities Co-ordinator. Carl is shocked at the wealth of engineering workshop equipment lying unused while the kids break the place up:

> **Carl**: Why isn't anybody using this gear?
> **Pauline**: Technology changes so fast these days. It's better for the kids to just to sit and sort of . . . wait.
> **Carl**: Yeah, but you could make some great stuff with this equipment!
> **Pauline**: Making things? I don't want to go on *Wogan* with a man who *makes* things! This isn't the seventies. Anyway, the CBI would never stand for it. If I catch you making things you'll be back inside pissing in a tin pot before you can say Amnesty International.

Carl finds that the policeman who arrested him (*another* police portrayal by Peter Richardson) now runs the community police – rounding the kids up and making them play cricket – while his brother Sterling is running a racket where the local kids steal every bicycle in sight (no matter what it's chained to – they are quite prepared to chop down telephone poles) so that Sterling can respray and resell them. (The police, being suitably remunerated by Sterling, don't interfere in his private enterprise.)

The film deliberately draws on the atmosphere of Brecht's 1928 musical play *The Threepenny Opera*, which took an incisive look at the corrupt social conditions of its day and the criminal underclass which they created; Sayle even quotes Brecht's famous line, 'Which is the greater criminal – he who robs a bank or he who founds one?'

On his first day at the Youth Centre, Carl subdues the young hooligans by firing over their heads with a submachine-gun; while they cower on the floor he puts to them his own proposals, and the film's underlying message:

> **Carl**: Good morning, class. I am Mr Carl Moss, your Unstructured Activities Co-ordinator. Today we will do Lying On The Floor. You will lie on the floor, you will continue to lie on the floor, and if you move a single muscle, I will kill you. Now, while you're lying on the floor, I would like to put to you a very simple proposition. Consider the ways of the anaconda. It strikes but rarely. It bides its time. It waits for its moment. Then, it strikes. Sometimes, it misses, and bangs its head on a tree. It's a horrible slimy thing, anyway. Consider this proposition. Who is the real criminal – he who steals bikes, or he who makes them?
> **Girl**: Or she! . . . sexist crap!
> (*Carl fires a shot.*)

Carl: Now, you are scum. Filth. The lowest of the low. Petty criminals, nicking bikes for my pus-bag brother. Now I too have dedicated my life to crime, and as a recidivist criminal, I ask you this simple question: Is crime right, or wrong?

Girl: Right.

Carl: Wrong. (*Fires a shot.*) Ethically, philosophically, politically, morally and mathematically, criminals are wrong. Why? Because they are anti-social. They are people of limited brain-power and even less will-power, who break the laws of society when they should be doing the real work, which is to *change* them. Criminals are people who steal from, cheat on, grass and betray their own kind, their own family, their own friends, their own radio-cassette-players, their own nice shoes and their own heated towel rails! You might think I'm talking rubbish, but ... (*inspiring music starts softly under him*) my brother Sterling will betray you, just as he betrayed me. Is there no answer to this dilemma? Yes – there is an answer. There is an answer. For I had a dream, my friends, I had a dream. I dreamt that all over this great nation, and all over the great nations of the world, there was machinery like this, rotting and wasting in schools and factories and community centres ... and I dreamed that there were people, people with skills and talents and abilities, that like the machines were rotting and wasting. (*The music builds up.*) And I dreamed of taking those resources – those people, those machines – and with them, forging a new spirit in the world – a new spirit of trust and co-operation and enterprise and creativity – oh, yes, I had a dream my friends, I had a dream. And I dreamt that this new spirit would seize the imagination of a generation until everywhere this new economy was the only economy – oh yes, I had a dream, my friends, I had a dream – then suddenly my dream changed, and I was in a swimming pool, and the swimming pool was full of small brown puppies – and each of the puppies had the face of a nineteenth-century politician – and one of the puppies, that had the face of Lord Palmerston, suddenly started shouting at me, 'Where's the spoons, where's the spoons, where's the bloody spoons?' (*The music has stopped.*) Any questions?

Girl: What happens if we don't take any notice of what you say, ever? (*Carl fires off several shots.*) Yes, I see.

Boy: Well then, what is it we're going to build?

Carl: Bicycles.

Carl's legitimate business provides unwelcome competition for Sterling, who attempts to close him down by violence, but comes off worst. ('You should always put a dead badger on a head wound,' says his solicitous mother, doing exactly that.) Sterling, Ms Sneak and the police set out to get Carl; eventually the brothers meet, and only one of them lives ... but is it Carl or Sterling? There is a subtle clue (though it was unplanned and is simply a felicitous trick of the light): it has already been established that there is a psychic bond between the brothers; in the final confrontation scene Sterling's eyes are blue while Carl's are brown; in the film's last close-up the surviving brother has one brown and one blue eye. As his mother claims him and they leave his bemused enemies (who cannot arrest him in case he *is* Sterling), he asks himself in Sterling's voice, 'Didn't you kill my brother?' – and answers himself in Carl's, 'Shut up and keep walking.'

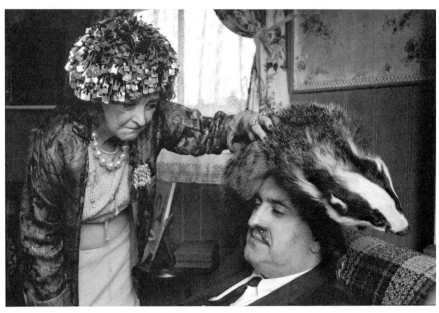

Didn't You Kill My Brother? – Beryl Reid and Alexei Sayle

Building on its Brechtian traditions without overplaying them, the film combines a social message with a sharp comedy which binds the whole story together. There is a song for Sterling – 'Crime' – complete with dancing henchmen, which works effectively and leads one to wonder whether the film might not have benefited from a longer running time and more songs to make it, perhaps, a *Threepenny Opera* for the eighties.

At the end, having decided that there is something to be said for the legitimate bicycle business, Carl/Sterling turns to the camera and delivers the film's moral:

> And now, our story's finished
> Our tale is almost told.
> But can we find a moral
> In the story of the Moss brothers so bold?
> Well, this country's based on stealing
> The poor are on the rack.
> But men like me will always be
> Plotting to steal this country back.*

*Didn't You Kill My Brother, Comic Strip, Channel Four.

With its blend of political standpoint and barbed comedy, *Didn't You Kill My Brother?* is one of the best of all the Comic Strip films; the 1988 series as a whole stands up well and mostly justifies the longer running times.

Perhaps encouraged by the experience of making his film, Sayle abandoned his normal distrust of television long enough to make a six-part series of half-hour programmes, transmitted on BBC2 starting on 13 October 1988, entitled *Alexei Sayle's Stuff*. Using a loose documentary format, and blending new material neatly with sections from his various stage acts, he dealt with a wide range of subjects, including Ancient Greece, bereaved ventriloquists' dummies, wigs, gerbils, triffids, Leslie Crowther, cinema intermissions, Tandy home computers and Einstein's theory of wave particle formation (the last explained in a George Formby song). Some sketches were surprisingly similar in atmosphere to *Monty Python's Flying Circus* – not an imitation, but a demonstration of the difficulty of avoiding their shadow when dealing with television presentation. The overall effect of the series – which was co-written with Andrew Marshall and David Renwick, and produced and directed by Marcus Mortimer – was a satisfying melding of Sayle's individual approach with the range of subjects and approaches which the loosely structured format made possible; Sayle's political viewpoint provided an underpinning for some of the material but was never allowed to obtrude. With the series, Sayle demonstrated how effectively he could use television in his own way, away from his Comic Strip colleagues.

The Comic Strip meanwhile continues as a film production company, offering the chance for its members to put ideas into practice; it is, of course, very largely a Peter Richardson organization, because he more than any of them has the drive to make the whole thing work. (There is – and one or two of them would admit it – perhaps some truth in the suggestion that it is largely laziness which allows this state of affairs.)

Certainly the Comic Strip periodically goes through introspective meetings where the members wonder whether it should carry on; happily, it always does. Adrian Edmondson has reservations: 'It's got very stupid in the Comic Strip, everything's got too close – everyone's going up their own arseholes in the end – writing, directing, starring – there's no extra input anywhere. And our ability to criticize each other seems to have waned, because we've become such good chums – and we are a genuinely chummy group. I think we like each other's work no matter whether it's good or bad.'

In view of Edmondson's remarks it is interesting that Sayle and Melville's first work for the Comic Strip should produce something

269

so effective. For Peter Richardson the value of the Comic Strip is the chance to be constantly different: 'People are keen to use the Comic Strip as a way of keeping their independence and doing things it's not expected of them to do, as opposed to doing a series that works and then dropping that and doing another one. We're individually more famous than collectively – I think Channel Four quite likes that, something where people get together to do something they feel proud of. I think everybody feels that the best work they do is with the Comic Strip.'

Certainly the opportunity for its members to explore odd one-off ideas is the strongest reason for the Comic Strip's existence; it is to be hoped that future series can maintain the range and quality of their work.

Although most performers would shy away from the 'alternative comedy' label – some would deny that the phrase has any meaning – Jenny Lecoat had occasion to work with a performer from the long-established northern club circuit, and comments: 'It was very fashionable a couple of years ago to disown "alternative" as a word; then you meet someone like that and you realize that there *is* a completely different world out there, a completely different circuit of doing the summer seasons, Pontin's, Butlin's. . . . There's still very much a division between that and us – it's largely an age division. I couldn't play that circuit – they'd tear me limb from limb as soon as I mentioned a swear-word on stage!'

Sad to say, that mainstream circuit still leans heavily on precisely the sort of racist and sexist jokes which the early Comedy Store performers were determined to kill off – humour which exists largely by confirming the audience's prejudices.

The so-called 'alternative comedy' field has become extremely wide, and there is consequently a wide range of attitudes amongst the performers. At one end of the scale are those who aim simply to be funny without any particular social or political message – for example John Hegley or Norman Lovett. Many others will make points in the course of their comedy; Jeremy Hardy, for example, operates by making wry comments on life in general – while Peter Richardson's filmic exercises in comedy frequently take a sardonic look at the state of the country. However, none of these people would see themselves as overtly bringing a message to their audiences; the principal aim is simply to be funny.

Rik Mayall takes the 'non-racist, non-sexist' attitude as something which doesn't have to be stated: 'My comedy is a lot less pointed than other people's – the meaninglessness of my comedy is really the message. There's hardly ever any constructive message in there – except that I am morally offended by this Tory administration; but I hope that what I do is much more general than just a piece of agit-prop. I don't deal in words and rational ideas; I deal in the unusual, the exciting, the very personal – people laugh at me because they've seen themselves do something like that.'

Because he is so widely known, as a result of his stage tours and *Saturday* and *Friday Night Live*, Ben Elton is widely seen as polemical; but he insists that this perception gets the political aspect of his work out of proportion: 'I do what I do in order to be funny; but I have faith in myself that in doing so I won't be sexist or racist. And I will sometimes use my personal abhorrence of sexism and racism to raise laughs, not to make a point – and it's a lovely side effect that I might get a hundred letters ... but the gag won't be funny unless it's true.'

For Tony Allen it is the message, the challenge and the danger of comedy which is important – one of his gags goes: 'The future of comedy is with Ben Elton – and it's in safe hands.' He is prepared to risk not being funny in order to make his point: 'Comedy is sort of incidental – it just happens that I've always made people laugh with my opinions. I do believe in change, and I know you can change people. And I know that things are changing all the time. We changed the face of comedy to a certain extent – not very well; the original idea was to change the world, and to stop people doing Irish jokes and mother-in-law jokes ... now people give lip-service to that. He who follows the innovator does exactly the opposite of what the innovator does.'

Tony Allen is unusual amongst the politically committed end of the scene in not being left-wing (or indeed any wing); Roland Muldoon has always seen comedy as an offshoot of political theatre which for the most part takes a left-wing standpoint: 'It must be a battle for yuppie hearts and minds – trying to say, "This isn't right, voting for selfishness." I've seen people in the countryside watching Ben Elton on *Saturday Live*, and they didn't know that anyone else was ever saying anything like that – it was a revelation for them to hear abuse of the system coming from a comedian. Tony Allen's built his career on saying "Down with Socialism" as much as anything else, and I often say that what he amounts to is a right-wing anarchist ... but nevertheless he was part of that phenomenon in the early 1980s that said that they didn't go along with Thatcher. They didn't change anything, but the point that it exists, that it is oppositionary, and that people flock to it, is important.'

Certainly the 1987 election killed any developing ideas of a comedy-inspired political or social revolution. Jenny Lecoat comments: 'If you're talking about comedians changing the world, you're wasting your time. *That Was The Week That Was* actually had some political clout in its time, if it really went for a particular political figure. I would like to see programmes like *Spitting Image* going more for that, and less for the "balanced view". To get political clout you have to have a point of view – otherwise you end up about as revolutionary as *Private Eye*. Up to a point it's possible to have an effect – but you're only going to get that sort of clout with people who are well-known, who are well-established and who are doing consistently good work. People like us going round the circuit and doing jokes to students doesn't make a blind bit of difference. It's easy for our circuit to become cosy and reassuring to the people we're performing to – you know, "Fuck the police, fuck Mrs Thatcher, up the revolution" ... it's a converted audience. Sometimes someone will do a political gig which is particularly poignant, particularly sharp, and makes you think about an aspect of that issue you hadn't considered before. That's the most you can ever hope for. If you really want to change the world, you don't go into comedy – you learn to fire a gun and you go and fight in El Salvador.'

There are other desirable changes than political. Simon Fanshawe is among those who have attempted to improve the acceptance of gays; as we have seen, he has found effective ways of putting his point of view over – but there is a long way to go. This aspect of his act has got him booed off at Jongleurs; more seriously, the government itself seems to be trying to shift the climate of opinion back to the anti-gay attitudes of thirty years ago.

He comments: 'If you're gay, you are fucked up for a long while – because society isn't geared to make it easy. You spend hours thinking, how do I cope with it? *My* way of coping with it is comedy – it's much cheaper than therapy! And it's exciting for gay people to come and see me on stage, having the whip hand, being the powerful person in the room, and being gay.'

The difficulties of gays are at least well-known to exist; the oppression of women has been less obvious, and one of the things that alternative comedy has done is to open up the field – to some extent – for women. In the previous – Monty Python/Oxbridge – generation of comedy there were practically no women; and in previous generations most women comics had to work within men's perceptions of them. In alternative comedy there have been a handful who have firmly stated a feminist point of view, and others who have simply gained acceptance as themselves.

However, those who imagine that there are large numbers of women comics are deluding themselves. Ben Elton saw many performers while sitting in on the research for *Saturday Live*, and comments: 'It's not true to say there's a vast army of women comics, although lots of TV producers desperately want it to be that way.... We all want it to be that way – people say to me, "Why aren't more women doing it?" – well, why aren't there more women doctors? –

It's because we live in a sexist society. It doesn't help to lie about it – there's only a handful ... but it's coming along.'

Gradually more women performers are appearing – although there is still a tendency for groups in particular to do very old-fashioned anti-men material; but the best of them are now making their points with more subtlety. Journalistic attempts to concentrate on the fact that performers *are* women – to the exclusion of their actual abilities – don't help matters; Jenny Lecoat: 'I've done so many interviews with people who particularly wanted to concentrate on the aspect of "Women and Humour" and "Women Comics" ... basically we're comics; we don't want to be called "comediennes", we don't want to be called "female comics", we want to be called "comics".'

Helen Lederer is less concerned about the labels: 'If you start getting worried about things like that it's counter-productive. You can't change things by being seen to be too aggressive on things that don't matter as much as things like respect, and having a voice – things like that are more important.'

The most successful women to emerge from the alternative scene, French and Saunders, were never interested in the 'women in comedy' label. Dawn French: 'We were never "women in comedy". We knew that our advantage in the beginning had been that there were no women about, but when we fell in with the Comic Strip, nobody was making a point to us about us being "the women". I really am glad that there are more women doing comedy – it's so refreshing ... but I think that if anything the people who have broken down the barriers were people like Victoria Wood who never intended to, who were just doing their job like anyone else.'

The major achievement might one day be a complete acceptance of women as just performers, with no one bothering to make comparisons or count numbers. Interestingly, the level of penetration by alternative comedy into black culture – and vice versa – has been practically nil. There are literally only one or two black performers on the circuit, and it is rare to see a black face in the audience. Maria Kempinska: 'We rarely get blacks in the audience – there are some, but most of them don't go to *any* venue. I've asked why, and they're just not interested; they're out doing their own thing – nor do they want whites to go to their things either ... they've got their own brand of humour anyway.'

The ghetto-ization of humour seems to work in both directions – although it's not a case of white venues discouraging blacks – and, given the long-standing difficulties of integration and the charged emotions attached to them, it is not surprising that there is little cross-culture; but it is a pity.

The cabaret circuit is, of course, an enclosed little world of its own. Outside is mainstream humour – which means largely television. It is difficult to assess whether alternative comedy has really had any effect on the mainstream. Jean Nicholson's years running the Crown and Castle have given her a broad view of the field; she comments: 'I think alternative comedy has had an impact on mainstream comedy – that is slowly becoming clear with various comedians. Some of the values have rubbed off on the more sensitive mainstream comedians – certainly making people think before they stick racist or mother-in-law jokes in.'

Obviously there is no major change, but even a minor change is something to be pleased about. Tony Allen: 'What I really like is that we won over people like Jasper Carrott – he got a lot of energy from what we were doing – and Lenny Henry, who was doing silly black man jokes about himself . . . they're still mainstream, but it was nice that those sorts of people realized they were in the wrong generation. It's shifted the mainstream a little bit – but to move the mainstream just a little bit you have to get over there and go *HEAVE!!*, and I think that's what we did.'

More insidious are the effects of the mainstream upon the performers; in the nature of things television requires compromises – if only in language – and the decisions between compromise and success can be difficult to make. Those who won't compromise at all – like Tony Allen – remain outside television; and those who compromise a little have to take care not to be absorbed into television's attitudes.

Alexei Sayle, until he was able to make a series on his own terms, steered clear of television; he comments: 'A lot of what was good about alternative comedy is being used by people who have middle-class attitudes – all this Channel Four crap – it's very middle-class, very preachy, very "educational". It's not what I'm about. It's an inevitable process – if something edgy comes up, it's assimilated as quickly as possible. And the performers conspire in that assimilation – they killed off punk in about two years, and they killed off alternative comedy in about the same time – unless the performers are very aware of that threat, and why should they be? And a lot of the performers court that threat – a lot of these supposedly "edgy" performers very much want to be establishment stars . . . waving the red flag to defeat the red flag.'

Jim Barclay, whose own stand-up material is rather too political for television, adds: 'A lot of them have never set out to be particularly subversive. They set out to be new and original, but that's not necessarily the same thing. They're not being taken over because they were never anti-Establishment figures.'

Barclay, like Andy de la Tour, Mark Arden and several others, is not totally dependent upon the comedy scene, and can move between straight acting and stand-up as the occasion arises. This gives him a greater power to choose what he does, and at the same time less dependence upon the vagaries of producers and audiences.

Jeremy Hardy, on the other hand, is a performer who is largely dependent on his stand-up work; his close and regular contact with the audiences has led him to some depressing conclusions: 'I think there's something spreading in our society – people are just becoming hedonists, they don't want to think, they don't want to have ideas, they don't want to change, they just want to get into a groove and be debauched. And nobody wants to know about politics any more – even people who aren't particularly bigoted one way or another don't really want to hear about it. People have got used to the idea that there's a certain regime in this country which doesn't seem to be going to change, and people don't seem to want to think about anything any more. The last [1987] election just reinforced that – people just thought, oh, what's the point? And people who are prone to conservative views are used to the idea that this is how things are, and any criticism of it is just some kind of petulant whingeing.'

The audiences' reactions to the comedy itself seem to be changing; the battle of the Comedy Store – to expunge racist and sexist jokes – seems to have been lost again, according to Jeremy Hardy: 'There was a traditional club comic got up at the Comedy Store and was racist, and sexist, and anti-gay, and he just stormed. The audience might like me as well, but they would be quite happy to see Jim Davidson and Bernard Manning. You get quite a lot of extremely bigoted and reactionary people at the Comedy Store – and the abuse that women attract is quite horrifying. There's a whole male feeling which takes over, which I'd only really experienced when I went to see Roy Chubby Brown [not at the Comedy Store] and there was a ninety per cent male audience absolutely baying to hear the word "cunt" said repeatedly. There's that element at the Comedy Store.'

The broadening of the audience for many of the cabaret circuit gigs inevitably brings in an undesirable element (and the Comedy Store, with its central position and late-night licence, is notorious for attracting them); but many gigs retain the more friendly and sympathetic atmosphere of earlier days. What *is* happening is that the whole scene is settling into a familiar pattern; of course the excitement of something being new cannot be maintained when the something has become familiar, and if the existence of a network of live comedy is not new, at least it is there and a reasonable percentage of it is worth watching.

Although most of the raw energy of the early days of the Comedy Store has gone, the effects of its opening in 1979 have been considerable. Television has certainly been affected – it would have been too much to hope for really major changes, but the best of alternative comedy on television has been worth having and has achieved something useful in the way of livening up a field which can all too easily become moribund.The resurgence of live comedy in London and elsewhere is of real value; as to any changes in political and social perception caused by alternative comedy, we have seen that these are slight; but any change for the better is to be welcomed. The disparate grouping of young performers included in the rather dubious label of 'alternative comedy' have perhaps widened the audiences' perceptions of themselves and the world by a small amount, have perhaps expanded the conception of what comedy is and what it is for . . . in fact, to coin a cliché, have refreshed the parts that other comedy cannot reach. When he opened the Comedy Store in 1979 Peter Rosengard started comedy on a new road; let us hope that it still has a long way to go.

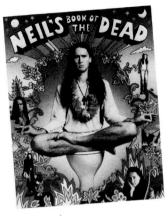

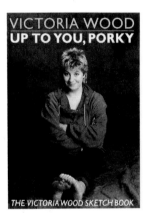

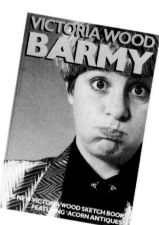

Appendix: Comic Strip Films 1982–88

Original transmission date (Ch4)	*Television films*
2–11–1982	**Five Go Mad in Dorset,** written by Peter Richardson and Pete Richens; directed by Bob Spiers
3–1–1983	**War,** wr. Richardson and Richens; dir. Spiers
(10–1–1983	Repeat of **Five Go Mad in Dorset)**
17–1–1983	**The Beat Generation,** wr. Richardson and Richens; dir. Spiers
24–1–1983	**Bad News Tour,** wr. Adrian Edmondson; dir. Sandy Johnson
31–1–1983	**Summer School,** wr. Dawn French and Jennifer Saunders; dir. Johnson
cancelled	**An Evening with Eddie Monsoon,** wr. Edmondson, French, Planer, Richardson, Richens and Saunders; dir. Spiers
2–11–1983	**Five Go Mad On Mescalin,** wr. Richardson and Richens; dir. Spiers
7–1–1984	**Dirty Movie,** wr. Rik Mayall and Adrian Edmondson; dir. Johnson
14–1–1984	**Susie,** wr. Richardson and Richens; dir. Spiers
21–1–1984	**A Fistful of Travellers' Cheques,** wr. Richardson, Richens and Mayall; dir. Spiers
28–1–1984	**Gino – Full Story and Pics,** wr. Richardson and Richens; dir. Spiers
4–2–1984	**Eddie Monsoon – A Life,** wr. Edmondson; dir. Johnson
11–2–1984	**Slags,** wr. Saunders; dir. Johnson
3–11–1984	**The Bullshitters** (*not billed as a Comic Strip film*), wr. Richardson and Keith Allen; dir. Stephen Frears
1–1–1986	**Consuela,** wr. French and Saunders; dir. Frears
2–1–1986	**Private Enterprise,** wr. and dir. Edmondson

20–2–1988	**The Strike**, wr. and dir. Richardson and Richens
27–2–1988	**More Bad News**, wr. and dir. Edmondson
5–3–1988	**Mr Jolly Lives Next Door**, wr. Edmondson, Mayall and Roland Rivron; dir. Frears
12–3–1988	**The Yob**, wr. Keith Allen and Daniel Peacock; dir. Ian Emes
19–3–1988	**Didn't You Kill My Brother?** wr. Alexei Sayle, Pauline Melville and David Stafford; dir. Spiers
26–3–1988	**Funseekers**, wr. Nigel Planer & Doug Lucie; dir. Baz Taylor

(*The 1988 series, except 'Funseekers', had a limited release in cinemas in Autumn 1987.*)

Cinema films

11–1985	**The Supergrass**, wr. Richardson and Richens; dir. Richardson
11–1987	**Eat The Rich** (*not billed as a Comic Strip film*), wr. Richardson and Richens; dir. Richardson

Index

284